Alternative U.S. Futures

Stahrl W. Edmunds

UNIVERSITY OF CALIFORNIA, RIVERSIDE

ALTERNATIVE U.S. FUTURES

A Policy Analysis
of Individual Choices
in a Political Economy

GOODYEAR PUBLISHING COMPANY, INC.
SANTA MONICA, CALIFORNIA

Library of Congress Cataloging in Publication Data

Edmunds, Stahrl.
  Alternative U.S. futures.

  Includes index.
  1. United States—Economic policy—1971-
2. Policy sciences. I. Title.
HC106.7.E35   338.973   77-28093
ISBN 0-87620-006-4

Current printing (last digit):
10 9 8 7 6 5 4 3 2 1

ISBN: 0-87620-006-4

Y-0064-9

Editing, interior design, and production supervision: Brian Williams
Photo research: Genoa Caldwell
Cover design: Michael Rogondino
Cover photo: Tom Tracy

Printed in the United States of America

To DEWEY, LAURA, AND ROLLIN

that they may realize the Jeffersonian dream of designing an alternate U.S. future for their own generation in which they may live their own lives.

CONTENTS

vii

Prologue

SOUTH CHICAGO, A.D. 2020

One day an architect-engineer named Jack Workman traveled via the Sky Shuttle from New City, which he had helped design, to Chicago to talk to officials there about a redevelopment concept for the South Side. He was accompanied by his wife, Joan, who worked as a school principal, and his fourteen-year-old son, Bobby. As they approached the city, his wife mentioned that South Chicago was still on the old-style elementary-secondary school system.

"What's an old-style school, Mother?" Bobby asked.

"Well, it's a bit hard to explain," she said. "See, children used to be taught words, and words became the things. Then they were taught how the world is, in these word-things, as geography, history, government, business, literature, and science. So children ended up with a great, abstract idea of the world about them as words and things, but without much experience or feeling about life."

"But that's backwards," Bobby said, who in New City attended a "work school," which welcomed the opportunity for students to work on real projects outside of school. "How did they know how the world feels or how one feels about the world?"

"Well, that came hard under the old system, if it came at all. That is why we changed to Three-Tier Learning."

"What's the difference?" Bobby asked.

"The lower tier is the Seeing School, the middle is the Measurement School, and the upper is the Concept School. That's the way we think children learn. They learn first by seeing and doing what is around them; they learn first in images and pictures, not words. So in Seeing School we teach art, painting, design, dance, handicrafts, and languages. These are all ways of expressing feelings and images. In the Measurement School, you learn mechanics, mathematics, computers, simulation, and natural sciences. Then in the third tier you learn concepts for putting all you have learned together—physical science, systems theory, mission analysis, human purpose, humanities, history, social science, logic, philosophy."

"Why was education done in reverse before? What changed it?"

"The change came after the Tax Reform Act of 1990 and after the Constitutional Convention of 1995," replied his father. "Before that, people were mostly employees, and education was geared to serving employers, things, and institutions. Now most people are self-employed, as I am, and people needed to see for themselves how to deal with the world, so education had to change."

"Didn't you live in Chicago once and work for someone else?" Bobby asked.

"Yes, for many years, I worked for a big corporation as a construction engineer. I could never save enough money to start a business for myself until the Tax Reform Act of 1990."

"How could that law make such a difference, to change over the whole country from employees to self-employed?"

"It eliminated all income-tax deductions for corporations and individuals except for the self-employed savings-investment credit. That ended the bottling up of capital by big corporations, and it enabled me to save money to go into business for myself."

"But why didn't you stay in Chicago?"

"Well, you know, the federal and state governments used to be huge and unmanageable, and sometimes of questionable ethics. But the Twelve Amendments to the Constitution, passed in 1995, put the fiscal power of government back into the hands of citizens and local government, which caused decentralization of population and government. The country villages were repopulated again, and new towns like New City grew up all over the country."

"Then, why didn't Chicago decentralize like everyone else?"

"Well, most big cities like Chicago had powerful political machines that wouldn't let go. It's taken a long time, for example, for the South Chicago Capital Reallocation Agency to be created, which is where I'm going today."

The shuttle car came into the dock at the Chicago terminal, and shortly afterward they were traveling in a cab along Outer Drive, looking at Lake Michigan and the skyline.

"What a beautiful city," Joan murmured. "That lake is so blue."

"Yes, it's one of the great waterfronts of the world," Jack said. "But wait until you see where we're going."

They drove into the South Side, past hulks of derelict buildings, broken windows, houses empty and stripped. Garbage, junk, and abandoned cars littered the streets.

"Boy," said Bobby. "Looks like there was a war here."

"But of course there hasn't been a war since Vietnam," his father said, "not since the Twelve Amendments were passed."

"Sure looks like war pictures of a bombed-out city."

"It's called urban decay. It started in the 1960s. Some neighborhoods were vandalized and looted like this, and the blight gradually spread all over the South Side. The area's been going downhill for nearly fifty years."

"Why didn't someone do something?"

"Well, the federal and state governments tried urban redevelopment for many years, but it never seemed to work—no motivation by the people to build up the area, I guess."

"Why not after 1995, like New City?"

"By then there were too few people remaining here and they were too old and too poor. We need to do something to bring new people here—young people, self-employed people, who want to save and build. That's what I'm here for."

"But, Dad, redevelopment did not work before on the South Side," said Bobby. "Why would it work, now?"

"The old redevelopments were before the Tax Reform Act of 1990 and the Twelve Amendments of 1995, which created self-employment and put government back into the hands of the people. See, people have to do things for themselves in order to learn, to be motivated, to be rewarded. The United States got away from that, sort of went on a wrong course for half a century or so up to 1980. Big institutions took over, did things for people and to people that they would not have done themselves. Wars, inflation, unemployment, and poor government made people lose confidence. People lost allegiance. People have to believe in what they are doing for themselves, otherwise they don't care anymore."

Introduction

CHOOSING AMONG ALTERNATIVES BEFORE US

The last grand design of the American political economy was made nearly two hundred years ago, when the Founding Fathers drafted the U.S. Constitution. Since 1787, however, no Constitutional Convention has ever been convened, although the Constitution makes provision for calling it. Nor has anything resembling what might be called a "system design review" of the Constitution taken place, except, perhaps, in 1791 with the enactment of the Bill of Rights and after the Civil War with the addition of the three amendments guaranteeing equal protection of the laws. Since then, one hundred years ago, only six amendments have been passed, and those in piecemeal fashion. Periodic elections cannot be considered to constitute a design review of the American political-economic system, for election issues revolve around the immediate needs of the electorate and the reelection motivations of the candidates, both of which tend to narrow issues to personal interests rather than to reviews of the sociopolitical design.

During this century, however, America has changed more than at any other time in its history—from being 70 percent farmers to 95 percent nonfarmers. Because of this great change from an agricultural to a postindustrial society, we are at a point where we need to review our own design—where we have been and where we may go.

Since early in the Republic, from Jefferson to Eisenhower, we have been admonished that individuals must retrieve authority over their own lives even from the best of institutions—even, Jefferson said, from the Constitution he helped write—and certainly from the worst. This advice tells us that we need some new means of adaptive change, ways of achieving a feasible compromise between institutional responsibility and individual authority. If we can create this adaptive-change process, it can alter us from predestined courses and the replaying of old, tragic scenarios.

The adaptive process contains several elements. Mission analysis and scenarios are a means of looking at the lives of individuals, peoples, or nations in an understandable way—a way that tells their story, where they came from, where they are, and where they are going. *Mission analysis* is a story of purpose, what people want. The *scenario* is a story of how people achieve that purpose. The events and actions which achieve a purpose are capable of being chosen by the actors; and it is in this sense that Carl Jung speaks of people "living their own legend." Living one's own legend is a form of self-fulfilling prophecy. People become what they choose to be. Taken together, the mission analysis and scenarios constitute a form of *policy analysis,* which portrays the spectrum of issues and policy choices citizens make by their actions or default. The structure of these policy choices becomes the *system design* for the social economy.

The point is, we can construct the social design of the United States *incrementally,* bit by bit, toward some unknown destiny as the Romans and Greeks did, or we can take a whole look at our individual and social preferences, as our Founding Fathers did in writing the Constitution, which was their scenario for their time, and seek to live our own lives as we wish to live them. This book takes the latter approach. That is, we need to speculate about alternative futures. It is a form of choice; it gives us scenes and scenarios we might choose to make happen—a choice among self-fulfilling prophecies. Nor should speculating about alternative futures be left to the "experts," whoever they may be; it is creative democracy at work, a game in which all citizens can participate. Futures are in the minds and acts of the actors. What citizens do now—how they vote, what they hope, how they regard each other—determines tomorrow's alternatives. If more adults drop out of society and join the youthful subculture (having already adopted its dress, hair styles, and some of its alienation), future U.S.A. will take one course. If they gird their work ethic to implement the destinies seen by multinational corporations, it will take quite another. Which direction should it go? This book is intended to illustrate several choices—and in doing so to encourage the restoration of hope and allegiance in the United States through the rediscovery of identity, purpose, mission, and inquiry about ourselves.

The art of becoming what one chooses to be is, at the individual level, the psychology of being—of realizing one's own identity. At the institutional and societal level, the becoming of what one chooses to be is the art of *management*. That is, management selects objectives (missions) and then organizes to achieve these objectives (writes a scenario, in effect; that is, outlines a word model of what one wants to happen). The *policy* side of management is concerned with defining the values and final ends; the *operational* side of management is concerned with achieving those ends. In government, for instance, politics is the art of selecting objectives (missions) for the whole society and program management is the operational skill (writing and performing the scenario). In this book, we are concerned with the missions and scenarios of the whole American social-political economy, not just the narrower interests of groups or institutions such as business corporations, universities, hospitals, or the federal government, for the objectives of institutions cannot be evaluated except in the context of the whole of human needs they are supposed to serve.

How might we foretell alternative futures? There are two ways. One is by extrapolating from the past. The past is prologue, and we can look at our present policies and institutions in the context of past policies whose outcomes are known to us. We are not so different physically, mentally, or culturally from those who have gone before that their experience is without value to us, even though technical skills may have changed the form of our lives. What our forebears set in motion as social practice and what momentum we ourselves add by recent acts form a trajectory into the future.

The second way is by devising social inventions for the future which are speculative and untried. The question is, do we have the creativity to invent new ways to manage change, to alter events now predestined by extrapolation from the past?

As an illustration of alternative policy choices and of policy analysis at the societal level, this book is useful for students of social sciences and of different forms of administration. It will also be of interest to anyone who would like to see a map of the social evolution of the United States—where it has been, where it is, and where it may go.

How the Book Is Organized

The book begins with a discussion of how authority has been and is being used in the United States, because this use of authority sets the framework for a policy analysis of the choices open for our decision. Decisions, public and private, form a pattern over time that is shaped by the values of decision makers, their mission, and their socialization. I have analyzed the range of value choices on thirteen major issues, from inflation to war, to show the extremes of choice on each issue and the consequences of the tendency of the United States to move toward one of the extremes. This analysis provides us with the set of policy choices that the United States is currently pursuing, which I will later compare with other alternatives and civilizations.

In Chapter 2, I examine the American policy choices in terms of their tendency to inspire allegiance or alienation. Allegiance is a mutual pact in which authority and loyalty are granted to those decision makers who fulfill human needs. If human needs go unmet, allegiance is withheld and alienation and dissent from authority occur, and dissent causes disorders. Hence, disorders are evidence of unmet human needs. Human needs are the foundation of what is called *mission analysis*—that is, what purposes and objectives should be fulfilled to satisfy unmet wants and to balance social interests. In war games, mission analysis starts with threats from abroad and the game's objective or scenario is to show the means for countering this threat. In domestic affairs, the threat is from within; that is, the threat of internal disorder, violence, and crime stems from the accumulation of unmet needs among some segments of the population. Chapter 2 raises the question of whether there are such unmet needs and tendencies toward disorder and violence in the United States.

Having seen what unmet human needs may exist, we are then ready to ask how we got that way. To see this, we must first have some reference points. These are examined in the structure of social change in Chapter 3.

The scenario of past and present U.S.A. is described in Chapter 4. This tells the story of how we got where we are today, for better or worse, and begins to suggest the choices we have for the future. I have told the story not as a history of the American people and not as a novel of individual lives, but as a map of the distribution of authority and functions, which is a way to describe the sociopolitical economy in which we live. That is, if we want to make choices about the future, we have to ask ourselves, what choices have we authority to make? If we do not have authority ourselves to make choices over our lives, we must then ask who does, whether we like the choices being made for us, and, if not, how we can shift authority so that society responds to what we want.

A variety of alternative futures or social outcomes are possible for American society, depending on where various authorities reside and what choices are made. One plausible outcome for the future United States is to "replay" the Roman destiny. This is done in Chapter 5. The parallels of the United States to the Roman society are more than striking—they appear rather prophetic. In my opinion, we are well on our way along the Roman trajectory, unless revised authority distributions and choices are made.

A replay of the history of ancient Greece, discussed in Chapter 6, is also a possibility although it seems less likely than a Roman scenario, since the elements of direct democracy have long since disappeared in the United States. However, one important likeness with ancient Greece is that the U.S.A. is a producing-trading economy (which Rome basically was not), and it may be that our economic destiny will override our Roman-like political structure and carry us along the plot of Greek tragedy.

A medieval replay, described in Chapter 7, is another, perhaps less plausible scenario for our future. We might solve our current disorders and conflict problems by segmenting society into localized units, united by some dictum or dogma. American society is gradually segmenting itself—in the separatist movement of minorities, the walled-off condominium communities, the exurbanite refugees, and the like—but it is hard to see where the unifying doctrine might come from, unless it is from science. However, science likes to think of itself as value-free. A value-free doctrine deals with things, not with people. Hence, the dogmatization of science would seem most plausible in combination with other fortuitous events. As we shall see, such concatenations of events are, at times, the stuff of history and social change.

Most likely we will not want to replay the Roman, Greek, or medieval scenes, since their outcomes were not entirely enviable. Why not write our own play? To do so, we must have a plot, a mission, a future, where we want to go. Chapter 8 is such a plot maker's guide to the future.

Chapter 9 is a discussion of a plausible set of purposes for the future United States based on concepts of the Founders of the U.S. Constitution. Chapter 10 is my own scenario of how we may choose to live—only one of many possible alternative futures, of course.

By this point, you will be ready to write your own alternative future. Although the writing of scenarios and the visualizing of the future are imperfect arts, their main value lies in putting into currency ideas of where we as a civilization might go. Other writers, too, have considered this question and developed alternative scenarios of their own from different perspectives and assumptions. Instead of proliferating scenarios beyond the four I've presented, in Chapter 11 I have examined how these scenarios compare with those of other observers. This chapter is a brief state-of-the-art review of alternative futures in recent writings and is intended to be representative of different perceptions rather than comprehensive of all the literature.

The writing of scenarios to illustrate the future may take many forms, the most elaborate including economic projections, technological forecasts, cultural extrapolations, as well as estimates of institutional change, actions, threats, and coalitions. Such scenarios are appropriate for short-term projections of a new technological system or in planning new institutional programs, where the focus can be narrowed to a limited number of events over a few years time span. I have not found this approach to be feasible for writing a scenario about the social process as a whole, over indefinite time periods, because of the limitless influences, possibilities, and combinations of events that come into play. Thus, I have adopted a somewhat simpler framework for the scenario by asking what different combinations of major policies may be plausible. The scenarios, then, are built around alternative sets of policy choices, and the consequences unfold as the choice is made to move toward one end of the spectrum or the other. The implementing means by which the policy choices are carried out are necessarily simplified to show the direction of choice, and the consequences are necessarily speculative since they lie in the future. This approach gives the scenarios some of the characteristics of parable or fable, which are venerable forms of learning. My intent is that these imaginative scenarios be taken as plausible (but not prophetic) illustrations of the serious policy analysis in the balance of the book. Documentation for the historical parallels will be found in the Greek, Roman, and Medieval appendices.

Acknowledgments

Much of this manuscript was written at Villa Serbelloni, the Bellagio Study and Conference Center, Italy, for which I gratefully thank the Rockefeller Foundation. I also thank the University of California for the sabbatical leave which made possible the completion of the work.

Riverside, Californa   S.W.E.
November 1977

Alternative U.S. Futures

Boston Stock Exchange. *(Photo by Peter Southwick/Stock, Boston.)*

Chapter One

THE CHOICES
BEFORE THE
UNITED STATES

In any country, the use of authority, whether private or governmental, expresses itself in decisions. Over a period of time, these decisions form a pattern shaped by the values of the decision makers, their purpose or mission, and how they acquire the behavior of a social class. Historically in the United States, a major mission of decision makers has been economic expansion. The principal means for this expansion has been intensive investment in capital equipment (productive equipment) to increase economic productivity. Indeed, this process of developing a capital-intensive society has become not only the modus operandi but the very means of survival of the United States. As such, some con-

1

tinuance of this process is important to the welfare of all of us. The real question, however—and one central to this book—is how capital-intensive the process should become, for capital expansion (the increase of production equipment and facilities) is achieved at a human cost: the sacrifice of labor and the saving of money which delays consumption until a future point.

Such human costs of capital expansion are few as long as resources are cheap and easily available. Coal near the surface, for instance, is easier and cheaper to mine than coal that lies deep in the earth. But as resources become scarce and high-priced, more effort is required to use them and so a diminishing rate of return on the productivity of capital is felt. That is, more and more capital has to be invested for less and less social return. For example, in minerals or petroleum, once the easy resources have been exploited, the extraction costs become higher, wells and shafts must be driven deeper, the quality of the mineral diminishes, the processing costs increase, and the pollution wastes become greater.

These mounting costs mean that larger aggregations of capital are needed to keep the expansion going. A whole array of institutional dele-gations and management practices have to be devised to pull together the financial and human capital for these intensifying investments. The capital-intensive society then becomes a capital-*intensifying* society. Its mode of survival has to be systematically intensified—economically, technically, politically, institutionally—to keep the expansion process going.

This intensification of the means is what exacts human costs, because the means become so difficult to achieve that the means become ends—for example, the mechanization of coal production becomes a more ur-gent problem than does the condition of the miners. What French philosopher Jacques Ellul calls the "dehumanization of technique" oc-curs.[1] Human needs for individuality are set aside by institutional deci-sion makers intent on still further capital intensification to eke minimal expansion from the diminishing returns. As the search for coal inten-sifies, for example, the work and tasks of the individual miner are de-termined by the machine, whether it is bigger, faster, more dangerous, or more routine.

At what point do we stop and ask, is it worth it? Are the human costs becoming higher than social return? Is there a better trade-off?

These are questions we must ask of present U.S. policy choices. We need to see which policy issues require decisions, what choices are open to us, and what are their consequences. We need to understand what set of policy choices have led us to where we are and what would give us new options on how we wish to live as a society.

[1]Jacques Ellul, *La Technique* (Paris: A. Colin, 1954).

POLICY ANALYSIS OF THIRTEEN ISSUES: THE CHOICES
BEFORE THE UNITED STATES

To illustrate the decisions the United States may make, I have identified thirteen policy choices before the nation. The basic choices before us are the extent to which the nation will fulfill unmet individual needs, discussed in Chapter 2, which are currently leading to alienation. *Policy analysis* is the examination of alternative choices and means. The policy analysis here examines thirteen issues, showing the choices open to us together with their consequences. These choices are shown in Table 1–1.

If you read down the consequences column of the table, you will see that these policy issues are highly interactive—that is, the choices are interrelated—which makes it difficult to analyze any one issue separately from the others. However, the first two policy issues, fiscal and income policies, are influenced heavily by government and constitute the most generalized authority controls over the social structure. Thus, they influence everything else and so provide a reasonable starting point.

To understand the policy stance of the United States on fiscal and income policies, we must be aware of the public and governmental attitude toward growth and development. Since frontier days, the U.S. government has pursued a highly developmental policy,[2] applying cheap labor to free resources in order to convert labor into savings and capital (for example, in homesteading of the frontier, when farmers turned raw land into productive farms with their toil, by clearing the land; building fences, houses, and barns; and by saving to buy equipment). Today, because labor is no longer cheap and resources no longer free, the process has become to amass savings by tax incentives and high incomes into capital-intensive technologies (as in the use of depletion allowances to encourage oil exploration). The laws and authority distributions to achieve this result have been accumulated over the past century into a highly articulated set of rules providing incentives to research, borrowing, saving, technical development, stabilizing prices, capital aggregation, and large-scale investment. These practices are so woven into the economic and social fabric of the nation that they would be extremely difficult to unravel, even if that were known to be a public policy choice.

The policy question we are asking, then, is not whether this intricate social policy should be unraveled and restructured but whether it should tend to more or less capital intensification. The question involves the

[2]For more details, see Stahrl Edmunds and John Letey, *Environmental Administration* (New York: McGraw-Hill, 1973), chs. 3 and 4.

TABLE 1-1. Policy Analysis of Thirteen Major Issues
Confronting the United States

Policy issue	Extremes of choice spectrum	Consequences of choice
1. Monetary-fiscal	Balance	Equilibrium
	Unbalanced (expansion)	Inflation
2. Income distribution	Normal	Equitable
	Skewed	Rich–poor extremes
3. Capital distribution	Open markets	Less concentrated
	Institutionally channeled	More concentrated
4. Competitive distribution	Open	Smaller units
	Oligopolistic	Larger business
5. Price policy	Free	Competitive, unstable
	Administered	Profit maximized, stable
	Rationing	Welfare maximized, stable
6. Living standards	Internalize cost	More amenities, less government
	Externalize cost	Less amenities, more government
7. Employment	Labor intensive	Service-oriented economy
	Labor extensive	Capital-intensive economy
8. Educational distribution	Wide	Adaptable individuals
	Narrow	Specialized individuals
9. Technological distribution	Wide	Open competition
	Narrow	Competition of the few
10. Barriers to entry	Lowered	Equitable incomes
	Raised	Skewed incomes
11. Voting	Wide issue	Direct democracy
	Narrow issue	Oligarchy
12. Internal order	Participative	Restive conflict resolution
	Coercive	Policing order
13. International order	Participative	Political flux
	Coercive	Military control

possible trade-offs between capital and people: capital versus labor-intensive, technologically defined jobs versus individually defined jobs, high investment versus underemployment, high growth versus limits to growth, high pollution versus low pollution, and so on.

Let us now consider each of the thirteen policy issues.

1. MONETARY AND FISCAL MANAGEMENT: BALANCED VS. UNBALANCED

The federal government manages the economy with two very gross means to try to balance growth, stability, and equity—namely monetary policy and fiscal policy. They may be used separately or together, either one being balanced or expansionist. Used separately they may become counterproductive to each other.

Monetary policy is a determination of the amount of money that shall flow into the economy relative to goods. The principal means for increasing such money flows is by increasing borrowing, particularly government borrowing, which the government must do when its expenditures exceed its tax revenues. Fiscal policy is concerned with the management of the federal budget, how much and which tax revenues to collect relative to how much and which expenditures.

There are four main policy options to government decision makers: (1) A neutral or free-market policy, of balancing the fiscal budget and constraining the money supply to the rate of change in goods, tends to leave the economy in equilibrium and let change take place by internal reallocation of resources in the private economy. This option is seldom used, because adjustment may come slowly and be accompanied by underemployment. (2) An expansionist monetary-fiscal policy increases the money supply by deficit spending (overspending), which tends to increase employment and inflation. This policy is commonly used to stimulate growth. (3) A restrained expansion policy seeks to tighten the money supply and simultaneously expands the deficit (a counterproductive policy) to reduce private spending while increasing public spending for welfare purposes. This is a common policy of the past three decades and has led to present inflation rates, because the government deficit gets built into the future money supply which is unleashed eventually. (4) A tight fiscal policy (balanced budget) with an expansionist monetary policy was the principal policy prior to 1930 but has been unused since, because of its cyclical effects (expansion and contraction in government is induced simultaneously with business).

Economic changes must come. The only question is, how shall they come? The basic policy choice in the United States has been between gradual economic adjustment (with underemployment) or inflation. The United States has historically been inflation-prone, but inflation eventually leads to a depression and unemployment, too. That day is deferred, however, perhaps for years, which is why politicians prefer it, for they can get reelected in the meantime. Hence, the trade-off really comes down to short-term versus long-term consequences, incremental versus catastrophic economic adjustment.

---

2. INCOME DISTRIBUTION: NORMAL VS. SKEWED

Government policy toward income distribution is influenced by the tax structure and the type of transfer payments (income shifted from one group to another) it makes among citizens. This policy may favor either a normal (narrow-range) distribution of income or a distribution skewed in favor of higher incomes (and savings).

An entirely equal distribution of income to everyone is an unlikely possibility, both historically (except in primitive subsistence economies) and practically, because of the differing risks and effort assumed by individuals. Nevertheless, it is possible to confine these differences into a distribution of narrow range, so that the differences between high and low incomes are small. This policy would result in equitable income distribution; that is, distributed relatively equally in proportion to risk and effort.

A policy option that encourages high savings rates among individuals and institutions by using tax incentives to induce investment will produce income and wealth skewed in favor of high-income groups. The skewing of income distribution to the high side has the consequence of increasing the income range and the number of both high- and low-income families. The government may seek to offset this adverse effect of inducing low incomes by transfer payments and public welfare programs to help the poverty groups. This form of tax-expenditure policy is counterproductive, in the sense of reducing taxes on high incomes to produce savings at the same time that it uses tax revenue to support low incomes, thus putting a double drain on the Treasury (or forcing the government to borrow).

The first policy choice of narrow-range normal distribution avoids this tortuous problem of trying to manage both ends of a skewed income distribution scale (that is, keeping the savings and welfare transfers in balance and at a steady rate). Welfare equity and stable savings are built into the first policy, but the savings may be at a lower rate. Thus, capital investment and economic growth would be at lower rates.

The trade-off between these two policy extremes is then the choice between an equity-equilibrium state of the economy or higher expansion rates. Historically, the choice has been toward high expansion rates, and this is favored by tax incentives, loopholes, and tax-avoidance means. Indeed, corporate business as a legal form (in contrast to pro-

prietor or partnership forms) may be viewed as a means of institutionalizing tax avoidance, because it avoids the higher end of the personal
income tax rate and avoids a portion of death taxes (because the corporation does not terminate). Other forms of tax avoidance are the deductions for interest expense, depreciation, rapid amortization, depletion,
and research and development. These legal authorizations make it possible for corporations to hold wealth in large amounts over long periods
of time, and for individuals to increase their savings and reduce their
tax liability, to the point where some people with extremely high incomes pay no taxes at all.

Perhaps this trade-off between the stability versus growth effects of
income distribution would be decided differently by members of the
public (if they understood it) than by elected representatives. Politically, the expedient choice is toward growth and higher income concen-
trations, for two reasons: (1) it stimulates expansion and employment,
which favors an officeholder's reelection, and (2) the concentrated
wealth makes it easier to raise campaign money. Again, we have a
short- versus a long-run choice. The short-run political climate favors
skewed incomes; the long-run public interest may favor narrow-range
normal income distributions. But tax policy and its effects have become
such a tangled skein that the public has difficulty being presented with,
or influencing, the basic choices.

---

3. CAPITAL DISTRIBUTION: OPEN MARKET VS. INSTITUTIONALLY CHANNELED

Capital distribution is determined by (1) the government's policy on
income distribution and (2) the marginal productivity of capital in the
private economy. On the first point, once income distribution and savings come into the hands of high-income individuals and corporations,
reinvestment of their funds results in further aggregation of capital and
wealth for them. As to the marginal productivity of capital, the private
economy will tend to choose investments that have the highest rate of
return until the last added capital investment in one use is marginally
equal to another. The private economy works fairly efficiently to allocate capital to its most productive uses, under conditions of open competition.

Competition for capital funds is open when all users have equal access
in a free capital market to bid for money and obtain it based upon paying
the highest money rate of interest for it. This open competition for funds
may be impeded or prevented by channeling funds within institutions so

they are never offered in the capital markets. Such an end can be achieved by internalizing capital flows within large institutions, in which the institutions exercise their own reinvestment options without making the capital available in the market. These internal capital flows of large corporations have become large enough to dominate the capital allocation process. For example, the retained earnings and depreciation allowances of corporations, which they use themselves without making them available to others for higher bid in the capital markets, make up two-thirds of all savings.

The basic trade-off, then, is, where shall the capital allocation decisions be made—in smaller economic units or in larger businesses? The smaller the economic units, the more likely they are to respond to individual work interest (especially if the individuals make the capital decisions for themselves). The larger the economic units, the more capital-intensive the investment is likely to be to maximize profit and growth. Again, the political process favors the expansionist choice, because of its short-run benefits to employment and reelection.

---

4. COMPETITIVE DISTRIBUTION:
OPEN VS. OLIGOPOLISTIC

The competition among firms may range from fairly open to fairly closed. The economic ideal of pure competition has seldom been achieved, the closest perhaps being the English textile industry of the fifteenth and sixteenth centuries from which Adam Smith drew his hypothesis. To have pure competition requires (1) infinite divisibility of capital equipment, (2) equal access to capital, and (3) no barriers to entry. Capital equipment is not infinitely divisible because complex technology dictates minimum economic sizes of capital equipment, which may often be quite large. Capital is not equally accessible to all, once the government has decided to skew income distributions toward high incomes and savings and to internalize capital flows within large institutions. Size and capital access are themselves barriers to entry, but other barriers may be erected by business through price competition or limiting access to technology, which in the end closes competition to all but a few. This condition, competition among the few, is called *oligopoly* and it is prevalent in today's American economy.

The policy choice, then, is competition among the many versus competition among the few. On the symbolic level, it has been U.S. government policy to encourage competition among the many, and this is the basis for the antitrust laws. But though they have been a century in operation, the antitrust laws have not been effective in increasing competition among the many; on the contrary, oligopolistic competition among the few has become more and more prevalent. The antitrust laws cannot be made effective unless policy choices are made (1) to equalize income distributions, and (2) to deinstitutionalize internal capital flows. But, for reasons of the politics of economic expansion, these choices have already been made, in favor of high incomes and institutionally channeled investment.

Thus, we see again how interlinked these decisions are: the decisions about income and capital distribution have dictated the competitive form of the economy, and legislative intent (such as antitrust laws) can no longer change that oligopolistic form. On the realistic level, therefore, the policy choice of the United States has been to favor competition among the few, as an instrument for realizing the politics of economic expansionism.

---

5. PRICE POLICY: FREE VS. ADMINISTERED VS. RATIONING

The policy on price is determined by the policy on competition, which in turn depends on the policy on income and capital distribution. Symbolically, the United States stands for free-market prices, but realistically the policy choices have been for administered prices. Administered prices are implicit in (1) oligopolistic competition among the few, and the few follow a price leader to maximize their mutual interests; (2) government subsidies and floors under commodity pricing; (3) government laws limiting price competition, such as the Robinson-Patman act; and (4) government contracts that negotiate (administer) pricing.

During periods of high inflation, administered pricing fails to keep the economy in adjustment, because large oligopolistic corporations have the power to raise their prices as fast or faster than costs, and certainly faster than worker incomes. This means that consumer buying power and living standards fall in inflationary periods. Public pressure causes the government to intervene and institute price controls or rationing. Again, these are counterproductive measures because, having once given business noncompetitive pricing authorizations (through income distribution and capital preferences), the government now seeks to restrict the use of these economic decisions by business. The effect is to limit the price-profit-capital flows in the business corporations, slow the economy, increase unemployment, and limit the capital available to increase supplies. The consequence is simultaneous inflation and stagnation ("stagflation"), which are the logical outcomes of the two counterproductive policies. This has recently been the price policy decision in the United States.

6. LIVING STANDARDS: MORE OR LESS AMENITIES VS. MORE OR LESS GOVERNMENT

Living standards are adversely affected by the inflation-stagnation phenomenon, because inflation limits buying power as prices rise faster than incomes, and stagnation increases unemployment so many former employees are without work or income. Government officials and politicians are then forced, by the threat of disorder and diminished prospects for their reelection, as well as humanitarian considerations, to support and subsidize the unemployed, through unemployment compensation, welfare, or food subsidy. These become large government costs and increase the size, scope, and authority of government. So now what we observe is former business costs (for employed labor) becoming a social cost (for government subsidy of unemployed labor).

This shift of costs from private enterprise to the public purse is called the *externalization* of costs. That is to say, unemployed labor costs are treated as external to business. The only labor costs business assumes are the short-term costs of labor directly applicable to their current output. This is an accounting convention, but this short-term accounting for labor-input costs enables business to maximize profits in the short run. Then all other labor costs are treated as external, social costs. This means government must assume the social costs, or leave people destitute. The failure of business to internalize total labor costs (employed and unemployed) has been a significant force in increasing the size of government to handle welfare problems.

Business has also tended to treat environmental costs as external or outside its short-term accounting costs. The act of dumping of industrial effluents and wastes into rivers, for example, presumes that water is a free resource. However, the public then has to treat the water to make it usable downstream, and this treatment represents a social, or governmental, cost to the public. The assumption of social costs by government, which properly belong to the internal costs of business, is a subsidy to business.

The inequity of this practice has led to environmental legislation that seeks to force business to internalize these costs by investing in equipment to clean up its own pollution. Some progress has been made to internalize environmental costs, but for the most part they still lie outside the business costing practice. Indeed, inflation, stagnation, and the energy crisis have provided businessmen with rationalizations for avoiding internalizing the costs, for some time to come.

The avoidance of these external, social costs by business has three effects: (1) It throws the burden of economic adjustment, such as unemployment, on the individual rather than on the business institution. (2) It increases the size of government expenditures to help absorb some of these social costs. (3) It reduces the living standards and amenities of life for the individual to the extent that government cannot (or does not) absorb the social costs. For example, the heaviest share of the burden of unemployment and pollution is still thrown upon individuals, despite the government's attempt to ameliorate the problems.

The ultimate policy question on this issue is, who shall bear the long-term costs of maintaining living standards? Or, as a trade-off, the issue is, does institutional maintenance take precedence over individual maintenance (living standards)? The policy choice in the United States has been to prefer institutional maintenance as a concomitant of economic expansionism.

---

7. EMPLOYMENT: SERVICE-ORIENTED VS. CAPITAL-INTENSIVE ECONOMY

A service-oriented economy uses labor intensively to provide goods and services to consumers, while a capital-intensive economy substitutes capital (productive equipment) for labor, thus reducing employment opportunities until a new expansion occurs.

As I stated above, treating labor as a direct, short-term cost forces the external and social costs of unemployment first upon the individual and then upon the government as an ameliorator. But there is another policy issue involved that is seldom raised—namely, what should be the balance or trade-off between capital intensification and labor intensification?

Hypothetically, at least, government incentives toward capital investment could be decreased and incentives for labor intensification could be increased. For example, rapid amortization (pay-back) of capital equipment could be eliminated, and rapid amortization of labor costs for employment maintenance in recession could be established. Both measures are forms of subsidy by government to business, but the second encounters more semantic difficulties in our psychological situation-set toward capital intensification. Rapid amortization of capital equipment sounds like we are buying future economic expansion, but this may or may not be true, for it may be sheer inflation of capital-goods prices or waste on an unsuccessful project. In contrast, a partial tax credit to business for keeping on labor that might otherwise be unemployed sounds like make-work, or money down the drain. In fact, the unemployed labor cost is going to be borne someplace anyway, so government might as well get as large a business contribution to it as possible.

The trade-off between capital-intensive versus labor-intensive uses of funds in the United States is biased in favor of capital intensification, owing to our expansionist syndrome. This is not as true in less developed countries, however, which are less specialized and have more diverse means of adaptability and stability. There public works may favor labor-intensive projects, and business bears higher social security or unemployment taxes as a means of reducing the unemployment burdens upon individuals. In South America, for example, road building is frequently done by hand rather than by machine, with the government employing the jobless from social security–type taxes.

---

8. EDUCATIONAL DISTRIBUTION: WIDE VS. NARROW

Educational opportunities in the United States have generally been widely distributed to most of the population through the land grants and public support for school systems. Until recently, education through the college level was available at low cost to most white males with ability. However, costs of all education have been rising, particularly at college levels, and part of these costs are being passed on to students, a move that in the future will narrow education opportunities somewhat.

Nevertheless, the distribution of educational opportunities has been narrow and limited as far as ethnic minorities and women are concerned and they have been narrow in academic range. Historically, ethnic minorities have been heavily discriminated against in educational opportunities, and recent attempts to rectify these inequalities have only been partial. Many public school districts are still semisegregated, with lower educational standards, and at the college level, educational opportunity is still limited by financial costs and inadequate financial aid.

The education of women has been historically limited as to level and type, with fewer women going on to higher education and being restricted academically mainly to the humanities and household arts. Although in recent years educational opportunity has been opening for women in all the academic disciplines, females are still underrepresented in the sciences, engineering, and the professions.

For all citizens, including white males, education has been of a somewhat narrow disciplinary scope—that is, relevant to the disciplinary research interests of the faculty rather than relevant to the needs of the students or society. Much of faculty research is necessarily highly specialized in order to be publishable, and college students tend to receive a highly specialized education that may or may not have use in the real world. Faculties will argue that this disciplinary training is the means by which knowledge advances, but even granting this argument, this does not require that all or even most education has to be highly specialized by discipline. It only means that those who want to be highly specialized should receive a disciplinary education, and this is surely a small portion of the student or working population. The crisis in higher education in the past decade has been mainly that too much specialized education—education not immediately relevant to society—was offered to too wide a segment of the population. Therefore, the seemingly wide educational opportunities have, in fact, been narrower than superficial enrollment numbers would show, in terms of the absence of minorities, women, or useful learning to the general population.

The major issue in education, then, has been: how research oriented or how useful should education be, and who shall decide? The trade-off is between the advancement of knowledge and the adaptability of knowledge to individual lives. Until recently, at least, educational policy has favored research and the advancement of knowledge, at least partly because it furthers technology, capital intensification, and expansionism in the economy. Most of the large research funds from the federal government have been for science and engineering to further military, space, and industrial development. The other crisis in education, besides its relevance to students, has been the disillusionment with research and the fading of research funds, particularly for the sciences. The decreasing returns from research expenditures, in terms of military or economic potential, caused national and state legislatures to cut research appropriations. While this has slowed the research levels in education, it has not yet significantly redirected education to the interests of individuals—that is, students.

---

9. TECHNOLOGICAL DISTRIBUTION: WIDE VS. NARROW

The distribution of technology has been much narrower than that of education. Much of the basic research of educational institutions goes into the public domain and is available to all. However, the research must be applied to become useful to decision makers in government or business. Applied research is put to use in new products, more efficient productive equipment, or more destructive military weapons. These results from applied research then are put into use by capital investment. Hence, applied research and development is a key link in providing new innovations for the capital-intensification process, which is intended to produce expansion in the economy (or military).

The funds for applied research are largely in the hands of the federal government and the large corporations. That is, research funds are institutionally channeled in the same manner as capital-investment funds. This provides for efficient coupling of the research and capital allocation decisions, but it also precludes open competition or availability of ideas. Technology is distributed, then, in the same oligopolistic pattern as are capital and competition.

The policy issue, then, is: to what extent should applied research funds and results be available to the few or the many? The trade-off is between proprietary research directed toward early (short-term) investment or diffused research directed toward eventual (long-term) opportunities for many. Economic expansionism favors the former, and so proprietary research for economic development has been the basic policy choice in the United States.

---

10. BARRIERS TO ENTRY: EQUITABLE VS. SKEWED INCOMES

Barriers to entry—by size of investment, patents, or proprietary technology—have the effect of keeping out new competition, maintaining existing institutions, and preserving the channeling of funds within existing institutions. Barriers are an important strategy for institutionalizing capital intensification and economic expansionism. The means for barring entry are many. Some have been discussed, such as preferential income distribution, concentration of capital, oligopolistic industrial organization, administered price policies, and restricted technological distribution. Other strategies are advertising, brand identification, horizontal market coverage (that is, number of outlets), planned product cycle of development and obsolescence (whether of computers or clothing fashions), territorial distribution control, trademarks, patents, mergers, and buying out of competitors. For example, advertised brand names for aspirin make it costly and difficult for small firms to sell the same thing under the general name of salicylic acid.

The antitrust laws and prosecutions attack some of the more overt of these barriers—that is, those that can be proven with evidence, such as discriminatory price cutting, collusion, horizontal market power, and mergers that diminish competition. But these attack the periphery of the problem and, at most, have been staying actions against further monopoly power. Once the income-capital distribution choices have been made to favor large capital aggregations for investment and expansion, most of the rest of the barriers to entry become normal business practice—for example, the planned product cycle of development and obsolescence. These barriers are not prosecutable, nor could they be made so without stopping the expansion process.

The policy issue is whether barriers to entry should be raised or lowered. Business managers of large corporations will incrementally raise the barriers as part of their accepted decision process. Lowering barriers takes specific and overt government intervention, which is difficult without changing many of the ground rules of the business operation. Barriers to entry have not become an active policy issue, nor does it show signs of surfacing. However, the trade-off is between increasing institutionalization in the hope of intensifying expansionism, or the diffusion of economic opportunity and flexibility by placing more self-determination back in the hands of individuals or small units.

---

11. VOTING: DIRECT DEMOCRACY VS. OLIGARCHY

We have noted that barriers to entry has not surfaced as a policy issue in the United States. The same is also true of income, capital, competitive distribution, price policy, and technological distribution—they have not surfaced as policy issues because the public arena is not organized to bring them out for public debate. These issues are intricately intertwined with each other and with existing laws, some quite historic, with the weight of precedence from another era behind them. The fact that eras have changed and new generations have new needs is not easily reflected in the political process. The U.S. Congress has specialized into committees, dominated by seniority (past eras), to deal with the specialized pieces of new legislation for fine-tuning the existing political-economic process. The result is the continual suboptimization of goals, largely for the maintenance or strengthening of present institutions. Congress is not organized to look at human needs systematically, nor does it have the leadership structure to do so. Moreover, the institutional lobbies are ever present to oppose, with voice and funds, such systematic revision.

The President is in a slightly better position to recommend systematic changes in legislation, but he faces at least three constraints: (1) His influence over Congress is modest, especially when it is dominated by the opposite party, and he must continually trade (from his viewpoint) less-priority legislation for higher-priority legislation, with the result that he is also forced to suboptimize. (2) His party leadership depends on keeping together a coalition, which means he can deviate from the support of only a few of his large supporters for part of the time, and this also forces a piecemeal, suboptimization of policy. (3) He must accommodate campaign backers for his reelection.

Because this political structure has so many accommodations, the public can seldom vote or express itself on a single policy issue, unless it is a crisis such as war or large unemployment. The issues are obscure in the elections; the vote can only express preference for a point of view or a man. It is said, somewhat disparagingly of voters, that they merely "vote their pocketbook" or for charismatic figures, but in fact they do not have a chance to vote for anything else. The issue basis in American elections is exceedingly narrow.

What would happen if people could vote independently for themselves on measures designed to raise and implement the ten issues I have already discussed? Would they vote for inflationary monetary-fiscal policies, having experienced galloping price inflation? Would they vote for continuance of tax-avoidance loopholes, which skew income and capital distribution to the wealthy and to large corporations? Would they vote for open competition or closed competition? free prices or administered prices? more government or less government? applied technology in the private or public domain? raising or lowering of barriers to entry? These issues do not emerge because the prospect of direct democracy is frightening to an institutionally stabilized world. Belief in democracy is nominal among oligarchies, and the means of restricting democracy is by obscuring the issues and having narrowly similar choices before the public.

The policy issue, then, is whether voting should widely reflect public choices on key issues after the manner of direct democracy, or reflect obscure attitudinal postures of oligarchy. The trade-off is between turbulent adaptability to individual needs or stabilized alienation. The policy choice of the United States has been for political stability. But alienation is itself a destabilizing force (as we will see in Chapter 2), and the tension between stability and alienation is difficult to maintain. Other civilizations have not been able to maintain the uneasy tension (as we will see in the chapters on Roman, Greek, and medieval replays).

The trouble is that stability requires authority intensification along with capital intensification. Authority and use of force to preserve existing social institutions need to increase incrementally to contain the accumulating alienation, until the disaffections spiral out of control into disorder. Again, we are back to short- versus long-run effects. In the short run, political stability by institutional control is less trying than wide-issue democratic change; in the long run, however, it is more violent in disorders.

Politicians live in the very short run, and we as citizens must choose whether we are willing to endure the tumult of change in our time or let alienation and disorder accumulate for our children's generation.

12. INTERNAL ORDER: PARTICIPATIVE VS. COERCIVE

The first appearances of disorder—petitions, apathy, demonstrations, strikes, riots, crime—present the society with two major approaches to deal with the conflicts: coercion by force or direct confrontation of the parties to try to resolve the conflict by participative negotiation. Coercion by force is the simplest short-term solution. Confrontation, negotiation, and participative decision making are stressful and time consuming. Still, most people prefer a conciliatory approach if it appears workable. Business executives, especially, have the instinct and skill to confront problems directly; however, the issues they are apt to confront are narrowly defined among the goals of their institution.

Social issues are more diversely fraught and more time consuming, and patient negotiation is not a notable American trait. Having won the Korean War, the United States came close to losing the peace over impatience in negotiations. We have negotiated somewhat more patiently to extricate ourselves from South Vietnam and in the Middle East, owing more to obdurate opponents than to our own wishes. The American West is perhaps still too much with us, where horse trades (and car trades) take only a few minutes and a deal is a deal. This is an efficient business procedure when parties agree but potentially dangerous when parties widely disagree.

In the 1960s, blacks and whites differed widely over civil rights, and college students and the public differed over institutional responsiveness and property rights. A certain amount of confrontation was tolerated while there seemed early hope of settlement. But when settlements were not easily reached, impatience led to violence, military force, and shootings. The killing of citizens by military force is a ghastly act not easily reconciled with democracy, because it is a confession of the inability of due process and participative negotiation to work under stress. The use of coercive force in these circumstances is a signal that similar stress will be dealt with by similar force. Actually, the force would have to escalate, for civil rights and student disagreements are minor issues with relatively few participants compared to what would happen if there were accumulated alienation over the twelve policy choices we have been discussing. Either the force must escalate or the negotiation machinery must improve, as more and more profound disaffections in our society come into conflict.

The mechanisms for participative negotiation are few in American society. The courts settle disputes of small groups under a code of law. Labor negotiators deal with labor disputes but not with civil rights or student disaffections. Corporate executives deal with business disputes, but these are usually contractual, where parties have similar perceptions of ground rules and business goals. That is nearly the whole participative apparatus for conflict resolution. Congress and the President do not negotiate conflicts, but they make the rules and, indeed, become part of the problem by ruling in favor of one side of a dispute (as for business over environmentalists or vice-versa). We might try public arbitrators like Solon and Cleisthenes as the Greeks did. We might try a Constitutional Convention as our forefathers did. We might reward negotiating administrators with patience instead of firing them. But the improvement of our internal peacekeeping machinery is scarcely perceived as a need, much less a public issue. And *that* is the forbidding part about the American future, for we take it for granted that coercive force will be applied when needed to settle disputes.

The (nonexistent) policy issue, then, is whether conflicts involving internal order shall be settled more by strengthening participative negotiations or more by coercive force. The trade-off is the amount and cost of coercive force that is needed to settle disputes quickly versus the amount of human liberty that is lost by failing to negotiate conflicting needs. This is another short-term versus long-term choice. Force is quicker in the short run, but its alienation and disaffection can cause greater violence in the long run.

---

13. INTERNATIONAL ORDER: POLITICAL FLUX VS. MILITARY CONTROL

When conflicts appear in the international scene, we can respond similarly by coercive force or participative negotiation. The human and economic cost of military force can be very high over minor disputes, as we learned from its use in Vietnam. The military cost of policing the world is beyond even the U.S. capability. Thus, we rely on treaties and alliances, in part, to maintain a combined military and negotiating posture vis-à-vis adversary nations such as Russia, China, or Cuba.

However, the predilection of the United States has been and is toward bilateral negotiation, between two parties. We try to make quick deals to settle two-party disputes. But in doing so we undermine our alliances and treaties, which depend upon multilateral consultation and negotiation, and we appear to our allies to be high-handed and self-interested by making side agreements on a bilateral basis without consulting them.

One reason why multilateral participative negotiation is difficult in international conflicts is that, here too, the negotiation and arbitration machinery is very weak. The League of Nations, the World Court, the United Nations, and NATO have successively tried to assume some negotiative role, but their influence in peacekeeping has been short lived. The other major mode of settlement is through diplomacy.

In foreign affairs, the United States is much given to personal diplomacy, despite its dubious record. Personal diplomacy is expedient. It fits into the economic and political expansionism of America, to keep things moving. The business analogy is that expansionism is moved by a big man making decisions, and this big-man concept of expansionism carries over to foreign affairs. The difficulty with this analogy is that the big man in business is the only sovereign authority in the corporate arena. In the international arena, there are many sovereign authorities, who are very diverse in view and who greatly resent one- or two-sided decisions.

Another difficulty in international order is that the United States tends to deal with other nations by "sides" or adversary proceedings. Adversary proceedings are not consistent with a systematic view of the American sociopolitical economy. As an operating system, the American economy includes all those who play a part, who have an interest, in the production-exchange-consumption process—all its producers, consumers, participants, and interest parties everywhere. Thus, the American economy has no territorial bounds. The Arab oil supplier is just as much a part of the U.S. energy system as is the Louisiana supplier. Venezuelan iron is as much a link in the economic process as is Minnesota iron.

The fact that the social system of the United States is larger than its decision-making (political) jurisdiction causes real problems, for some participants—say foreign oil producers—have no voice in a political process that affects them. Moreover, there is no arbitration apparatus to negotiate conflicts that they have with us (except by building commodity cartels, like the Arab oil nations in OPEC, which give them bargaining power). The only avenue for settlement, other than commodity cartels, which the United States opposes, is by adversary proceedings in bilateral discussions. But bilateral settlement presents foreign participants in our system with conflicts among other countries who have not been consulted. The difficulty is that the decision-making apparatus is not as big as the system.

The policy issue, then, is whether the United States should expand its concept of national sovereignty and participative negotiation to include the entire American system with all its foreign interactions, or whether to deal nationalistically with others by adversary bilateral proceedings backed by coercive force. The trade-off is between tumultuous international bargaining and prompt settlements through the balance of power (political, economic, and military). The U.S. policy during the past fifty years has been basically to seek settlements through the balance of economic and military power. Again, this is a short-term choice predicated on the expedience of expansionism.

THE PRESENT POLICIES
OF THE UNITED STATES

The American pattern or value set of policy choices on these thirteen major issues is summarized in Table 1–2. As we shall see, the consequences of this set of policy choices, shown in the right column, is almost identical with the contemporary problems causing disorder that I shall discuss in Chapter 2. To state it as directly as possible, alienation in the United States is traceable to a systematic set of policy choices aimed at expansionism. This expansionism is achieved institutionally by capital intensification and the centralizing of authority. The consequence is that individuals are left with diminished means and latitude for their own self-development, as they are left without resources to deal with their underemployment or self-employment.

TABLE 1-2. The American Policy Choice on Thirteen Major Issues

Policy issue	The American choice tendency	Consequences of choice
1. Monetary-fiscal	Unbalanced (expansion)	Inflation
2. Income distribution	Skewed	Rich–poor extremes
3. Capital distribution	Institutionally channeled	Capital concentration
4. Competitive distribution	Oligopolistic	Large business oligopoly
5. Price policy	Administered	Profit maximized, stable
6. Living standards	Externalize costs	Less amenities, more government
7. Employment	Labor extensive	Unemployment, capital-intensive economy
8. Educational distribution	Semiwide	Semispecialized individuals
9. Technological distribution	Narrow	Oligopoly
10. Barriers to entry	Raised	Skewed (concentrated) incomes
11. Voting	Narrow issue	Oligarchic republic
12. Internal order	Semiparticipative	Limited conflict resolution
13. International order	Semicoercive	Use of economic-military power in conflict resolution

Probably the United States did not make this set of policy choices consciously and deliberately. The United States happened by circumstance—the circumstance of abundant resources—upon a mode of survival, and that mode of survival was economic expansion through capital-intensive development. Custom, law, habit, attitude, and social drill have all accumulated into a logically consistent set of expansionist policies, whose great merit is that they have worked to expand the economic base of society but whose great demerit is that they have institutionalized the economic base to the point of denying some individuals their human potential, by leaving them underemployed, on welfare, or without access to capital for self-employment, as we shall see in Chapter 2.

The American set of policy choices has, then, become adverse to many individuals, especially to the one-fifth of the economy underemployed or on welfare. The question is whether these adverse policy choices shall run their course to their logical consequences, as in other societies, or whether systematic change in the policy sets is socially feasible. The remaining chapters will explore the alternatives involved in relentless evolution versus managed change.

If there is hope for systematic revision in the U.S. policy set, we need to choose consciously where change in society can most effectively occur. The more decisions and resources can be decentralized to smaller social groups, the more likely that individuals can influence decisions and adapt economic activity to their needs. That is, individuals need latitude (authority and resources) for adaptive change. If they do not have latitude, change can occur only by institutional (government and corporate) decision makers.

Institutions have limited capability for adaptation, because their goals emphasize institutional maintenance and survival rather than human individuation, the realizing of each individual's human potential and maturity. As a result, institutions tend to insulate themselves against change to ensure their own continuance. Business institutions, for example, avoid competition and free-market prices. Governments avoid direct democracy and wide issue voting.

By insulating themselves against change, institutions throw the whole burden of change upon individuals without the resources or authority to cope with it. This is the cause of frustration, disorder, alienation, and despair.

There are three major places where adaptation can be built into the society: (1) into the economy by competition and free prices, (2) into the political process by voice and vote on specific issues, and (3) into the individual by providing him or her with authority and resources for response to experience.

The U.S. set of policy choices shows that the economy is largely foreclosed from change in the areas of pricing, competition, capital allocation, structure of income distribution, and technology access. That means the major avenue left open for economic change is through unemployment, and that burden falls on the individual.

The principal process by which government ameliorates the unemployment burden of individuals is by more expansionism through inflation, which again adversely affects us all at a later date. Moreover, the government is largely foreclosed from change in these thirteen basic policies; it changes mainly in personnel or in increasing or lessening expansionism at any point in time. Issues do not surface as specific policy choices, because there is little voting opportunity on specific policies, and because the apparatus for participative conflict resolution is very limited.

The economic and political avenues for social change are limited by institutional maintenance and self-protection. With the economic and government avenues substantially closed to change, adaptation is thrown almost wholly on the third alternative—individuals. Individuals, however, must try to cope with rapid change without adequate means to respond—this is the dilemma of American society. To the extent there is hope in finding our way out of the dilemma, it lies in looking at the pattern of policy choices to see where authority can be dispersed to facilitate adaptation.

One way to examine the alternative sets of U.S. policies is to look first at contemporary problems of order and disorder, then at past societies to see what policy choices they made and where they led. Then perhaps we can learn from experience, avoid mistakes that have already been made, and find some new adaptive set of policies for ourselves.

Antibusing rally. (Photo by Arthur Grace/Stock, Boston.)

Chapter Two

THE TENDENCIES
TOWARD DISORDER

In the previous chapter we saw how authority, as expressed through decisions, is used in the United States. Now let us examine the relationship of authority to allegiance—that is, order versus disorder.

The distribution of authority, functions, allegiances, and tasks within the social process to respond to individual needs is the means by which a society organizes itself. If they are flexibly distributed and are responsive to changing individual needs over time, the society tends to be orderly and harmonious. If they are not, the society tends toward disorder and conflict; that is, deprived segments of society attempt to regroup authorities into a more responsive pattern, as happened in the American and and French revolutions.

One test of the viability of a society, then, is whether its social outputs—that is, services that fill individual needs—are tending to produce order or disorder. This is a test we can apply to contemporary affairs and ask ourselves whether American (and Western) civilization are tending toward order or disorder. We can then compare, on a scale of order to disorder, our pattern of social outputs with those of past societies to see what the likely outcome may be. We may also then devise alternative scenarios as to what changes in authority distributions need to occur, if we wish to change an expected outcome. In this way, we will have constructed a map of social evaluations, past, present, and future, to see whether we are indeed headed where we want to go.

Let us now consider the contemporary tendencies toward order and disorder, in the United States, the institutional and systematic character of the disorders, and the general evolution of American society.

TENDENCIES TOWARD ORDER

The orderly characteristics of the United States are most readily apparent in the industrial economy and in the social organizations of the upper income groups. There are seven social outputs that are responsive to the needs of individuals in these groups: economic growth, rising living standards, orderly capital investment, security through property rights, technological progress, educational attainment, and decision authority over their own individual economic progress. We will examine each of these social outputs and see how they relate to the needs of individuals in this interest group.

The upper-income interest group consists of a coalition of large property owners, professional managers, and members of the professional technostructure (engineers, scientists, economists, programmers, marketeers, financiers, and so on) that runs the industrial economy. This whole interest group comprises a large decision-making complex that is able to function in unison through carefully articulated laws, rights, regulations, customs, and practices. The practices are management methods. The methodology generally entails intensive capital investment in technological innovations to achieve economic growth for the social economy at large and for this interest group in particular.

Economic growth as a social output is measurable by productivity and the Gross National Product of society. Economic growth is distributed as income to the upper classes in the form of rents, profits, return on investment, salary incentives, and bonuses. These forms of compensation maintain this interest group at the high upper end of the income distribution.

Rising living standards are an implicit benefit to the upper classes as a result of their preferential income distribution. These rising living standards are shared, to an extent, through bargaining arrangements or legislation with the larger society in the form of union wage contracts, cost-of-living and productivity increases to nonunion workers (to keep them nonunion), and taxation that redistributes income to the poor and the elderly. To the extent that economic growth is partially shared, even through the income distribution is highly skewed in favor of the decision-making classes, social order is maintained by giving enough social output to the lower income classes to satisfy their expectations.

The maintenance of *orderly capital markets* is the principal means for economic growth. These intermediary financial institutions funnel savings from all classes into new plants, new producing machinery, new technologies, and new products. As long as this capital flow is maintained, the upper-class decision group has the functional means to channel funds into uses for its primary benefit. Orderly capital flow is, then, a social output that denotes stability in the society.

Property rights are one means of maintaining an orderly capital flow, as well as a means of maintaining preferred income treatment. Property rights (through legislation) grant to the owner a contractual privilege to use capital according to his or her own decision and to retain the earnings from that capital. Protection of property rights is, therefore, an essential requirement for the upper classes to maintain their authority and their security. This is why the threat to property, as in the race riots and college-student dissent of the 1960s, was so gravely regarded by conservative (upper-class) groups. "Law and order" is the social output that protects property rights and preferential incomes, and thus law and order was a critical, emotional issue of that time.

Technological progress is a necessary condition to capital investment and economic growth because there must be a flow of new innovations to achieve productivity gains. For this reason, research and technology are highly subsidized by public funds for the benefit of the high-income groups. One form of subsidy is the use of tax revenues directly for contracts and grants to pay private and public institutions to do research. Other subsidization is achieved indirectly by tax-avoidance incentives, such as depreciation allowances to increase institutional cash flows, and the capitalization, or direct expensing, of research costs to reduce taxable income. The subsidization of a high level of technological expenditures is a social output that is indicative of order in an industrial society.

Educational attainment is the means by which technological progress is made possible (in addition to subsidy). The professional and managerial classes have higher levels of educational attainment than do members of the general population, and such technical knowledge provides the passport of entry into the upper middle classes. College and professional educations give such people the technical skills to make the industrial society work. These educations also serve to socialize them into accepting the assumptions, customs, and practices of the social system of which they have chosen to become a part. The educational passport to the upper middle classes has been avidly sought, especially by those without property, as a means of economic progress and security. Although the oversupply of college-trained people in the last decade has raised questions about the value or relevance of the educational passport, nevertheless a steady supply of a selected number of trained managers and professionals is a social output necessary for the order and stability of a complex industrial society, which is one of the reasons why education is also heavily subsidized.

All of these social outputs—economic growth, rising living standards, orderly capital markets, property rights, technological subsidization, and educational achievement—are the means by which *decision authority* can be exercised by the upper classes for their individual economic progress, maturation, or individuation. That is, the social order is arranged to provide members of this interest group with the means for their own fulfillment.

The size of the propertied-professional interest group is limited in number. The sizes of segments of society vary, depending on the definitions used, but perhaps one-tenth of society may be regarded as consisting of large holders of productive property or entrepreneurs large and small. This group has the most at stake and is the greatest beneficiary of the complex industrial process as it is organized. Perhaps another fifth or sixth of the population has a sufficient professional or managerial role to be a substantial (though not primary) beneficiary as well. About half the population, workers and employees, derive benefits in the form of rising living standards as dependents; that is, as long as the income gains are shared. This leaves about one-fourth of the population, made up mainly of the unskilled, youth, racial minorities, single mothers, and elderly, who are essentially outside of the economic process. They represent persons in persistent underemployment or poverty who exist largely as dependents on society through welfare or other forms of assistance.

Now, if the social process is organized so that one-fourth of the population are primary beneficiaries of the industrial system and one-fourth are excluded as beneficiaries from the system, then the order and stability of the society rests with the remaining half of the population—that is, the workers and employees whose individual needs depend upon how widely income gains of society are shared. That is, the workers and employees are dependent upon the wisdom, beneficence, or political pressure that causes the upper income classes to share the economic gains, which they control, with the working half of the population.

What is happening to this big employee class? Are there signs of order or disorder in the social processes and events which affect it?

TENDENCIES TOWARD DISORDER

There are twelve problems that confront the employee population and that have been evidence of conflict and disorder in recent decades: war, inflation, unemployment, impaired living standards, poverty, consumerism, environmental pollution, equal opportunity, educational irrelevance, falling birth rates, alienated subcultures, and barriers to entry into the complex industrial process. Let us consider each of these.

Wars are fought by members of the middle (employee) classes; they provide the manpower. Three major wars in three generations (the two world wars and Vietnam), plus almost constant smaller military actions in between, have levied heavy losses on this group in terms of dead, wounded, unemployed, and psychologically impaired. These heavy human losses, plus the persistence of wars and the elusiveness of peace, have created a doubt about the leadership ability of the United States in international governance. This doubt about our competence to exercise world leadership implies doubts as well about the American way of life and the ability of the federal government in domestic governance. If the Vietnam war achieved little or nothing abroad for world leadership or peace in Southeast Asia, despite its enormous costs in human life, suffering, and domestic conflicts, then what is the wisdom of governance (in three administrations) that incurred so much dissent, repression, and discord for so little value either to the United States at home or to world peace? Was it just a mistake? Was it human error? If so, then how do we account for so persistent a series of mistakes over the period of a decade, over three administrations, over all the congressmen, senators, Presidents, political leaders, lobbyists, and industrialists who influence policy? Wise governance learns from mistakes and corrects them. Not to correct mistakes is a sign of inflexibility in the social process. Are there signs of persistent error in governance and public policy?

Persistent *inflation* is a sign of persistent error in social management. Persistent inflation contributed to the crumbling of the Roman Empire. The United States has had persistent inflation for at least sixty years, and it has appeared in disruptive form after every major war. Some public officials in this decade have said that the causes of inflation are difficult to determine and inflation is not controllable. Economics defines inflation as the expansion of the money supply relative to available goods, and it is the government that inflates the money supply by overspending (spending beyond taxation). The United States government has had a budget deficit (overspending) for every year, except one, in the past fifteen years (to 1976). The cumulative deficits were nearly $200 billion, of which about 40 percent was credit the government borrowed from banks and added to the money supply, causing a 60 percent price inflation. The economy has had uncontrollable inflation because the government has an uncontrollable budget, and an uncontrollable budget raises severe questions again about the ability of the federal government to govern.

Unemployment is, in part, a consequence of inflation, because every inflation is followed by a partial deflation, recession, and unemployment. Unemployment affects the working and employee class, which is the half of the population dependent upon the members of the decision-making classes for their income distribution. When economic security is denied to the working classes but assured to the upper classes, a schism of interest begins to open up. The employees are no longer reassured of benefiting from the social process, and their interests begin to diverge from the established system.

Impaired living standards are another consequence of persistent inflation, because wages and salaries do not rise as fast as prices. In contrast to the wage earner, owners, managers, and professionals are able to raise prices as a means of maintaining their real income. Inflation is a form of taxation, initiated by government in failing to raise its revenues enough to meet its expenditures, and it is a form of taxation that is highly regressive, falling heavily on members of the employee class by reducing their purchasing power, and most heavily on the poor. The fact that the controlling classes (government, property owners, managers, and professionals) allow inflation to happen is a breach of the social contract by which the coalition between themselves and the other half of the population (employees) is maintained. Inflation is a message that says that the upper classes are willing to throw the whole cost of war and social burdens on employees, while maintaining their own preferential income distribution. That message, which gets louder as inflation persists, is a signal for conflict and dissent rather than order. It says that the employee population must defend its income by strikes, demonstrations, or voting blocs against the upper classes. This is, again, a sign of disorder in the social processes.

Persistent *poverty* is an important sign that the social process has failed to meet the needs of a portion of the citizenry. In the 1930s, President Roosevelt said that one-third of the nation was ill-housed, ill-clothed, and ill-fed. Today, after more than forty years of the longest prosperity in the economic history of the United States, about one-fourth of the population is *still* near or below the poverty level. The persistent exclusion of a portion of society from sharing in economic gains is another sign of conflict and disorder.

Consumerism, a recent social phenomenon, is a form of organized protest against the pricing and product practices of business, asserting unfairness in the cost, quality, or representation of products. Consumerism has emerged in the past decade and is another sign that dissent is felt in the half of the population dependent upon the decision makers.

Environmental pollution, also emerging as a problem in the past decade, has led to organized protest against decision makers who ignore the amenities of living and destroy the quality of the environment or the ecology. The prevalence of pollution, particularly in air and water, has been caused by business failure to recognize the health and social costs of emissions and effluents from industrial products or processes. As the environmental quality of life has diminished, the mass of the population has suffered another form of loss in its living standards.

Equal opportunity has become an issue particularly for women and ethnic minorities, who have sought to emerge from poverty and reap the benefits of the social process. Racial minorities were encouraged to believe that equal educations would enable them to enter the social process, and some have become managers and professionals by this means. But to many if not most minorities, additional education did not open additional jobs. Now minorities, including women, are trying to force equal opportunity through political pressure, lobbying, and regulation. The affirmative-action program, with the force of federal law and regulation, is opening additional employment to such people but certainly not at a rate that would provide equal employment opportunity during our generation.

Educational irrelevance is another indicator of dissent and disorder. Education has been a disillusion not only to minorities but also to a large portion of the white youth from the middle class. Middle-class white parents have historically looked to education as the means by which, lacking the benefits of property ownership, their sons and daughters may progress farther than they. The only route into the upper classes for youth with brains but without capital has been education. Today, the oversupply of educated youth means that college education is no longer a passport to a better life. College-trained youths must look for their fulfillment in manual work, political action, or dropping out—none of which they are trained to do well. Hence, education has become irrelevant to getting jobs, political reform, or doing one's own thing. This irrelevance is an indicator of disorder in the social process.

Alienation and falling birth rates have become part of the youthful subculture and morality. This is superficially explainable by the availability of birth control pills. However, the use of birth-control pills is volitional, and their widespread use implies a profound attitudinal malaise—namely, that young people do not want children. The youthful subculture obscures this fact by an easy morality, which offends members of the older generation, who attribute the motivation to mere pleasure seeking. But the denial of so basic a biological motive as reproduction connotes a profound tension. It is painful to see life in such a way as to not want children.

The seeing of the world as not a worthy place to bring newborn babies is an expression that life is not worth living—not for the babies, but for those who foresee the lives for their unwanted babies. Perhaps this is the bitterest alienation of them all, that life is no longer fit for the living. A life so unfit can be turned off in many ways—by dropping out of it, by drowning it out with loud music, transforming it to fantasy with drugs, by temporarily distracting the pain with pleasure seeking. These are the mores of an *alienated subculture* within the social process of the United States. How could young people have written more boldly or more obviously that some terrible disorder affects their souls? Or that the schism in their souls reflects the social disorder in which they prefer not to live?

Barriers to entry into the established social process diminish the will to live because these barriers deny to the individual person the means to make decisions over his or her own life. The principal barrier is the denial, except to a few, of access to capital. In early America, capital was widely available by homesteading land or staking out natural resources. In mid-American history, capital was decentralized and dispersed throughout small enterprises and available to small entrepreneurs with will and enterprise. Today, capital requirements for most enterprises are large, and capital flows are concentrated in huge conglomerate business corporations. Access to capital by ordinary people is very limited, and without capital they cannot do their own decision making in a capitalistic industrial system. Moreover, if education no longer provides entry into that decision system, they have little opportunity to make the decisions that shape their own lives.

Dissent, demonstration, and disorder are reactions arising from the limited ability that the vast majority of individuals have to shape their own destinies. The enveloping institutions that surround them have assumed direction over individual lives because they control the capital flows, which in turn determine the pattern of prospective enterprise and the activities of individuals. If individuals have little opportunity to decide upon their own work content, they have little scope to pursue their life interests and individuation. Such persons are psychologically deprived of maturation and tend to express their disaffection by demonstration and dissent.

THE SOCIAL INSTITUTIONS CAUSING SOCIAL DISORDER

This list of twelve disorders indiates, obviously, that corrective measures are needed to reduce social conflict and restore integrity to the social process. This restoration of integrity—that is, achieving consistency with human need—will be possible when changes are made in existing institutions, although delegations of authority to institutions, by law or practice, tend to be timeless, and institutions resist changes in their timeless authorities. Still, let us identify which institutions are responsible for which functions causing disorder.

There are three types of social institutions: voluntary, business, and governmental. Voluntary institutions are those that deal on a personal basis with human needs, usually at the option of the individual and in small groups, such as schools, hospitals, colleges, churches, and community organizations. Business deals with the economic affairs of society, usually on a mass contractual basis. Government is a public body of last resort that redelegates authorities or rectifies injustices on a minimal, mass basis. The kinds of contemporary disorders each are mainly responsible for are as follows:

Voluntary institutions:
1. Equal opportunity
2. Educational irrelevance
3. Alienated subcultures (falling birth rates)

Business institutions:
1. Unemployment
2. Consumerism
3. Environmental pollution
4. Barriers to entry

Governmental institutions:
1. War
2. Inflation
3. Impaired living standards
4. Poverty
5. Demonstration and dissent

Let us briefly consider these three kinds of institutions and the problems they cause.

Problems of Voluntary Institutions

Schools, clubs, familial groups, churches, and community agencies are among the first to reflect acceptance or nonacceptance of individuals—that is, equal opportunity or discrimination. The sense of equality in a community is reflected in how much access everyone has to all of the community activities and functions.

Ethnic minorities and women have frequently not had such access, particularly to education or jobs. The opening of educational institutions to deprived individuals has seemingly improved their opportunity to enter the social process. However, as education has become less relevant to jobs and job placement, many minorities, as well as growing numbers of educated white middle-class youth, have been excluded from jobs and a place in the social economy.

The consequence of exclusion is alienation. Thus, youths and minorities are turning away from that which has rejected them and are trying to find some separate lives of their own. This separate lifestyle creates the subcultures alien to the main society, which at best creates frictions and at worst violence. The primary responsibility for this alienation—that is, inequality of opportunity and educational irrelevance—lies with the voluntary social institutions.

Problems of Business Institutions

Business does not exist merely to create profits, as is sometimes assumed; it exists to satisfy human economic wants. The unwritten but understood social contract, as expressed in legislation, is that the profit privileges of business are its compensation for productive activity in satisfying human needs. One such human need is employment, and business has the responsibility to create employment for the purpose of productive output, creating purchasing power, and enabling worker-consumers to purchase goods and services to meet their needs. The failure to provide employment, then, is a failure of the business system.

The consumer and environmental movements are dissents against business, which seek to force it to provide quality goods at fair prices, and to prevent despoliation of the environment. The past indifference of business to such obligations has caused legislators to assign these responsibilities explicitly to business and to enact penalties for noncompliance.

Barriers to entry have arisen against individuals and new enterprises to prevent them from entering into the industrial process. Massive mergers and conglomeration of corporations have created highly centralized business institutions capable of controlling capital, markets, and supply, erecting serious barriers to entry by new entrepreneurs by severely limiting their ability to obtain capital and pursue endeavors that would fulfill their interests.

Problems of Governmental Institutions

Government is an institution of last resort expected to correct inequities, injustices, and to regroup authorities that deny equal opportunity to individuals. The government has alleviated some of these inequalities by progressive taxation and by welfare programs, but these measures redistribute only a small portion of income, and they do not redistribute savings or capital, which is the key to equal opportunity. For example, corporate savings have remained about twice as large as individual savings for fifty years, despite government attempts at redistribution. Thus, the government has maintained and reinforced present institutional rights, which perpetuates inequalities at home and necessitates the defense of trade abroad.[1] The result is that foreign policy leads the United States to war to defend its foreign trade, investments, and vital economic interests. The interactive chain of events among institutions, as we have already seen, leads to war, inflation, impaired living standards, poverty, alienation, falling birth rates among educated, underemployed youth, and dissent.

The array of contemporary problems points to failures by institutions to respond to the human needs for which they are assigned responsibility. The persistence of this inflexibility and nonresponsiveness presages continuous conflict.

THE INTERRELATEDNESS OF OUR SOCIAL DISORDERS

Our examination of contemporary disorders has shown that they are interrelated. The fact that they are systematically interlocked is a clear signal that not just some social tendencies but the entire social process is misaligned with human needs and that authorities and functions need

[1]See Kenneth Boulding, *Economic Imperialism* (Ann Arbor, Mich.: University of Michigan Press, 1972); Michael Hudson, *Super-Imperialism* (New York: Holt, Rinehart, and Winston, 1968); Arthur C. Pigou, *The Political Economy of War* (New York: Macmillan, 1941); Lionel Robbins, *The Economic Causes of War* (London: Jonathan Cape, 1940).

regrouping to become responsive again. This systematic disorder may be illustrated by comparing five elements of the social structure with the different roles of institutions in an orderly and a disorderly society.

This is shown in tables 2–1 and 2–2 below.

An orderly society (Table 2–1) is one in which individuals are accepted by voluntary social groups, without discrimination, and accorded equal opportunity and access to all the activities of the community. Since individual needs are many, social institutions are adaptive and creative in initiating whatever new activities respond to changing human needs. The functional means for exercising authority is mainly by moral suasion. In such a society, the members act cooperatively. Strong allegiances run to the community, which nurtures and protects the individual.

In an orderly society, business provides full and equal employment, so that those who wish to work can find work of their choice to fulfill their talents. Business authority is decentralized to give opportunity, means, and capital to individualistic talents. The functional means by which business achieves individualistic employment or enterprise is by diverse technical knowledge and productivity. Allegiance of the members is to general economic growth, which is achieved by the process of widely accessible capital.

The government of an orderly society is concerned with the equitable distribution of incomes and widespread opportunity. Government authority is minimal and dispersed to allow wide opportunity for individual differences and enterprises. The means of government are financed by equitable taxation. In such a society the allegiance of the citizenry is to law, and the process of the society is orderly governance.

An orderly society, such as that described above, may be utopian in

TABLE 2-1. The Orderly Society

Elements of social structure	Voluntary institutions	Business institutions	Governmental institutions
Individual needs, grievances, or mission	Equal opportunity	Equal employment	Equitable incomes
Institutional authority	Adaptive	Decentralized	Dispersed
Functions and tasks (means)	Morality	Technological productivity	Equitable taxation
Allegiance or alienation	Community	Economic growth	Law
Process	Cooperation	Accessible capital	Orderly governance

degree, but some civilizations (including the United States and Britain in the early ninteenth century) have approached it at least for a time. The distinction of such a society is clearly that the set of relationships among its members—their needs, authority structure, functions, and institutions—is systematically consistent and articulated, each reinforcing and harmonizing with the others.

A society tending toward disorder is, in contrast, not articulated and is systematically in conflict. In such a society (Table 2–2), individuals have grievances because their needs are not met; minorities, women, older men, and the handicapped, for example, may face job discrimination. Social institutions are also nonresponsive to such grievances and instead, deal with the problems expediently—that is, by doing what is convenient for the institution, without regard for its effects on individuals. In these circumstances, individuals feel no allegiance to the institutions and are pessimistic about their grievances being redressed and about their own future. The result of this pessimism is alienation from the society.

In a society tending toward disorder, significant segments of the population are unemployed, underemployed, or unable to find employment suited to their interests and abilities. Business authority is centralized in large institutions that are nonresponsive to individualistic employment needs and that see their responsibility not in creating interesting employment for the general population but in making as much profit as they can for themselves. General Motors had a strike in its highly automated Vega plant, for example, because its work was boring to young, educated workers. The large corporations deal with each other both as buyers and sellers, and thus respect each other's financial power, preferring not to compete with or offend formidable buyers or sellers.

TABLE 2-2. The Society Tending Toward Disorder

Social structure	Voluntary institutions	Business institutions	Governmental institutions
Individual needs, grievances, or mission	Discrimination	Underemployment	Poverty
Institutional authority	Nonresponsive	Centralized	Power politics (war)
Functions and tasks (means)	Expedience	Reciprocity (collusion)	Inflation
Allegiance or alienation	Pessimism	Security	Crime or evasion of law
Process	Alienation	Oligopoly	Dissent and disorder

This leads them to reciprocity, or buying from and selling to each other by gentlemen's agreements, which in the extreme may become collusion in restraint of trade. Allegiance within these surroundings is to economic security. The process of business is oligopolistic competition, which tends to function as an economic in-group excluding new or outside enterprises.

In a disorderly society, poverty is persistent. Government authority is exercised in response to lobbies and power politics. Power politics, for the protection of "vital interests" (economic interests and investments) abroad, leads to frequent wars. Wars and subsidies cause inflation, which gradually impoverishes employee classes as well as the unemployed. Those who are alienated or impoverished resort to crime. Evasion of the law is general, led by the big companies and big politicians. A crime is viewed as being caught, not as committing violations of law. The process of government is one of conflict, dissent, and disorder, which is repressed when necessary by power, such as using military force against one's own citizens (as in the 1967 race disturbances in Detroit or the 1970 killings of students at Kent State).

Looking at the spectrum from the orderly to the disorderly society, we can see, as we will show in Chapter 4, that American civilization in its early development had many systematic characteristics of the orderly society. Clearly the American society is moving toward a disorderly state, and its problems are becoming systematically aggravated because the issues are interconnected and reinforcing.

Indeed, all of the interrelated problems are tied up in one great problem—namely, that authority has now become centralized and nonresponsive, whereas in early America it was relatively dispersed and adaptive. As Columbia University sociologist Robert Nisbet has pointed out (as have Tocqueville and Lord Acton), freedom in a society exists when there are many dispersed authorities, and the authorities must be closely united to functions that command the response and talents of members.[2] Today, large corporations and government agencies have become remote from individuals and too unknowing of individual needs to command the response and talents of its members. The members of the American community have many unused talents, about one-fourth of them are outside the social process entirely, and about one-half work at jobs not conceived by themselves for their own interests and talents.

How did all this happen, the remarkable shift from an orderly toward a disorderly society? To see this transformation, we need to look at the

[2]Robert A. Nisbet, *Community and Power* (London: Oxford University Press, 1953), pp. xii, 56, 189–91.

shift in authority patterns in the United States historically. In the next two chapters, we will discuss the process of social evolution and apply it to the United States past and present.

First vote. *(Photo by Owen Franklin/Stock, Boston.)*

Chapter Three

THE DRAMATIC PLOT
OF SOCIAL CHANGE

The remarkable shift of the United States from a fairly orderly toward a disorderly state has taken place over many decades, and this evolution is seen perhaps most sharply by contrasting the social structure and authority distributions of agrarian American with that of the postindustrial United States. The evolution of these two states could, of course, be chronicled here in much detail, but I would be repeating a lot of history that most Americans are familiar with. I shall therefore describe only the beginning and ending states of this evolution.

Before we can analyze these beginning and ending states, however, we need some framework with which to make the comparison. The framework will follow that described in Chapter 2, which showed that social organization may be understood systematically in terms of the distribution of needs, authority, functions, tasks, allegiance, and process. The change in these distributions accounts for social evolution.

We shall first consider how social evolution takes place in society in general and then, in Chapter 4, see how it applies in the United States.

HOW SOCIAL EVOLUTION TAKES PLACE

From historic times, thinkers have been tempted to liken the social process to the growth of individual organisms, and there are insights to be learned by this analogy. The Greeks thought of life and human processes in terms of *physis,* the growth and death cycle of plants. Sociologist Robert Nisbet has shown how this botanical analogy of birth and decay was converted by St. Augustine, in the fourth century A.D., into the idea of developmental progress. Darwin in turn converted Augustine's idea of progress into his ideas of human evolution.[1]

The evolutionary paradigm has also been used to describe social processes by a number of contemporary scholars—for instance, Walter Rostow, professor of economics at Harvard, who (somewhat like Oswald Spengler) looks upon societies as going through periods of birth, expansion, rapid development, maturation, and decay; Warren Bennis, president of the University of Cincinnati, who likens organizations to complex organisms adapting to environmental change; and Harvard psychologist Henry Murray, who postulates that ideas (which he calls "idenes"[2]) play the same role in society that genes play in forming organisms.

Enlightening as these ideas are, however, the organic-evolution analogy is deficient in one important respect—namely, that in an organism, a genetic code describes a limited number of alternative adaptations the organism can make. Instinctive creatures, such as birds and lizards, have very limited alternatives as to their form or behavior. Human beings have no alternatives as to their physical forms but a few as to their behavior.

Social organizations, by contrast, have few limits as to their interactive behavior. The larger possibilities of social organization lie, almost entirely, in the near-infinite linkages between humans and the surrounding ecological system. A society is the organized relationship of human kind with its environment. While a person's own behavior options are few, his or her relations with nature, other people, the food chain, the energy-nutrient cycle, natural resources, materials, and other ecological species are innumerable. For example, today we live

[1]Robert A. Nisbet, *Social Change and History* (London: Oxford University Press, 1969), pp. 22 and 66 ff.

[2]Warren Bennis, *Beyond Bureaucracy* (New York: McGraw-Hill, 1966), pp. 1 ff.

principally on about twenty food crops and primitive people lived on perhaps one hundred, but the edible potential of food crops is in the thousands. Obviously, the mere selection of twenty crops, whether it occurred empirically or by chance, dictates a large part of social organization—which lands will be used in which climates, the amount of rainfall required, the means of tillage, means of ownership, the forms of harvesting and distribution. Settle these few questions with twenty crops and much of a basic social structure has been determined.

There are three points to be made about organizations. First, environmental surroundings are not trivial conditions of social organization; they are, in fact, the independent variables, the determining conditions of organizational form and design. Moreover, these independent variables are of countless variety, which accounts for the variety of human experience and civilizations. Social organizations are, therefore, capable of innumerable variations, whereas botanical organisms are genetically limited to the few forms that have historically survived.

Second, despite this potential for variety, organizations have in fact been monotonously similar historically because of the human proclivity toward habit. Human beings tend to live and behave as their parents and teachers did before them, unless some dramatic necessity requires them to change.

Thirdly, the dramatic necessity to change in social organization appears infrequently in human history, but when it does, it is coupled with turmoil and anxiety, as well as opportunity. Major historical epochs in which social designs have changed have been in Greece in the fifth century B.C.; in Rome in the first century B.C.; in Western civilization in the fourteenth and ninteenth centuries; and the signs of such change may again be present today. These historical epochs have some remarkable similarities, owing no doubt to human habit, and we shall build some future scenarios for the United States based upon these similarities. These scenarios will show us what social trajectories we could embark upon if we extrapolate the organizational strengths and weaknesses already built into our social structure, which former civilizations have already lived out before us.

Before replaying old dramas with our future, however, we need to examine more closely how the social plot thickens.

THE STRUCTURE OF CHANGE:
THE SOCIAL PLOT THICKENS

Social evolution proceeds like a dramatic plot. Like any good drama, the plot thickens by foreclosing options until the protagonist has fewer and fewer choices left so that finally only heroic necessity must prevail. Likewise, societies develop by finding some practical means for survival which, by successful application, forecloses options until few choices other than heroic ones are left.

Many societies have not had the organizational means to make heroic changes or choices and so they failed. The question is, does the United States have the organizational structure for heroic decisions and changes? If not, can we learn, from past failures, how to make an adaptive structure?

This reasoning leads us back to structure, and we may now define social evolution in terms of structural change. The structure of society may be understood in terms of eight elements: its needs, mission, au-

TABLE 3-1. The Structural Evolution of Societies

Elements of social structure	Evolutionary periods
Needs	Fermentation and unrest
Mission	"Opportunity-creation-invention" phenomenon
Authority	Adaptive period
Functions	Formulation period
Tasks	Developmental period
Allegiance	Ideology emerges
Process	Socialization period or operative regime
Alienation	New needs go unmet—fermentation and unrest begins again

thority, functions, tasks, allegiance, process, and alienation. These structural elements have evolutionary counterparts in social development, as shown in Table 3–1. Let us consider the changes in these elements.

UNMET NEEDS AND SOCIAL FERMENTATION

Fermentation occurs when old institutions no longer meet new needs and members of significant segments of society are restless to the point of disorder, as they try to make the old institutions adaptive and responsive to their needs. Such restive periods have preceded each major epochal change in history, and as we saw in Chapter 2 we may now be in such a restive period again.

THE NEW MISSION AND THE
"OPPORTUNITY-CREATION-INVENTION" PHENOMENON

When the new needs are responded to by someone, often a new institution or civilization, there occurs what is called the "opportunity-creation-invention" phenomenon. This phenomenon brings together the needs with some new vision that sees, as *opportunity,* the means, design, resources, technology, and management to satisfy them. That vision is an act of social *creation*. The confluence of needs, means, resources, and management to carry out the vision are the social *invention* by which a new mission or social purpose becomes possible in the society.

The opportunity-creation-invention phenomenon is one of the least understood aspects of social evolution. Joseph Schumpeter, formerly Harvard economist, aptly called it, in the political economy, the "concatenation of events." A similar idea, in more colorful language, has been described as the garbage can theory of management science. What is meant is that human affairs are made up of long chains, linkages, or networks of events with such immeasurable possibilities for crossing, permutation, and combination that no rational cause can be found for their coming together, or concatenation. Thus, they are "phenomena," defined in philosophy as observable events known through the senses or observation rather than through rational thought.

Creators and inventors in these opportune times tend not to be thinkers but keen observers, who intuitively sense or see the significance of a fortuitous concatenation of events. They visualize what might be (a mission), a kind of design for the future. It might be any kind of design; artistic, technological, political, social. They see a role for themselves in making that design and living out the design (that is, live their own legend). If the design works, others follow and mimic the heroic effort. Thus, the adaptive period begins with mimicry, which is one of the foundations for social learning and education.

About the opportunity-creation-invention phenomenon we might also observe that, although it is mysterious as to how it occurs, it is almost always accompanied by an enormous expansion in new resources. This was true of the Greek, Roman, and Renaissance periods; each in its own way opened vast new resources. Perhaps one of the greatest of social inventors was Christopher Columbus, with his vision of a round, navigable earth. In creating his voyage, or mission, he opened more resources than the world had seen before.

On a much smaller industrial scale, the vision or invention of new technologies results frequently not only in new product development but also in the opening of new resources (in a displacement, or opportunity-cost, sense). For example, the invention of microcircuitry and computers displaced large cadres of computational labor and substituted for it silicon and metallic materials in cheap and ample supply.

Another characteristic of epochal change is that the new resources discovered or released by the opportunity-creation-invention phenomenon are channeled into new institutions, which then displace the old ones. The discovery of America, for instance, channeled resources of the New World into distinctively American institutions, and the old organizations of authority ruling from Spain and England withered away. Similarly, the computer invention resulted in new organizations, the electronics industry, which displaced manual and mechanical computational organizations with their intensive labor requirements.

THE ADAPTIVE PERIOD AND NEW AUTHORITY

Once the opportunity-creation-invention phenomenon has been demonstrated by its creator-inventor, other persons also see the potential of the new mission. They also see the resource potential, and the mimickers follow the mission of the inventor, with variations, in a scramble for resources. Thus, Columbus was followed by Cortes, Pizarro, Balboa, John Smith, the New England colonists, and the westward pioneers in the most massive land grab in world history. This land-grab syndrome during the adaptive period was, in fact, a vying for authority, a competition that often became bloody and took the form of jurisdictional disputes and conflicts over the right to rule.

The right to rule may be in the form of territorial disputes, as in the case of Cortes's conflicts with the crown; in the form of rebellion and civil war over sovereignty, as in the bloody battles among Pizarro's followers; or in the form of disputed property rights, as in the gunplay of the Wild West. The adaptive period is filled with buccaneers and robber barons, whose lust for wealth and power causes every authority to be tested and strained in old and new institutions alike, until a few of these authorites hold. Thus, throughout our history, rebels and freebooters have tested the tea tax, the British Crown, the Continental Congress, the Constitution, the Confederacy, the Union, the western sheriff, the antitrust laws, and the election-financing laws. Whenever authority gave way, power was usurped and old institutions died. When improvised organizations are able to settle conflicts, as did the Constitution and the western sheriff, new institutions begin. The institution-building phase of the adaptive period occurs as authority conflicts are settled and become imbedded into law, property rights, or decision-making privileges.

THE FORMULATION PERIOD AND THE DELEGATION OF FUNCTIONS

Once new authority is established, the formulation period follows. Here the decision maker uses his authority to delegate assignments or functions to others who work on his behalf. Cortes, for example, distributed land and mineral rights among his captains, who exploited it on his and their behalf. The American railroad tycoons delegated functions of roadbed construction, rail operations, and land sales to subordinates. The western rancher, with the settled authority of his property rights, delegated functions of ranch operations among his cowhands.

The formulation period is one in which organizational structure is defined hierarchically in terms of major responsibility and authority over functions of an institution. Thus, Cortes's conquistadors became the bureaucracy of New Spain; the railroad became a departmentalized operating organization; and the ranch became a management unit of related activities.

THE DEVELOPMENTAL PERIOD AND ESTABLISHMENT OF TASKS

The developmental period goes along with and after the formulation period. Once the organizational structure is defined, individuals assume tasks assigned to them. These tasks can be done in a variety of ways, depending on the technique or technology applied. Hence, the developmental period is one in which technological experimentation occurs to find easier, cheaper, or better ways to do organizational tasks, such as the development of Mexican silver mines, more powerful locomotives, or improved cattle strains.

ALLEGIANCE AND THE EMERGENCE OF IDEOLOGY

By this time, social evolution is far advanced. A broad mission or social purpose meeting new needs has been perceived by all. Authority distributions are settled; organizational structures are established and workable; tasks are being performed with advancing technical skills. The society has something to be proud about. It is working. It has adapted, survived, and may even be wealthy. The thinkers now give thought to what has been the nature of this marvelous social invention in which they live. They think up ideas, theories, descriptions, gods, heroes, symbols, rights, freedoms, legends, histories, philosophies, sciences, and metaphysics to explain it all and to command allegiance.

These ideas become enshrined in an ideology filled with shining symbols: "freedom," "democracy," "free enterprise," "free markets," "property rights," "economic growth," "rising living standards," "the American dream." Just to utter one of these expressions invokes a set of images about a societal style as vividly as does showing a caduceus, the American flag, or the Cross. The ideology, then, has symbolic meanings that can be elaborated into theories descriptive of the social process. Moreover, this ideology, being symbolic, is charged with emotion as well as rationalization, and thus it may be pitted against competing ideologies to command allegiance, including patriotism, sacrifice, and even death. Individuals associate the symbols with themselves, when they like their role and tasks in society, and thus yield their allegiance, even to the extent of sacrifice, for the society.

THE SOCIAL PROCESS: FIRST SOCIALIZATION, THEN ALIENATION

The emergence of ideology is followed by the socialization period, and the ideology becomes the social drill in which everyone is educated and taught to believe. Within the institutional organization believers are promoted and nonbelievers are ostracized. Ostracization takes many forms. In ancient Greece, it was banishment; in a modern corporation, it is being kicked upstairs, as with faltering executives, or being left unemployed, as with many American youth.

The socialization process has many advantages for it enables individuals to learn very complex, technical, and interrelated tasks. Without socialization, professions would be impossible. Socialization enhances the total skills and expertise of a society, causing it to evolve into more intricate forms—more intricate art, as in the Renaissance, or more intricate science, as today.

But socialization also has a danger in that it may ossify the social process. The technique of socialization becomes enshrined, as though it were an end instead of a means. Technique becomes so intricate, so beautiful, so demanding, so hard to learn, so rare, so removed, so incomprehensible to most people that it becomes a symbol in itself. The art technique becomes more important than the creative design. The elegance of the experiment becomes more important than the results. University disciplines become increasingly remote and theoretical, and only the practitioners can perceive the intricacy of their field. Art is understood only by artists, physics only by physicists. Economists speak only to economists, chemists write only to chemists. Knowledge becomes increasingly erudite, irrelevant, and useless to human ends.

People become preoccupied with their own technique because their niche in life is dictated by their acceptance by their technical colleagues rather than by the public. As a result, research becomes busywork, bureaucracy becomes red tape. Business services become indifferent. The public begins to fear science as a threat rather than a benefactor, to suspect medicine of malpractice, to regard politicians as corrupt, scholars as arrogant, businessmen as profiteers, public servants as drones. An era of mutual suspicion and alienation emerges because human needs are no longer regarded as the ends. Individuals come to feel powerless because of techniques they do not understand. Technique has become the end, and humans the means—just the reverse of the way the social evolution began.

The dehumanizing effects of technique have been lucidly portrayed by French philosopher Jacques Ellul.[3] The tasks of the institution, he points out, and the way they are done gain ascendency over the people in the institution, of those who are served by it. Human needs go unserved, new needs not recognized. But institutions do not falter, their technique does not change, their authority and resource prerogatives are too firmly imbedded in law and timeless delegations within the social process. Old institutions seldom change; rather, they are displaced. But the displacement requires new inventors, new resources.

The death throes of a civilization, which signal the beginning of a new cycle of evolution, are a long period of fermentation, restiveness, and disorder, followed by a new opportunity-creation-invention phenomenon. The concatenation of these events may take centuries, as in the demise of Rome, or they may occur suddenly, as in the opening of the New World.

To recapitulate, social evolution has an inevitable plot, as compelling as any drama, which is made up of structural elements corresponding to the emergence of its authority and decision-making pattern. Civilizations first experience a fermentation and restive period, in which new, unmet needs are visualized and new resources are released. Then, a new mission is conceived, and an adaptive period occurs in which there is a testing, straining, and struggling for authority, out of which a settled

[3]Jacques Ellul, *La Technique* (Paris: A. Colin, 1954).

pattern of authority distribution emerges. The new authorities assign and delegate functions among the organizational components available to them—in essence to do their work for them—and the organizational institutions in turn break up these functions into smaller, simpler, specialized tasks in order to spread out the drudgery among the powerless. If the powerless like their tasks or treatment, they yield allegiance to the institutions, and these allegiances become symbolized as ideology. If people do not like their tasks, they remain disinterested or disgruntled, without allegiance, until the next change comes along, soon or centuries later. The allegiances, few or weak though they may be, then become the indoctrination media for the socialization process. If the socialization process ossifies into nonresponsive behavior, alienation and disorder occur, and the cycle begins anew.

Where are we today in the social evolution of the United States? In the next chapter, we will contrast the needs, mission, authority, functions, tasks, allegiance, and process of agrarian America with those of postindustrial America.

Harvested fields. *(Photo by Harry Riddle/The Stockmarket.)*

Chapter Four

TWO SCENARIOS: THE U.S.A., PAST AND PRESENT

In comparing agrarian with postindustrial America, we will take the year 1870 as the demarcation line, for in that year about 70 percent of the population still lived on farms or in farm villages. One hundred years later, less than 5 percent of the population was on farms. This great mass migration from rural to urban living was caused by two social reorganizations. The first was the attraction of rural people and their organization into industrial factories; this took place between 1870 and 1940, until nearly half of the population was working in manufacturing. Since 1940, however, the proportion of people in manufacturing has declined, and American society has become a more technical, professional, service-oriented set of organizations—the distinctive characteristic of the postindustrial state.

MISSION ANALYSIS OF AGRARIAN AMERICA

Futurists use the terms "mission analysis" and "scenarios" to describe ways of looking at the lives of individuals, peoples, or nations in an understandable way—a way that tells their story, where they came from, where they are, and where they are going.

Mission analysis tells a story of purpose, what people want. It is an examination of the needs (or requirements or threats) that individuals feel impinge upon them from their surroundings, together with the alternative responses and authority that will accommodate these needs.

A *scenario* is a story of how people achieve their social purpose. The events and actions that achieve a purpose are capable of being chosen by the actors. It is in this sense that Carl Jung speaks of people "living their own legend." Living one's own legend is a form of self-fulfilling prophecy. People become what they choose to be. A scenario, then, is the narrative of how authority is converted into actions—that is, functions, tasks, allegiance, and process—that cope with the environment.

A scenario of agrarian America, 1607–1870, could obviously be a series of large historical volumes, but they would not serve the purpose of our policy analysis. We are interested in the essential authority distributions by which agrarian America adapted to its surroundings. This kind of mission analysis requires us to abstract the essentials of the social structure, for comparison later with other possible alternatives or social patterns. Such abstraction is clearly a delicate business because like making a good painting, it requires a high degree of selectivity and simplification to essential forms, and one artist's perception may, of course, differ from another's. Still, just as it is the privilege of those who differ to paint their own pictures, so it is ours to abstract our own social design of agrarian America.

Exhibit 4–1 presents, in abstract form, my own mission analysis and scenario of agrarian America's social structure and design. The exhibit and mission analysis are used, in the balance of the chapter, to describe how the authority structure of agrarian America emerged from individual needs, and then to compare the authority patterns of agrarian America with that of postindustrial America.

ECONOMIC AUTHORITY IN AGRARIAN AMERICA

Let us first examine the distribution of economic authority between 1607 and 1870 and its close ties to family relationships. Economic units

EXHIBIT 4-1. Agrarian America, 1607–1870. An abstract of mission analysis and scenario according to six elements of social structure.

NEEDS AND MISSIONS

1. To seek individual expression and wealth.
2. To open and develop new lands by individual or family enterprises.
3. To trade overseas for manufactured goods.
4. To develop domestic manufactured goods from rich resources.
5. To exercise political freedom and choice without oppression or regimentation.

AUTHORITY

1. Individuals acquired property rights to ample resources through land grants that gave them authority and capital to pursue their own occupational choice.
2. Family authority assigned functions within farming and small business enterprises.
3. Merchants and sea captains had contractual authority by law to conduct mercantile trade.
4. Localized manufacturers converted resource capital into products by their own or hired labor.
5. Political authority was dispersed to small units of government, where issues were few and were influenced by local votes or hearings.

FUNCTIONS

1. Individuals produced goods and services by their own labor, with marketing and financial assistance from other local enterprises.
2. Regional and international trade were carried on by competitive units in open markets.
3. Manufacturing was done by crafts applied to local resources, using small capital equipment and tools.
4. The federal government was sharply constrained, and self-government in small units prevented political regimentation.

EXHIBIT 4-1 (continued)

TASKS

1. Craft tasks were self-determined and self-taught or taught through apprenticeship.
2. Technology was commonly and widely available by father-to-son training or extension services of land-grant universities (county agents).
3. Trade tasks ensued from free-market price and exchange, with individual contractual liabilities.
4. Manufacturing tasks were generally to craft whole products and were not finely specialized.
5. Citizens voiced needs in town-hall meetings and voted in single- (or few-) issue elections.

ALLEGIANCE

1. Strong allegiance ran to the family and the family enterprise, which formed both a filial and economic unit.
2. Individuals gave allegiance to the free-market system as a necessity in order to exchange output for needs.
3. Freely available capital bred support for the capitalistic system.
4. Local-government responsibility stimulated loyalty to representative government.

PROCESS

1. The economic process was one of individual ownership of one's occupational enterprise, familial economic units, free-market prices, and freely available resources.
2. The political process was one of self-determination through local government and a highly circumscribed central government.
3. The social process was family and community centered.

were generally small and in the form of single proprietorships, where owners themselves and their families worked the land or the mercantile business. Aggregations of capital were few, except with some Southern plantation owners and some New England sea captains dealing in the rum-slave trade. The few aggregations of capital were well outnumbered by individual property holders working their own enterprises, and economic authority was diverse, distributed, and widespread.

This dispersal of economic authority was augmented with each opening of new lands to the West, and thus for two and a half centuries, the United States had a constant source of replenishment of its diverse property ownership. In spite of the tendency for the older regions of the nation to develop wealth aggregation and a rich-versus-poor class structure, the availability of new lands provided free access to capital, which enabled individuals to pursue their own activities, and so the expanding West always replenished and swelled the numbers of small, independent property owners and gave them decision authority over their own holdings and their own lives.

As long as economic diversity, dispersal, and distribution of authority renewed itself, the potential concentration of political power never seriously threatened, except on a few occasions, as when James Fisk cornered the gold market and Mark Hanna made presidents from his front porch in Ohio. Indeed, the exceptions put us ahead of the story, for Mark Hanna's political machinations came into being only after the business trusts had begun to concentrate economic power through corporate organization.

Before corporate organization, the largest economic units were partnerships. Like individual ownerships, a partnership has unlimited legal liability, which makes individual managers very responsible for their acts, since they could lose all their business and entire personal fortunes by one management mistake. Unlimited legal liability for one's acts is the ultimate in accountability, and it tends toward a certain integrity of behavior. All economic enterprise, prior to 1850, was in proprietor or partner form.

With the coming of the Industrial Revolution in the mid-nineteenth century, partnerships began to get larger, and in Britain complaints were voiced against them because it was no longer always clear with whom one was dealing. Theoretically in law, every partner is an agent who commits the personal liability and wealth of every other partner in the firm. But legal enforcement was costly if people made contracts with one partner in a large firm, and then, when they sued the partnership for breach of contract, found that the partnership contested liability for a partner's acts. In the 1850s, the problem of assigning or avoiding liability in large partnerships caused Parliament to pass the first incorporation acts for business and industry.

Incorporation had existed for nonprofit and quasi-public institutions prior to 1850, because the corporate form is derived in Roman law from the incorporation of municipalities. The Roman municipium was the legal incorporation instrument for the governance of its colonies overseas. Britain applied municipal incorporation law to the modern, limited-liability business corporations, and the United States soon followed.

The coming of the American Civil War, with its industrial mobilization, expansion of the railroads, and burgeoning of iron, steel, coal, and mechanical industries, brought an explosive era of business incorporation which within just a generation changed the legal form of economic enterprise. By the 1870s, only twenty years after incorporation became common, trusts had become so large, among coal, sugar, steel, railroads, and oil, that railroad rate and antitrust regulation had to be legislated to try to control these new centralized authority structures.

The incorporation of American business brought two new eras—from 1870 to 1940 that of industrialization or large manufacturing, and from 1940 to the 1970s that of corporate aggregation into large-scale service enterprises. Thus, this century of change transformed the authority distribution patterns from being dispersed and decentralized among individual ownerships, to being conglomerated and centralized into large corporate entities.

POLITICAL AUTHORITY IN AGRARIAN AMERICA

The early colonists to the New World were agriculturalists settling the land, and they brought with them from Great Britain to New England a peculiar form of land holding which affected local governance—namely, the village or local town government. The first land-holding pattern in America was the New England village in which land was owned in common. Although separate fields were assigned for individual cultivation in areas surrounding the town, after the manner of tenant farmership in England, the central town area was used in common as open field by all the citizens. Each citizen was a property holder in common, and each property holder had a vote in town meetings. Each citizen in town meeting voted for himself, as he saw his own decision requirements, without a representative as his intermediary. Hence, the New England town was a true direct democracy, after the manner of Athens or the Villanova tribes (precursors of the Roman civilization); and the essence of democracy was that governance was tied to the land and its use.

The gradual change, which came over America from democracy to republican governance, was influenced in significant part by the treatment of land as an exchangeable commodity, because this separated governance from economic usage. The Southern colonies were settled in quite a different manner from those in New England, being occupied first by landed aristocrats who were given huge land charters by the British crown. The first workers of this land were not slaves, as they were later, but rather indentured servants, debtors, minor convicts, and the persecuted. To attract such labor, land was granted to each individual settler in small parcels as an economic incentive, and these land grants were known as "headrights." The headrights were what we now would call title in fee simple, and as such they were saleable.

Many settlers had neither the capital nor skill to farm small parcels, and so they sold their headrights to pay off their debts, indentures, or cost of their voyage. The result was that sea captains and speculators became major land holders in the South, along with the landed aristocracy, and farming moved toward the plantation system and serfdom (much as in Rome). In the South as in the North, it was traditional that only property holders could vote in elections, and the result was that the electorate was limited to members of the elite, who became legislative representatives for the disenfranchised as well as for themselves.

Thus, governance in the South was that of a representative republic, whereas in New England it was that of a direct democracy. These two forms of government were merged in the U.S. Constitution to provide a Senate representative on an area or land basis (Roman) and a House of Representatives organized on a population basis (Greek *deme*). By happenstance or quirk of history, therefore, the United States recreated almost exactly the Roman Republic, with a Senate made up of the landed aristocracy and an Assembly representative of the disenfranchised plebes (nonproperty owners). Even more striking in similarity, the framers of the Constitution established that the President should be elected by the people (first through the legislature and later directly) and have a term independent of the legislature, just as the Tribune of the Romans was elected by the plebian Assembly.

In Rome, the Tribune was the change agent in the system, because only he could intercede for the people with clemency or could initiate reform. The Senate in Rome was the stabilizing agent in the system because it could veto reform. The American President was granted the clemency powers of the Tribune (or the king's mercy). Also, as the sole nationally elected official in the government, it was felt that only he could presume to represent the whole public interest in change or reform. But the President's reform, or legislative proposals, had to receive legislative approval, in which the Senate (as in Rome) had a veto. Thus, as in Rome, the American Presidency is the change agent in the system and the Senate is the stabilizing agent.

The U.S. Presidency, as Tribune reincarnate, has given the American civilization a different trajectory than that of the nations of Western Europe, which evolved parliamentary government. European governments for centuries experienced tyranny through usurpation of power by the king. Parliamentary government was devised as a protection against such usurpation, and authority and governance was apportioned collegially in the representatives and the king's ministers. Although the king may dispose of an uncongenial minister from time to time or even an unruly representative, it is difficult for him to dispose of all of them at once. The collectivization of political authority in a common legislative-executive body in Western Europe is the same safeguard as the reforms Cleisthenes utilized to check the tyrannies of Greece in the sixth century B.C.

In modern times, the workings of the parliamentary versus the tribunate system of government have produced startling differences in results. During every crisis in the United States, whether it involves war, inflation, energy, unemployment, strikes, or riots, the American Presidency assumes more powers, granted by Congress, to deal with that crisis. But these emergency powers are seldom withdrawn; they become timeless delegations of authority. The sum of the accrued emergency powers of the President are potentially despotic. Thus, President Kennedy was able to use emergency military powers to police a minor incident in Indochina, which later unfolded into the longest war in American history, when supposedly only Congress had the power to declare war.

Every major crisis in parliamentary forms, by contrast, appears to weaken the government, because there is no independent change agent with authority for action. The lack of a focus for action, and the diversity of parliamentary views, causes the government to temporize in the face of crisis. The result is that, under crisis and stress, parliamentary governments, tend to fall into the hands of a strong man. The fall of parliamentary government before Hitler and Mussolini, the weakness and repeated change of the French government before De Gaulle, the repetitious dictatorships and military coups in South America, all are illustrative of weakness in crisis.

Only the parliamentary government of Britain has endured without failing, in spite of weakening, and this might be attributed to its own form of romanism. That is, Britain is a highly homogenous, class-structured society, in which governance traditionally is in the hands of an elite or aristocracy. The class-structured elitism of England is itself a stabilizing influence in crisis and is a means of coalescing action. Hence, the elite in Parliament can function (like a Roman Senate or Greek Aeropagus Council) to preserve the constitution and precipitate action in a way other Western nations have found to be difficult.

The political structure of the United States, then, began as dispersed authority and direct democracy in New England, and ended up as a highly centralized tribunate, as in Rome. Moreover, the centralization of economic authority and political authority have stimulated and rein-forced each other. Since 1870, the United States has had an unstable, cyclical economy, owing to the herd behavior of large corporate and financial managers. Eleven financial panics and depressions (in 1870, 1892, 1907, 1921, 1929, 1937, 1949, 1954, 1959, 1969, and 1974) have had the effect of increasing the power of the Presidency and central government in order to ameliorate the suffering of the unemployed. The federal government and Presidency have been granted large fiscal, monetary, and spending powers to offset the contractions in the corpo-rate business economy. But these economic powers of the federal gov-ernment are now so large that often the government, by miscalculation, causes depressions or inflations while trying to cure them (for example, large government deficits led to the 1972 inflation followed by the 1974 recession). And these grants of power do not have terminal dates upon them; hence, they are timeless and additive, and the power grows.

The availability of power tempts its use, for good purposes, of course, and so the government expands education, research, science, technol-ogy, investment, depreciation, tax incentives, all to the good end of creating more jobs or raising living standards. But the flow of funds must go through contemporary institutions capable of using them. Hence, the funds go to the large corporations, large universities, large research institutes, all again to the good end of creating jobs or raising living standards. But each time, these institutions become larger, ac-quire more funds, gain more authority. Each time the flow of funds and availability of capital to ordinary people become less.

Herein lies the principal contrast of agrarian with postindustrial America. In our agrarian society, the capital flows were freely available to the common man; in postindustrial America, the capital flows are channeled away from ordinary people (their taxes and savings) to the institutions, which make decisions for them.

MISSION ANALYSIS OF POSTINDUSTRIAL AMERICA

The needs of individuals in postindustrial America, 1940–1970s, reflect their employee status. The needs are to raise living standards, receive an equitable distribution of income, obtain individualized services that meet their unique needs, and to have satisfying and creative work that fulfills their individual identities and maturation.

But notice that few of these needs can be met by individuals themselves as employees—and more than half the population are employees. Employees cannot raise their own living standards, determine their own income shares, supply their own services, nor create their own jobs. These authorities lie elsewhere, in large institutions. Hence, our mission analysis for the postindustrial United States, shown in Exhibit 4-2, shows an incongruity between individual human needs and the authority distributions capable of responding to those needs.

EXHIBIT 4-2. Postindustrial America, 1940–1970s. An abstract of mission analysis and scenario according to six elements of social structure.

NEEDS AND MISSIONS

1. To raise living standards.
2. To provide equitable distribution of income.
3. To deliver services, as well as goods, responsive to unique (rather than standardized) human needs, which are increasingly cultural.
4. To provide satisfying creative work, fulfilling individual identities and maturation.

AUTHORITY

1. Economic growth, living standards, and income distribution are determined primarily in large technical corporations.
2. Services are delivered mainly by large institutions and government in standardized form.
3. Work is defined by tasks needed by the institutions, rather than originating in individual interest.
4. The change process is in the hands of a representative central government, in which the individual has no discrete vote on key issues such as war, inflation, or unemployment.

FUNCTIONS

1. Growth and income are generated by capital investment in technological means.
2. Services are performed by professionals, who evaluate their own colleagues with little public appraisal.
3. Intricate technologies are subdivided into networks of simple tasks, which are given to workers who have little knowledge of the whole process.
4. Representative government legislates change in response to lobbies that are professional or bureaucratic power blocs, rather than in response to individuals.

TASKS

1. Research, education, science, and technology are the task environments for generating techno-economic growth.
2. Capital-intensive investments for big technology are agglomerated from small savings and small accounting tasks, which consolidate into large-scale finance and capital flows.
3. Services are performed by specialized professionals, who are expert in treating part of a problem.
4. Tasks assigned by institutions appear as work-in-process to the individual, who has little cognizance of the final product.
5. Campaign and fund-raising tasks enable the individual to influence the selection between two like politicians, whose behavior is unpredictable on crucial issues after the lobby-bargaining process starts.

ALLEGIANCE

1. Individuals tolerate large institutions to the extent their own economic well-being is advanced.
2. Services are sufficiently impersonal so that individuals are indifferent toward most service organizations.
3. Job satisfaction is rare except at high professional levels.
4. The political process appears nonresponsive and ungovernable, with many nonvoters indifferent to who is elected.
5. Allegiances run largely to the isolated, nuclear family (and profession, for those who have one).

EXHIBIT 4-2 (continued)

PROCESS

1. The process of education, research, and technology is highly advanced and articulated, with institutional maintenance.
2. The capital-formation process is controlled by large institutions, which make capital-allocation decisions for institutional maintenance.
3. Services are performed by professional organizations concerned with institutional maintenance.
4. The government is run by elected officials, whose principal goal of reelection is realized with financial support from lobbying groups.

AUTHORITY PATTERNS CONTRASTED

The mission analysis for the postindustrial United States is, perhaps, self-explanatory to those of us living contemporaneously within the social system. Clearly, the authority distributions are highly centralized in the federal government and large institutions. The result is that functions, tasks, and the social process are determined institutionally rather than by individual choice or decision. Since institutions exist first to maintain themselves and secondly to serve their clientele, the nonresponsiveness to individual needs increases as institutional authority encompasses larger and larger segments of human life.

The authority patterns in America today differ sharply from those of nineteenth-century agrarian America. Then authority was dispersed, diverse, and decentralized. Individuals could respond largely to their own needs, because they had the means in available capital resources to decide and act on their own behalf. They had authority and self-determination because they had resources and capital and could make their own capital allocations. Today, individuals (employees) cannot exercise such authority because the capital flows are channeled not to individuals but to institutions.

Notice, too, in contrasting the present with agrarian America, that there are few allegiances today and they are mainly to the isolated family, with no economic foundation, and to one's occupation to the extent that one shares in equitable income distribution and rising living standards. These are weak allegiances, for the family has no pervasive authority and one's income share depends upon institutional wisdom or largesse.

The ideology of America comes largely from its agrarian form. Read the allegiances of the agrarian scenario; they ring of Americanism itself. But these allegiances are gone, departed with the conditions of self-determination which made them possible. That is why America has moved from the orderly to the disorderly state. The present institutions, their authority, their responsiveness, do not sufficiently meet the needs of the people. Allegiance is a two-way social contract. When authority responds to needs, the people grant allegiance to the authority. When authority is nonresponsive to individuals, individuals are nonresponsive in their allegiances.

If you compare the scenario of agrarian America with that of the orderly society shown in Chapter 2, you will notice, in both cases, the close congruency of authority and function distributions to individual needs. If you compare the scenario of present America with that of the disorderly society in Chapter 2, you will notice the lack of congruence and articulation between (a) the needs and (b) responsiveness of authority patterns.

The critical policy issue of the United States is to bring authority patterns back into congruence with human needs, either by making institutions responsive or by returning authority to individuals so that they can respond on their own behalf. The scenarios we have given suggest that one crucial element needed to restructure authority and make it more responsive is to change the capital flows from the institutions back to the individuals. Legislatively, this reversal of capital flows would be relatively simple, merely by taxing corporations identically with individuals. Politically, such a measure is practically impossible, because the corporate lobbies have most of the political campaign funds, and therefore in tax legislation before the legislatures they have the votes and individuals do not.

In addition, opponents will argue that the reversal of capital flows from institutions to individuals is economically infeasible, for several reaons: First, economies of scale make the fragmentation of capital impossible. Second, technology requires massive research expenditures and capital investments. Third, there is greater managerial expertise in large organizations than there is with ordinary people. Fourth, such ordinary people do not understand technology and its implications. Fifth, ordinary people do not understand the social process and its complex interrelations. Sixth, national security requires large organizations to support military preparations. Seventh, never change horses in the middle of the stream; organizational change is too traumatic to consider.

These are good reasons, and they have been used repeatedly to justify the continuance of present practice against heroic choices required to make change. But whether they have foundation in fact or not, it is the assertion of this book that if such good reasons prevail, the social evolution of the United States will continue along its inevitable course to the same dismal end that other civilizations have reached. Do we wish to diminish as the Greek, Roman, or medieval societies did? These scenarios are all available to us, and the next three chapters will show that, to the extent there are elements of Roman, Greek, and medieval society in American society, the United States will follow the same dramatic plot to the same climactic end. Reading these scenarios and replaying these old dramas are like browsing through one's alternative obituaries.

However, no course of events is inevitable. As I have already stated, the potential relationships of humankind with its environment are innumerable. If we do not like Greek or Roman tragedies, perhaps we can write a scenario based upon a whole new set of assumptions and see how the plot logically unfolds.

Let us suppose, for example, that the seven assumptions above regarding the infeasibility of reversing capital flows are false. I am not asserting that they are false, because the difference between truth and falsity is very obscure even to the wisest. However, we can bring out counterarguments that are just as plausible as the seven "good reasons" given above: First, economies of scale do not limit the ability to reverse capital flows into smaller units because such economies apply only to mass-production industries, which account for a minority of the national output. Second, massive research expenditures produce decreasing returns, and the major innovations of our time have been produced by the lone, or small-scale, researcher rather than by big research. Third, managerial expertise is widely distributed and, with education and training, ordinary people can learn to be more responsive to individual needs than can large institutions. Fourth, if ordinary people cannot understand the implications of technology, the technology is irrelevant. Fifth, ordinary people may not understand the complex interrelations of our intricate social system, but neither apparently do our present political or managerial leaders. Sixth, national security is more a matter of allegiance than of massive armament. Seventh, if you do not change horses in the middle of the stream, you may never get to the other side.

We may inquire whether one set of assumptions is as plausible as another's, at least to see what may happen on paper, because the truth is indeed obscure. Can we not then, write a scenario that reverses all the assumptions that repeat the plots of old dramas? Of course we can, and in due course we shall. But first we need to see where events might take us if post industrial America sticks with all the "good reasons" for pursuing the status quo. As we have seen, today authority has gravitated upward to large institutions and central government, to the point where the society appears nonresponsive and ungovernable to many people. Their lack of ability to influence the social process and their lack of access to capital flows cause them, at best, to be indifferent and, at worst, alienated from the society. The result is lack of allegiance, loyalty, or morality and a tendency toward disorder.

Where will this restiveness lead? The alternative futures are many. In the next chapter, we shall see how we would do as the Romans did.

Old and new Rome. *(Photo by Bela Kalman/Stock, Boston.)*

Chapter Five

THE FUTURE
OF THE U.S.A.:
THE ROMAN REPLAY

American society has a number of striking similarities to the ancient Roman society, some of which have already been noted in the previous chapter. Indeed, a replay of Roman history is one of the more plausible alternative futures for the United States, which is why I shall describe it before the Greek and medieval possibilities. Of course, there are also differences, and the purpose of this chapter is to clarify these similarities and differences. However, we will assume here that the similarities in social structure will dominate the future of the United States and that our social evolution will follow the same trajectory as Roman history. Although the setting, players, technology, and customs will provide Future U.S.A., Roman style, with minor variations in the

69

scenario, the institutional similarities are assumed to dominate the drama, bringing us to a similar logical climax.

Sometimes we forget how long the Roman state lasted. It existed for nine centuries under its own identity and another ten under that of the Roman Catholic church. We should be fortunate to last as long, since other nations and empires have frequently run their course in much shorter spans—perhaps only three centuries or less. The Roman scenario is not a very happy one, but it meets the tests of durability and survival.

Replaying this scenario is difficult without a sense of Roman history, but since a rereading of history would be quite tiresome for most people, I have simply written Roman Replay U.S.A. straightaway, as though everyone recalled what Roman history was all about. The appendix, however, provides a chronology, abstract, and mission analysis of the Roman society, and this appendix might fruitfully be read in parallel with the scenario. (In a sense, the appendix is the documentation from which the replay scenario is drawn.)

SIMILARITIES BETWEEN AMERICAN AND ROMAN SOCIETIES

Besides their similar political structures, which have already been discussed, the most striking parallel between the United States and Roman society is in the dispossession of the farmers of their land and capital, together with all the social consequences of this dispossession. In both instances, it caused the society to shift a majority of its members from an independent to a dependent class, of plebes or employees and of the urban poor. In turn both societies built ever larger institutions to respond to these dependent classes or to protect the elite from them. The consequences issuing from this chain of events provide most of the similarities, as shown below.

Dispossession of Farmers

The strength of the Roman legions lay in their property-owning farmer, conscripted to military service, who fought for their own lands and livelihood as well as for the state. The Etruscan and Latin wars, by which the Italian peninsula was conquered, were intermittent, regional wars to consolidate the security of the Roman society and the farmer's land. Moreover, the farmer-legionnaire could, with his family's help, attend to the crops sufficiently to retain the farm. But with the Carthaginian and Macedonian wars from 265 to 168 B.C., the interminable overseas campaigns severed the farmer from his land by military service, neglect, or indebtedness.

Similarly, American farmers were dispossessed of their land by industrialization, the attraction of manufacturing wages, the marginal nature of small farms, erratic commodity prices, World War I, indebtedness, and the massive farm-mortgage foreclosures of the Great Depression.

Growth of Institutional Authority

In Rome, the farmer was displaced by large, corporate estates called *latifundia*, owned by landed aristocrats who bought up land cheaply during the generations of war and who operated them with slaves captured by military conquest. The main business of Rome was carried on in the *latifundia*, the procurator enterprises that supplied the army, and the military organizations themselves. These institutions all grew to large size and scale as conquest expanded.

The American farmer was displaced by the large business corporation, which expanded from manufacturing into agriculture, trade, finance, services, and multinational operations.

Uniform Administration of Law or Fixed Policy

The military conquests brought so many geographically dispersed colonies under Roman control that they could not be run from Rome. Since Rome's economic growth was based upon tribute rather than production, these colonies had to be exploited efficiently. Hence, Roman municipal law was formulated to provide a codified set of rules for running colonies, and the law was administered by a Roman prefect.

The United States is geographically dispersed and, before today's rapid communications media, needed to be administered effectively by closely articulated local, state, and federal regulations. These were codified into law or judicial precedent and formed common administrative practice among the several states. The rise of decentralized and multinational corporations required similar consistency of practice, which was accomplished by fixing uniform corporate policy.

Large Scale of Institutions

In both Rome and the United States, institutions were (are) large and with centralized authority, compared to other contemporary societies.

Similar Political Structure

Both societies had bicameral legislatures, one house intended to represent the people, and the other to represent the elite. In Rome, the executive was selected independently from the legislature in the form of consul or tribune (counterpart of U.S. President). The executive and the people's assembly could initiate reform. In Rome, the senate, judiciary, and military could veto reform.

Destruction of the Family

The Caesars deliberately set out to destroy the family by removing its economic base (farm and capital), forbidding any associations, and instituting *tribuncia potestas* in which Caesar assumed the powers of the father. Thus, the family became wholly dependent upon the state. In the United States, we have bemoaned the loss of family but have nonetheless continued to undermine it inadvertently or covertly by denying it capital and economic function and by instituting welfare measures to keep it dependent upon the state.

Unarmed Nature of Dissent

The nature of dissent was the same in both societies, taking the form of unarmed protests against nonresponsiveness, inequality, or injustices. (The exception, perhaps, is the Sparticus slave revolt.) In Rome, the form and legal means of dissent was generally by demonstration, to signalize the issue, and by reforms introduced in the people's assembly. The frustration of reform was in senatorial or executive veto or in nonexecution.

Rise of the Military

In Rome, international wars and local dissent required an enlarged military establishment to fight increasing wars abroad and to intervene with force (including killing citizens) in domestic disturbances.

Emergence of Oligarchy and Representative Plutocracy

In Rome, the landed aristocrats, with military assistance, suppressed local dissent and used the senatorial veto to neutralize the plebian assembly. The senate and the military granted increasing powers to the consul and tribune to deal with revolt, to the point where the consul became dictator. In the United States, the cost of elections, particularly after the rise of television, has made electoral campaigns prohibitive to the ordinary person, so that representation has come increasingly from the wealthy, those with a family name, or candidates of the lobbies. Plutocracy, oligarchy, and elitism have emerged because mainly well-financed candidates from big institutions or name families are capable of running for office.

Centralization of Power

In Rome, the combination of dissent, military suppression, oligarchical rule, large institutions, and emergency powers to the executive all combined to form a highly centralized regime.

DIFFERENCES BETWEEN AMERICAN AND ROMAN SOCIETIES

If it seems that I have overdrawn somewhat the similarities between U.S. and Roman societies for the sake of emphasis, the differences will also be sharpened (if only to make it possible to write a Greek and medieval replay). The main differences are:

Basis for Economic Growth

Roman economic growth was based upon military expansion and tribute, whereas the U.S. is based upon industrial productivity and trade. Rome was unable to provide even its own food supply from production in Italy, especially after the dispossession of the farmers. When the military mines around the Mediterranean began to run out, Rome faced grave material shortages.

Technologies

The Roman construction, textile, metal, and shipbuilding industries and agriculture and military preparation were comparatively advanced for the time. American technology, on the other hand, has excelled in manufacturing, communication, science, and advanced weaponry, but between 1955 and 1975 the United States exported a considerable part of its competitive edge.

Corporate Style

The corporate style of the *latifundia* was largely that of plantation overseer with absentee owners. The U.S. corporate style emphasizes strategic planning, finance, and technological advancement, all provided by members of a professional technostructure hired by absentee owners.

Labor Contract

The Roman labor contract was slavery. The American labor contract is wages. The American employees have had only minor influence on keeping wages in line with prices, but at least they can quit their jobs.

Family Authority

The Roman family was patriarchal, with the father having final authority, even over revenge and death. In the American family, the decision process is one of concurrence, with the father acting as chief advisor and arbiter.

Local Government

The municipium-prefect system made local government a direct line of command from Rome. In the United States, even with all the subvention and subversion of local government by federal grants, some vestigial authority and local self-determination remains.

THE BEGINNING OF FUTURE U.S.A., ROMAN REPLAY

The similarities and differences between Roman and American societies may be compared in a simple table (Table 5–1). The similarities are numerous, basic, and impressive, especially in power structure, dissensions, and tendency to resolve the class conflicts unilaterally and by force. The differences, while seemingly fewer, may be fairly compelling in the long run for our analysis, particularly as regards the family structure and the means of economic growth. However, for the time being, we shall ignore the significance of these differences, if only for the purpose of developing the plot of our scenario.

TABLE 5-1. Comparison of American and Roman Societies

Similarities	Differences
Dispossession of farmers	Basis for economic growth
Growth of institutional authority	Technologies
Uniform administration of law	Corporate style
Large scale of institutions	Labor contract
Political structure	Family authority
Destruction of family	Local government
Unarmed nature of dissent	
Rise of military	
Emergence of oligarchy	
Centralization of power	

Now let us start unreeling the scenario. It begins in the 1970s in the United States, a time period assumed to be roughly equivalent to 50 or 60 B.C. in Rome. Sulla has exited the drama, Pompey is on stage, and Julius Ceasar is in the wings. Table 5–2 shows the benchmarks leading up to the present point.

For those familiar with Roman history (see appendix), the chain of events in the Roman society will become quite clear. Briefly, Julius Caesar, the last of several military generals (Marius, Sulla, Pompey) to quell internal riots at the request of the Senate, established himself as personal ruler over the wealth of the empire by the municipalization of the colonies; that is, by making the municipal administrative authorities responsible to himself, rather than to the Senate, or consuls. This usurption was part of the "ambition" that later caused his assassination. Mark Antony, after pursuing the assassins, sought a de facto division of empire between East and West, with Antony and Cleopatra ruling Egypt. Octavius defeated Antony and consolidated power again.

More than any other, Octavius, later Augustus Caesar, had the political craft to institutionalize the power of empire by seemingly letting it remain a symbolic republic while in fact converting it to a monarchy. He did this by several shrewd moves: (1) placating the Senate by returning the "peaceful" municipia to its rule, but retaining the "rebellious" colonies (also the rich ones) under military rule directed by himself; (2) instituting a constitutional reform naming himself first in presiding over the Senate; (3) instituting another reform declaring himself equal and superior to elected consuls; and (4) instituting a third making himself Tribune of the people, which placed reform and clemency in his own hands. Rome continued to have all the panoply of a republic governed by the Senate, but Octavius held all the key offices.

Some clarification of events in the United States are also needed. The

TABLE 5-2. Chronological Parallels Between American and Roman Societies

Event	Roman date	U.S. Date
Foreign sovereignty over colonial development	800–509 B.C. Etruscan	A.D. 1607–1776 British
Founding of the republic	509	1787
Enfranchisement and legal protection of nonproperty owners	450–367	1880–1960
Ascendency of juridical law	396–265	1840–1905
Dispossession of farmers	265–146	1870–1940
Rise of corporate organizations	265–30 Latifundia	1870–1970 Corporations
First populist dissent	133–121	1870–1900
Second popular revolt	118–90	1930–1940
Third popular revolt	60–40	1960–1970
Welfare reforms	133–118 Gracchan	1932–39 Roosevelt
Beginning of the dole	133	1933
Use of military to suppress citizens	118–40	1960–70
Rise of political oligarchy	118–30	1954–1970s
Alienation, immorality, dropping out, drug addiction, free fornication, birth control, depopulation	150	1960s
Rise of dictatorship and *tribunicia potestas*	30	?

legal protection of nonproperty owners began with revision of election laws in 1810 to 1850. Election laws (and the commercial code) are state prerogatives under the constitutional definition of powers. Early election laws franchised only property-owning males. The franchise was extended to all males early in the Republic, to women around the turn of the century, and to blacks by the civil rights acts of the 1960s. Debtor laws were similarly relaxed over time.

The ascendency of juridical law is taken to originate in the Dred Scott decision, asserting federal ascendency over state sovereignty, and to extend to the Standard Oil case in 1911, where federal antitrust laws were applied, for citizen protection, to the corporate trusts.

The first popular dissension is taken to be the Populist movement among farmers in the 1870s; the first labor organizations, such as the International Workers of the World; and the suppression of the first railroad strike.

The second popular revolt is regarded as the Farmer's Holiday of the 1930s, the violence of the truckers' union, and the sit-down strikes of the Great Depression.

The third popular revolt is taken to be Little Rock, Watts, and Detroit race riots and the Kent State killing of students.

The rise of political oligarchy and plutocracy is assumed to coincide with the advent of television, high campaign costs, and the election-financing laws. The names of the oligarchs can be read in the campaign finance lists of the 1972 presidential election.

So here we are, a Romanesque American society in the 1970s about to make the same decisions and mistakes the Romans made from 50 B.C. onward. Let us see what would happen.

ANALYSIS OF ROMAN POLICY CHOICES

The picture of the Romans' road to their destiny will become more sharply focused for us if we put their set of policy choices in the same analytical framework of thirteen policy choices that we did for the United States in Chapter 1. This is shown in Table 5–3. We have already noted that the Roman and American modus operandi for survival differ: theirs was military expansion, and ours is capital expansion. Their form of intensification of the social process, as they needed to establish control over internal disorder, was military intensification. As a military-intensive economy, Roman society applied both capital and technology to its military expansion. For example, road and mine operations were under military ownership and control, which meant that the technologies associated with construction, mining, communications, logistics, and weaponry were largely military. In the policy analysis that follows, then, Roman military intensification is treated as an analog to U.S. capital intensification.

The Roman policy choices, as nearly as they can be comparatively reconstructed, correspond with those of the United States almost exactly, with four exceptions: (1) theirs was a labor-intensive economy, based on slavery by military conquest, which left the freemen un-employed; (2) educational distribution was narrow; (3) internal order was maintained by military force; and (4) international order was main-tained by military conquest. However, these four characteristics of Roman governance were more conspicuous in the later phases (after 133 B.C.) of their evolution than in its early stages. Between 509 and 265 B.C., the society was fairly orderly and effective as a representative republic. The resort to coercion came after the dispossession of the farmers (265–

TABLE 5-3. Policy Analysis and Comparison of Thirteen Major Issues Confronting Rome and the United States

	Policy issue	Roman choice	U.S. choice	Consequence of Roman choice	Consequence of U.S. choice
1.	Monetary-fiscal	Unbalanced (expansion)	Unbalanced (expansion)	Inflation	Inflation
2.	Income distribution	Skewed	Skewed	Rich-poor extremes	Rich-poor extremes
3.	Capital distribution	Institutionally channeled	Institutionally channeled	Capital concentration	Capital concentration
4.	Competitive distribution	Oligopolistic	Oligopolistic	Large economic oligopoly	Large business oligopoly
5.	Price policy	Administered	Administered	Tribute maximized, stable	Profit maximized, stable
6.	Living standards	Externalize cost	Externalize cost	Less amenities, more government	Less amenities more government
7.	Employment	Labor intensive*	Labor extensive	Slavery, freeman unemployment	Unemployment, capital intensification
8.	Educational distribution	Narrow*	Semiwide	Ruling elite	Specialized technostructure
9.	Technological distribution	Narrow	Narrow	Oligopoly	Oligopoly
10.	Barriers to entry	Raised	Raised	Skewed incomes	Skewed incomes
11.	Voting	Narrow issue	Narrow issue	Oligarchic republic	Oligarchic republic
12.	Internal order	Coercive*	Semiparticipative	Police state	Limited conflict
13.	International order	Coercive*	Semicoercive	Military rule	Use of economic-military power

*Differences of Roman choices compared to those of U.S.A.

146 B.C.) and the first popular revolts (133 B.C.). From then on, the use of military force for internal coercion mounted (118–40 B.C.), until finally the military intensification led to dictatorship and police state under Octavius (30 B.C.).

Like the United States, Rome financed its military intensification by expansionist monetary-fiscal means. Inflation led to the abandonment of free prices first in grain (133 B.C.) and the use of government rationing to feed the poor. Inflation eventually became so uncontrollable that the Diocletian price control edicts froze prices and forced the economy into barter, which was the beginning of feudalism.

Capital distribution was institutionally channeled by tribute to the military and its logistics procurators, as well as to the landed oligarchs by the allocation of conquered slaves to the *latifundia*. By the time of Caesar Augustus, capital (land and military power) was reportedly concentrated in the hands of about 2,000 families, who formed the ruling oligarchy.

The political choice of this ruling oligarchy in Rome, when disorder erupted for the third time (60–40 B.C.), was to put the revolt down by military rule and to set up dictatorial power for maintaining existing institutions. This period of military intensification required increasing use of coercive military force in order to maintain order, with diminishing social returns; that is, the return in tribute at home and abroad did not increase proportionately to the military resources applied. By about the time of Octavius, Rome had reached diminished marginal productivity from military expenditures. The net gain in wealth from military exploits had been highest during the second century B.C. By the third century A.D., however, the resource demands for maintaining order had become so costly in terms of mounting military requirements that the Roman Empire began to cave in from the inside before it was conquered externally.

The Roman set of policy choices very closely approximates those of the United States. The Romans' disorders and time of troubles began, as have ours, first, when the forced expansionism of military (capital) intensification caused inflation, and, second, when institutional authority (military and *latifundia*) caused incomes and capital to be distributed into extremes of rich and poor. Unemployment, poverty, and declining living conditions (inflation, less amenities, more government) led to riots, which the Roman oligarchy chose to put down by military force.

Let us assume that the United States in the future makes the next logical, incremental decisions inherent in the choice patterns we have already established, and since our choice patterns closely approximate the Romans', let us assume that the United States evolves as the Roman Empire did. What would our future be like?

The United States experiences repeated periods of simultaneous inflation and stagnation (stagflation), as in 1975. Double-digit inflation is endemic to the United States, and incomes of employees do not keep up with rising administered prices. As incomes fall behind prices, living standards diminish, people are able to purchase less, corporation sales decline, more employees are discharged, unemployment increases.

Unemployment and decreasing living standards cause a public clamor for relief, since the burden is falling on individuals rather than on institutions. The federal government responds by reiterating past choices—that is, by expansionism through the increase of government deficit spending and bank borrowing (inflating the money supply). These expansionist tactics work temporarily, business improves, people are reemployed. However, small increases in demand, at home and abroad, upon the narrowing base of more costly resources, quickly cause the inflated money supply from the last expansion to be put to use as higher prices.

Each time this inflation-unemployment-inflation cycle repeats itself, the expansion has to be intensified, because of the decreasing marginal returns from capital. Capital investment has to be intensified to try to achieve some kind of minimal expansion to get out of stagnationunemployment. Large corporations have to aggregate increasing amounts of capital for each cycle. They do this partly by trying to increase profits through reducing competition, and partly by channeling savings from the public into their institutions. Capital intensification of this type requires authority intensification in the institutions and more control over prices, capital, competition, technology, education, and barriers to entry.

Private firms also seek to enlarge their profits (capital flows) by externalizing costs (such as pollution), excluding as many costs as they can from their own accounts and shifting them to the public or to the government. The government is forced by public clamor to ameliorate the social costs that business has excluded; hence, government has rapidly rising expenditures for environmental costs, medical costs, retirment, social security, unemployment, welfare, and food stamps. Government keeps getting larger, but the amenities and living standards for individuals keep declining.

At some point in this upward inflationary spiral, the net expansion by business through capital intensification is no longer able to increase productivity or output. Still, government costs keep rising and price inflation keeps galloping. Ordinary people become uneasy about keeping money because it falls in value so fast, but the government has no other new source from which to finance its rising costs. It cannot tax more, because living standards are already falling. It cannot get new revenue through capital productivity, which is declining. Capital intensification no longer works, but expenses go on rising. What to do?

The economy is so precariously on the brink of disaster that government officials hesitate to make reforms or changes, because their consequences would be unknown. Change takes at least a little time. Some margin of resources is needed to finance change, to pay costs for the transition time. But there is no margin of resources at this point, because the economy has been pushed too far. The capital-intensification process on which the United States relied is producing decreasing returns. It is costing money to try to intensify rather than yielding a social return.

With no policy options left, there is only one thing to do: exercise the institutional authority that remains. The government expands the money supply and its deficit again, knowing that there will be no expansion in the supply of goods. Prices rise immediately and sharply as more and more money chases fewer goods. The goods have become fewer because both individual and industrial buyers are hoarding, buying up everything they can which they can store. Supplies dry up, black markets emerge, prices soar higher. In panic, consumers buy everything available—houses, property, cars, clothes—to the point where sellers no longer sell but will only barter for other goods. Money is to be avoided, since it is nearly worthless.

Suddenly the middle class finds that it has been dispossessed. Life savings in banks, securities, and savings accounts are worth nothing. Retirement incomes will not buy enough food to eat. Taxes and upkeep are so high that people do not have enough money to keep their homes. Old people lose their houses. Young married people have no hope of buying them. Employee incomes lag so far behind prices that workers drop below a subsistence level.

The workers strike to keep their incomes up with prices, but unemployment is so high that strikes are only partly effective. The corporations have declining sales, low profits, and declining returns from investment. They say they cannot afford to pay higher wages; they can only afford to raise prices. The strikes get more violent, and are put down with police force.

The dispossessed middle class, the poor, the disadvantaged, the old, and the minorities join the worker demonstrations to show their own needs and despair. The demonstrations are massive but peaceful, the people unarmed. In one demonstration, the military militias trying to contain the crowd are few in number relative to the demonstrators. The troops try to move the crowd, to disperse it. Pushing and shoving starts, which soon leads to batons versus sticks, bricks and stones versus tear gas. The weight of the massive crowd pushes back the military. The troops retreat, and a few soldiers fall and are overtaken. The troops regroup to try to rescue their overtaken comrades. The soldiers have to jab into the crowd, but the mob will not move. The soldiers use bayonets, then rifle fire. The crowd scatters, leaving dead behind.

For days it is quiet. Individuals are home brooding, mourning the dead, grieved by their losses, wondering what to do. Petitions and political hearings do not work. There is no arbitration or settlement procedure for the conflict. More than half the population has little to lose, meager incomes, no life savings, few jobs, little hope. Nothing matters anymore. Any act, however desperate, is better than no act.

People organize clandestinely into guerrilla units with hunting rifles, pistols, and home-made gasoline bombs. They snipe at the militia, burn out trucks and tanks. The military brings in reinforcements, levels resistance, and searches out arms. The revolt is quelled. Martial law is declared, with military posts and surveillance of the population in every community.

Now two lines of government exist, the military command, which is maintaining order, and the former civil government, which is nominally in charge of nonmilitary affairs. The question is how to merge them. Open elections cannot be held, because the existing military government has no support, only enmity. The executive of the civil government, therefore, confers with the military (of which he is nominally commander-in-chief) about an approved slate of candidates who might stand for election from the two parties. The approved slate contains only names of candidates from the oligarchy that supports the existing regime. Both party candidates run on a platform of a return to law and order and a return to work. The elections are held and few voters appear, but a legally constituted government continues.

Now the government is faced with reconstruction. The first new piece of legislation is the Return to Work Law, which requires employees to go to work assigned by the government at wages negotiated for them between the government and the corporations. The second law is a monetary revaluation law, which exchanges a very limited supply of new currency for all the old money outstanding.

The effect of these new economic policies is to create a new kind of stability. Within a short time, almost everyone who wants to work is employed, and unemployment becomes negligible. Inflation is gone, because the money supply is tightly controlled and wages are frozen. Production increases, goods are available again. Employees can buy goods again at stable prices, but they find their standard of living is much lower than it was.

Two important social changes have occurred: first, the rich have become richer (and fewer); second, the middle class has become poorer, with lower incomes and no assets. A dramatic redistribution of income has occurred, skewing incomes even more to the high side. During the inflation, the rich who owned income-producing property bought up all the assets (life savings) of the middle class with worthless money. This concentrated capital into large holdings in fewer hands. Then the freezing of wages at low levels and conscripting of people back to work widened profit margins enough so that investment of capital again became attractive. In effect, the lower marginal productivity of capital was being subsidized by transferring income (through lower wages) to the owners of capital (via larger profits). The capital-intensification process could now be made to work again, by shifting income and capital distribution in favor of the few. The many paid tribute from their wages to the capital-intensification process run by the oligarchy.

Employees hate the government and job conscription but can do little about it. A minority of employees even feel that, despite harder work and lower living standards, the stable regime is better than inflation or revolution, even if it is a police state. These are mainly older employees; younger ones still conspire and scheme to overthrow the government, and periodically they disappear into labor camps run by the military.

The real strife is no longer at the bottom or between rich and poor. The conflict now breaks out within the oligarchy, among the rich, and between the rich and the government. The military and government officials feel that they are the ones holding the country together, maintaining order, redistributing income from the lower to upper income groups, but that they, the officials, are not getting any of the spoils— they are getting only a government salary and doing all the work, while the property owners are getting all the money. The military and government officials rectify this inequity by three means: (1) granting favorable rulings on wage-price decisions (profit margins), in exchange for stock or ownership in the corporations; (2) bringing conspiracy charges against uncooperative business oligarchs; and (3) as a last resort, expropriating corporate property, with the government officials then taking over the executive and stockholder positions.

The cupidity of government officials incenses the oligarchs, and they begin to conspire among themselves to remove the most avaricious of these officials by whatever means necessary, including assassination. The government-corporate oligarchy becomes a nightmare of intrigue and conspiracy, with counterespionage and informers throughout the oligarchy. The powerful cease to trust each other, and life becomes anxious despite their wealth. They seek order among themselves, and they find it in a military general who appears to be beyond cupidity.

The general begins removing from office all civil and military officials engaged in larcenous acts against the rich, which endears him to the corporate oligarchy. The oligarchy supports the general in assuming the duties of President, Vice-President, president pro-tem of the Senate, Chief Justice, and Speaker of the House, as well as remaining general of the military. This consolidation of offices has the advantages of (1) economy, since the general is willing to accept only one salary for his public duty, and (2) efficiency in decision making, because now all legislative, judicial, executive, and military decisions can be closely coordinated and made at one point. This "one-stop" decision making is demonstrated to be just as efficient and decisive as its analogue in the business corporation.

The news media, which retain a modicum of freedom as long as they do not incite insurrection, criticize this new arrangement as being extralegal and unconstitutional. The general agrees that this is a lamentable condition that should be corrected, and therefore is proposed, by the oligarchs, on the approved list of candidates to be elected as President, Vice-President, and Representative in Congress. Upon his election, he then appoints himself Chief Justice of the Supreme Court, Speaker of the House, Chairman of the Joint Chiefs of Staff, and he is, of course, presiding officer of the Senate through the Vice-Presidency.

The general (or General) is now the constitutional head of state, with all the powers of the three branches of government. The Republic endures. Indeed, the General qua President is very devoted to the ideals of the Republic, attends all his offices assiduously, holds elections regularly, passes legislation with dispatch, and executes the law with military precision, with seldom a dissenting opinion from the Supreme Court. The government has become a marvel of stability and efficiency, and the Republic is venerated for its harmony.

The General now turns his attention to scholarly pursuits. He creates a Science and Education Advisory Board, with the purpose of planning the future needs of the nation. This board evaluates new military weapons needs, basic scientific discoveries, and industrial applications. The board then distributes development rights among corporations by a license upon which the corporation must pay a royalty for its use. The royalty is geared to the profitability of the idea, as in any good business practice. Corporations find they have to bid for these royalties, and as the sources for innovations dry up (outside the Science Board), the bids and royalties become higher and higher, until all the surplus profits are absorbed by the payments to government.

The General, as head of the key offices of state, uses his own discretion on the use of these funds. It is alleged by some, prone to slander the General, that he has villas, yachts, and foreign bank accounts plied with these royalty receipts. The General calmly denies such slander and publishes a list of expenditures, which demonstrates the large sums that go into his educational selection program. That is, the bulk of the royalties can be shown to go into financing higher education for those given scholarship awards by the General's Educational Selection Board. Education is no longer open to anyone except those selected by the board. Moreover, there is no technical staff available to the corporations, except those allocated to it by the Educational Selection Board. The development rights under government license, with its royalty, carries with it authorization to requisition technical manpower from the educational system. Education becomes highly specialized, technical and skilled, and there is a waiting line for employers seeking to employ the graduates. The graduates have all been carefully selected for their technical and intellectual ability and loyalties, which run strongly to the General. The General has, without obvious cupidity, assumed control of the business process, by capturing its intellectual resources.

The nation is now serene. True, there is said to be alienation among the employees; but such an allegation cannot be demonstrated. The society functions well as an institutional organism, and if some individual needs go unmet, that is the price to pay for efficiency and security.

The General is persuaded in his latter years, after all these accomplishments, to appear on television before a panel of newsmen. He is asked how he came to his achievements. He replies: "As a youth, I studied the political craftsmanship of Octavius Augustus Caesar, and noting the similarity between the policy choices of the United States and those of Rome, I carried them to their logical conclusion."

Acropolis statues. *(Photo by Tim Carlson/Stock, Boston.)*

Chapter Six

THE FUTURE
OF THE U.S.A.:
THE GREEK REPLAY

Whereas the main similarities of the United States to Roman society are in political structure, the major analogies with ancient Greece are in the trading economies by which both societies achieved their economic growth.

The export trade of Athens flourished in part because of the supremacy of Athenian pottery, crafts, bronze, and precious metal work. Athens and the Ionians of Asia Minor also shared a seagoing tradition, which caused them to colonize first the Aegean sea and next in southern Italy, until finally the trade and colonization ranged from Spain to the Black Sea. This larger Greece, Magna Graeca, was tied together by the exchange of commodities, by cultural similarities, and above all by common commercial practices.

The adoption of coinage and currency by Greece from Lydia in the eighth century B.C. moved exchange from barter to a market system, in which settlements could be in reckonings of coin or bullion. The monetary exchange system of trade brought into being a whole set of laws and legal codes governing private commercial practice, such as contracts, liability, debt instruments, and the transfer of title to goods and property. The perfection of these exchange techniques made possible a swelling of international trade, the prosperity of Magna Graeca, and the wealth of Athens.

The existence of a wealthy commercial class of merchants, tradesmen, and craftsmen also affected the political structure of Athens. The landed aristocracy of Greece had tended to dominate the ruling Areopagus council. This council of magistrates was made up originally of aristocrats by birth, but the rivalry and conspiracy among the aristocrats was a cause of strife and instability in the city state, which was bad for business. The Solon reforms of 594 B.C. made the Areopagus a representative plutocracy by including wealthy merchants among the magistrates. The merchants had nearly the same proclivity to rivalry and self-interest as the aristocrats, however, and from time to time the government would be taken over by tyrants. The tyrannies were not popular reform movements but the usurpation of power by the wealthy for their own aggrandizement. The tyrannies were also bad for trade.

However, the townspeople, craftsmen, and guildsmen gained political experience under the Solon reforms at the same time as their wealth increased. By their demands, Cleisthenes was called upon to serve as an arbiter to settle differences and disputes among the classes. The Cleisthenes reforms of 508 B.C. proceeded to distribute more governing authority to the guildsmen, tradesmen, and townspeople at the expense of the aristocratic clans and the wealthy, who had abused their power by rivalry.

The basic reform was to create an electoral system based upon location of residence, called a *deme,* rather than clan. The *demes* were the foundation for democracy in Athens because they provided direct input on agenda and vote in the Assembly. Cleisthenes retained the Aeropagus Council as guardian of the constitution and hence achieved a set of checks and balances, decentralizing authority to diverse social groups and compartmentalizing it so no group could dominate. Athens thus became a direct democracy, whose only parallel in the United States was the short-lived New England town government. However, we have inherited from Greece the concept of checks and balances in government—and we are having about the same difficulty making the checks and balances work as they did.

As long as Athens was prosperous, which was from 508 B.C. to 404 B.C., the democracy with its checks and balances worked well. This period included the famous forty-year Age of Pericles (445–404 B.C.), in which most of the glories of Greece, as we know them, originated. Much of the wealth for this glorification came from the defense fund of the Confederation of Delos.

Between 546 B.C. and A.D. 466, Persia threatened to conquer Greece and its rich trade routes. Sparta, as leader of the Peloponnesian League (which Athens belatedly joined), fought the Persians to a standstill at Thermopylae and Plataea, but these defensive victories did not stop Persia. Sparta refused to counterattack or lead a foreign campaign against Persia, so Athens formed a naval coalition, the Confederacy of Delos, made up of the Ionian city-states and the Aegean islands. The Confederacy of Delos subscribed funds to build a fleet, which Athens was to command; Athens was to share in half of any booty recovered. The Confederacy of Delos destroyed the Persian fleet and army at Pamphylia in 466 B.C., and Athens used its half of the Delos fund and the booty for the glorifications of the Periclean Age.

The Athenians were rightly proud of their democracy and cultural achievements at home, but they were unable to conceive of extending democratic citizenship or equality of opportunity to other city-states. Quite the reverse, Pericles set upon an imperial course of military conquest, subjugating surrounding states, including Samos, which was a member of the Confederacy of Delos. This Athenian perfidy caused the other Greek city-states to seek the protection of Sparta, which led the Peloponnesian League to defeat Athens in 404 B.C.

Sparta kept the peace for sixty years, but as a land-based agricultural state it was unable to revive trade and empire. Athens made a comeback try but failed, and its defeat caused it to doubt itself and its institutions, to suffer a "failure of nerve." The oligarchs began fighting among themselves again, tyrannies returned, small landowners and tradesmen were dispossessed by take-overs and tight money, poverty increased, wealth became concentrated, the poor revolted and massacred the rich, oppression tightened, and Socrates was condemned to death for his individualism.

Demoralization of the rich as well as the poor accompanied these troubled times. Sexual libertinism, free unions, avoidance of motherhood, and depopulation began. Educated classes disavowed the state religion, denied parental authority, discouraged marriage, political, or economic responsibility. People bought their way out of military service and liturgy (service to the public). Athletes became professional, war mercenary, politics intrigue, and succession conspiracy. To the oligarchs, Socrates' free thinking symbolized this demoralization and decay, and he was blamed for the corruption of youth, which did not cease upon his death.

Philip of Macedonia had lived as a hostage among the Greeks and knew their demoralization and internecine strife, which he exploited by being a master of intrigue as well as of military conquest. Philip of

Macedonia bribed the oligarchs of some city-states to his allegiance and conquered the rest. Within seventy years after its greatest glories, the Greek tragedy came to its end, almost as though the society had willed its own death.

SIMILARITIES AND DIFFERENCES BETWEEN AMERICAN AND GREEK SOCIETIES

With this brief background (see the appendix for more detail), some of the main similarities and differences between U. S. and Greek societies become apparent. A summary is shown in Table 6–1.

Many of these comparisons are obvious, but explanation is required of a few. For example, the dispossession of small business in Greece occurred by usurpation and financial pressure, while in the United States it was by displacement through the normal competitive practices of mass-production manufacturers, chain stores, supermarkets, and discount houses against small proprietorships. The scale of institutions in the United States and Rome were massive, whereas Greece had more individualistic crafts and enterprises. The differences in technology and scale perhaps account for why the United States and Rome developed the strong executive concept in both public and private institutions, whereas Greece persisted with individual rivalries and tyrannies. The socialization process of building large institutions and their leadership, in the United States and Rome, may also account for the organization of elitism through education and experience, which caused both America and Rome to operate more with power blocs than with internecine strife.

TABLE 6-1. Comparison of Greek and American Societies

Similarities	Differences
1. Trading economy	1. Scale and size of institutions
2. Competition and rivalry	2. Strong executive concept
3. Codification of commercial practice	3. Technology (vs. craft)
4. Dispossession of small business	4. Organized elitism
5. Constitution	5. Federalism
6. Local government based in demes	6. Family
7. National security based upon coalitions and treaties	
8. Demoralization	

Federalism, too, is a concept related to strong executives, power blocs, and organized elites and so comes naturally to the U. S. institutional context. The absence of federalism is perhaps the fatal defect of the Greek social process; indeed, from our perspective, it seems astounding that, having applied the federal concept with triumphant success in the Confederation of Delos, Athens immediately turned upon its federated members to subjugate them, illustrating perhaps the differences between individualistic and institutional rivalries. Finally, some of these rivalry differences stem from the family structure, which in Greece still retained strong clannish rivalry, whereas the American family has become less clannish, more nuclear and internally cooperative.

THE BEGINNING OF FUTURE U.S.A., GREEK REPLAY

Again we make the assumption that similarities dominate the social evolution of the United States so that it follows the Greek historical pattern. The chronology of this historical pattern is shown in Table 6–2.

In the table, the Homeric period of the United States covers the odysseys of Columbus and John Smith to the heroics of the early colonial settlements. The colonization and expansion includes the interior settlement of the thirteen original colonies plus the expansion into the western territories. The mastery of coinage in finance in the United States covers the entire fumbling with the state banks and currencies down through the development of central banking and the underwriting for large capital-stock companies. The codification of commercial practice in the United States is taken to be not only the legal code, which only

TABLE 6-2. Chronological Parallels Between American and Greek Societies

Event	Greek date	U.S. date
Homeric period	1600–900 B.C.	A.D. 1492–1700
Colonization and expansion	900–700	1700–1700
Mastery of coinage and finance	800–700	1700–1900
Codification of commerce	700–600	1800–1900
Constitution	594	1787
Perfection of electoral system	508	1800s
Rise of the wealthy	550–450	1860–1930
National security based upon coalitions and treaty	500–445	1917–1970s
Imperialistic expansion	445–404	1900–1974
Defeat and failure of nerve	404	1965–74
Demoralization	400–338	1970s

recently has become a uniform commercial act among the states, but also the perfection of large corporate policy making. The rise of the wealthy is regarded as the first emergence of great family wealth, brought about by the Civil War, the first trusts, and the absence of a federal personal-income tax. U.S. imperialistic expansion started with Teddy Roosevelt's big stick and continues in the form of multinational corporations exporting capital and setting up new subsidiaries (financial colonies) abroad. The American defeat, failure of nerve, and demoralization occurred during the Vietnam war and the 1972 election-financing debacle and is manifested in the doubt of institutions and the youthful demoralization and dissent (discussed in Chapter 2).

ANALYSIS OF GREEK POLICY CHOICES

The ancient Greeks (especially Athens) evolved their mode of survival from the sea around them and the skill of their crafts. Theirs was an international trading economy based on craft production superimposed upon an agricultural, landed aristocracy. The landed aristocrats were wealthy and given to clannish rivalry. The trading merchants became wealthy as a result of economic gains made from competitive trading. The governments were small city-states, whose main functions were military defense and public order. Military defense was accomplished by levying drafts for manpower and funds upon the clans, later the *demes*. Order was maintained by a judicial system that heard cases of treason and conspiracy against the state but no private disputes. Private disputes were settled by private arbiters. Other public service was demanded of the clans and *demes* in the form of personal service (liturgy) of its citizens.

In these circumstances, the policy choices of ancient Greece, shown in Table 6–3, reflect preferences for a rather free and open economy. Of the thirteen policy issues, Greece appears to be unlike us on ten issues and like us on three. The three similar policy choices are (1) for skewed income distributions, with extremes of rich and poor; (2) for oligopolistic competition; and (3) for participative resolution of internal conflicts. The skewing of incomes to the rich occurred because members of the landed aristocracy were wealthy, with large, slave-operated estates, and because successful merchants could keep and reinvest their earnings without redistribution through taxation. In this sense, the merchant-financiers of ancient Greece were much like the U.S. financiers prior to institution of the income tax; they could pyramid their wealth by relending and reinvesting without intervention. The gov-

TABLE 6-3. Policy Analysis and Comparison of Thirteen Major Issues Confronting Ancient Greece and the United States

	Policy issue	Greek choice	U.S. choice	Consequence of Greek choice	Consequence of U.S. choice
1.	Monetary-fiscal	Balanced*	Unbalanced	Equilibrium	Inflation
2.	Income distribution	Skewed	Skewed	Rich-poor extremes	Rich-poor extremes
3.	Capital distribution	Semiopen*	Institutionally channeled	Less concentrated, market channeled	Capital concentration
4.	Competitive distribution	Oligopolistic	Oligopolistic	Economic oligarchy	Large business oligopoly
5.	Price policy	Free*	Administered	Competitive, unstable	Profit-maximized, stable
6.	Living standards	Internalize cost*	Externalize cost	More amenities, less government	Less amenities, more government
7.	Employment	Labor intensive*	Labor extensive	Service-oriented economy	Unemployment, capital-intensification
8.	Educational distribution	Narrow*	Semiwide	Ruling elite	Specialized techno-structure
9.	Technological distribution	Wide*	Narrow	Open competition	Oligopoly
10.	Barriers to entry	Lowered*	Raised	Equalize income	Skewed incomes
11.	Voting	Wide issue*	Narrow issue	Direct democracy	Oligarchic republic
12.	Internal order	Participative	Semiparticipative	Restive conflict resolution	Limited conflict resolution
13.	International order	Coercive*	Semicoercive	Military power and conquest	Use of economic-military power

*Differences of ancient Greek choices compared to those of U.S.A.

ernment did not intervene partly because, like pre-1915 U.S.A., it operated under balanced budgets.

The concentration of wealth and incomes among the landed aristocracy and the merchants tended to make competition oligopolistic, or limited to the few. Wealthy merchants reinvested on their own behalf, as well as acted as moneylenders in a semiopen market. Moneylenders then, as now, prefer to lend to those who already have money and a success record, rather than to those who do not. This tended to limit competition to the few.

Internal order was kept by private means, or the private settlement of disputes through arbiters. In extreme cases, the clannish settlement by revenge and blood money was used.

The differences in the set of policy choices by ancient Greece were many:

1. Monetary-fiscal policy was generally balanced, because military and public service was conscripted in kind.
2. Capital distribution was personally channeled rather than institutionally channeled.
3. Prices were free, competitive, and unstable.
4. Labor was used intensively in crafts and in a service-oriented economy.
5. Few costs from private enterprise were thrown on the public as social costs; hence, living standards tended to reflect the productivity of labor, and government intervention was small.
6. Education was private and narrowly available to those who could pay for it for themselves, which tended to create a ruling elite and oligopolistic competition.
7. Technology was craft oriented and widely available, and barriers to entry were lowered.
8. International order was uneasy and depended on military prowess and conquest.

The policy choices of ancient Greece favored those with personal power (as opposed to institutional power) gained either through land or trade, not unlike the economy of the free-wheeling West in the United States during the preindustrial period. This personal power was sometimes used to usurp the state, for tyrannies, or self-rule for self-interest, just as the United States had its land and robber barons. The Cleisthenes reforms of checks and balances were aimed at preventing these tyrannies.

The Greek penchant toward personal power and exploit was a destablizing influence throughout its history, but it was contained by government checks and balances, free markets, wide technology, low barriers to entry, and arbitration. These checks functioned sufficiently to maintain order as long as Greece prospered, but under disillusionment, stress, international conflict, and defeat, they failed. Rich exploited poor, poor massacred rich, city-states turned against each other, and internecine carnage opened the way to conquest by Philip of Macedonia.

THE FUTURE OF THE U.S.A.—THE GREEK SCENARIO

Americans stand today as the Greeks stood in 404 B.C., facing the future with failing confidence in our institutions. The United States experiences repeated cycles of inflation and stagnation, as in 1975, until the public has grown weary of the erosion of living standards through higher prices plus chronic underemployment. People are ready for a change, for a man of action who does not temporize as the head of state.

A right-wing Presidential candidate, with charisma and a full campaign chest, emerges who speaks nostalgically of the "good old days," when men were free and times were good. The time has come, he says, to turn the clock back to early America, to rugged individualism, and self-help. Should he be elected, he pledges, he will whittle away the big government and the big corporations. They are the cause of inflation and stagnation, with their deficit spending and administered prices. Getting the government out of people's pockets and the economy, he says, will give individuals back their freedom. Free competition will give everyone a chance and reduce big business down to workable size. The candidate wears Edwardian clothes and campaigns against backdrops of early Americana. The nostalgia is overwhelming, and he is elected to office.

The first act of the new government is to balance the federal budget and tighten the money supply. The only way to balance expenditures with revenues is to cut either the military or human welfare programs. Welfare programs are cut. People are now on self-help.

The second act of government is to enact a progressive, or graduated, corporate income-tax law. This makes it less advantageous for people to use the corporation as a holding company for wealth, since it is taxed similarly to an individual.

The third act is to file price-conspiracy charges under the antitrust laws against all corporations with similar pricing, but the government agrees to drop prosecution if the corporations will split up into smaller units to increase competition.

The attacks upon the corporations are popular, and they enable the administration to plead for time. The end of welfare and the new self-help philosophy impose hardships on the public, but competition is being restored, inflation has been checked, and economic revival of the economy under rugged individualism is on its way. The public, recalling the inflation-stagnation hardships, decides to give the new program a chance. But the unemployed have to eat. They are forced to double up with family, take odd jobs at any wage, start family gardens, and barter away possessions or work for food. It is humiliating, but it works. People do survive, and wage rates fall through all the new competition for jobs.

The corporations meantime do not fight the antitrust suits because the tax laws motivate them to disaggregate. They busily split themselves up by spinning off subsidiaries and demerging. This disaggregation is done by distributing stock in new, smaller enterprises to the shareholders of the older ones, so that no real redistribution of wealth occurs. The optimum size of corporations now comes to be that point where the progressive corporate tax rate coincides with the progressive personal income-tax rate of wealthy individuals. However, all of the tax-avoidance regulations still enable individuals in high-income brackets to save substantially.

Competition does appear to increase. There are more firms in the same markets, more products, more brands, more price differentials. The lower prices stimulate demand, and these firms begin hiring the lower-priced labor. Unemployment slowly diminishes. Self-help is working, albeit at lower living standards than before for the reemployed. Lower wages are being used to subsidize capital intensification. Firms with lower marginal productivity of capital are able to earn a minimal profit under low wage structures.

Wealthy individuals begin to find it in their interest to pay attention to management, rather than being disinterested absentee-shareholders as before. The tax trade-off between progressive corporate taxes and progressive individual taxes is very close, meriting minute examination. The wealthy find it to their advantage to sell off their stock in companies where they have a small interest, and to concentrate their investments in one company or a few. This consolidation of portfolio entails more risk, but it also makes the tax trade-offs more predictable and more manipulative. The wealthy are forced into active management of their own corporations again.

The wealthy owner-managers of the new, smaller corporations behave differently than their professional predecessors. They are more direct, decisive, authoritative. They are dealing with their own money. They get rid of overhead, staffs, and frills and cut costs. But they also take higher risks—on new products, new inventions, new marketing, and with competitive price-cutting, and they make more money. Profit margins expand. Wages are kept low by the competitive rate of the weakest firms. The new products expand markets and employment. The widening profit margins of the efficient firms generate higher capital flows. The capital-intensification process begins again—and the rich get richer.

The unions now demand a fairer share of the gains in productivity, and the smaller corporations are in a weak bargaining position relative to big unions using industry-wide bargaining. The Administration sees that with smaller government and smaller corporations unions also must become smaller to reduce their countervailing power. The Administration secures passage through Congress of an omnibus Human Development Act, which provides that (1) all education beyond junior high school shall be privately financed; (2) trade unions shall be responsible for apprenticeship and licensing of all craftsmen; (3) unions must accept all applicants for entry into the craft; (4) employers must hire licensed craftsmen; (5) the government will provide a grant-in-aid to individuals to cover part of the cost of apprenticeships; (6) trade unions shall be bargaining agents for all licensed members; and (7) the maximum size bargaining unit shall be that of a contiguous plant or firm, whichever is smaller.

This piece of legislation is vigorously opposed by the unions, but it passes anyway. Then the unions are faced with a dilemma—whether to resist enforcement of the legislations by bitter strikes to retain their industry-wide bargaining power, or whether to accept the reduced power and greatly expand their membership through apprenticeship licensing. The expansion of membership induces them to comply.

The trade unions, instead of schools, have now assumed the educational function for the working population. At one stroke, the government has dramatically reduced the cost of education, made education relevant, and reduced the power of the unions. The unions, bargaining in small units with small corporations, raise wages slightly, but no strike is big enough to be noticeable in restricting production. The union wage negotiations have to be geared to keeping the marginal corporations in business, otherwise the unions know they will lose members. The principal function of the unions becomes training and licensing. Craftsmanship improves in industry. Products are more finely and artistically wrought. The improved workmanship makes American products highly competitive in foreign markets, and the balance of international trade improves significantly.

Meantime, public senior high schools and universities have been liquidated, their faculties being given preference in transition into the crafts. Private preparation schools and private universities continue to serve the children of wealthy families who can afford higher education. Higher education has become elite again, to the satisfaction of the employed faculties, who have preferred elitism all along.

American society becomes remarkably vigorous in risk taking, creativity, and output. Employment is high, at low wages. The rich are extravagantly rich, and live that way. New mansions after the grand manner reappear at Newport and elsewhere. The rich patronize the arts, and the high craftsmanship of the populace produces fine arts for the decoration of the mansions and the public plazas.

There are a few problems. Business is very cyclical, and there are sharp ups and downs in profits and employment. Some owner-managers are harsh and dictatorial, with competitive practices that border on the illegal, such as kickbacks and discriminatory pricing. Such practices are prosecuted when found, which is rare, because they are surreptitious. The Administration naturally deplores these practices, but that is the price Americans pay for the vigor of the new economy.

The Administration now takes stock of what it has done to bring back rugged individualism into American life and is tolerably pleased. It has reversed the following policy choices of 1970 U.S.A.: (1) balanced monetary-fiscal policy, (2) rechanneled capital through private rather than institutional hands; (3) created freer market prices; (4) made employment more labor intensive and craft oriented, (5) reduced government; (6) made education elitist; (7) made technology (crafts) widely available; and (8) lowered barriers to entry. Only one additional measure is needed to complete the package—that is, make voting more wide issued and democratic. This reversal measure will have to be most artfully conceived so that it will affect the scope and activity of government, which is still too big, but will not disturb the preferential distribution of income and capital to the wealthy, upon which capital intensification and expansionism is built.

Cleisthenes's answer to such a problem was to leave the power of the oligarchy in the Senate and to diffuse the voting responsibilities of the House to the people. The Administration, with the help of a huge "educational" campaign fund contributed by the wealthy, secures adoption of a Constitutional amendment that provides that the U.S. House of Representatives shall submit a balanced budget to the people on a referendum with line-item by line-item appropriation approval, before appropriations become effective as legally authorized expenditures. This new amendment has startling effects because it turns out that citizens are much less ready to spend their own money than are members of Congress, who had looked upon tax money as a way to buy votes for reelection. Under the referenda, the authorized appropriations of government are greatly reduced, and government shrinks again in size.

Now all is well, the United States has been set aright, and the rugged individual has returned to the American scene. Critics say that this is not an equitable society, but proponents say that it is even better for it is efficient.

As long as resources are available, rugged individuals efficiently exploit the resource base. The world populations have greatly expanded, rugged individualism abroad also seeks resources, and expectations for living standards are rising worldwide.

The scarcity of resources begins to cause difficulties in rugged America. Gasoline is scarce to run automobiles. Fuels are scarce for electricity. Wheat is scarce in world markets. The price of ferrous and nonferrous metals rises. Worldwide demand is pressing on a narrow resource base. The rugged individuals find that if they cannot get materials they cannot make a profit nor maintain the richness of their lives. Materials must be had at any price, or better still without a price. Reputable companies take up a new business practice called "diversionary shipment," which is to divert a competitor's supply to oneself. This has to be done very carefully lest they be prosecuted as hijackers, and hence diversionary shipments are practiced very secretively. A few timid firms hire the Mafia to do their diversionary shipments for them, but this proves very expensive. Besides, it becomes clear that the small owner-manager corporation is ideally suited to clandestine operations. There are no committees, stockholders, staffs, or technocrats to consult. The wealthy owner-manager merely consults with his procurement agents covertly as to where the next hit shall be made.

As long as diversionary shipments are conducted within the United States, the problem remains manageable. The government prosecutes violations of the law when it can, but business learns to look out for itself by improving the quality of its espionage and enforcement squads. The rich are stealing from the rich and the more ruthless prevail, but then, that is what rugged individualism is in the end.

The trouble really breaks out when there are no longer enough resources, even for the most ruthless, among the rich stealing from the rich. Some corporations become so desperate for fuel to keep up their operations that they hijack oil supertankers on the high seas. Foreign companies and nations write stiff protest notes to the United States demanding recovery of the hijacked ships. When the United States investigates, ships are found moored in American habors with their cargos gone, and there is no trace of where the oil was discharged. The United States returns the tankers with apologies but says it cannot locate the perpetrator of the crime.

The diversionary shipments of foreign commodities—not only oil, but coffee, minerals, and fibers—increases to epidemic proportions. Foreign protests become stern and demanding to the point of ultimatums. The United States answer, that it is unable to apprehend or stop the pirates, is regarded as frivolous and irresponsible. The United States government makes a major effort to stop piracy, but the law-evasion skills of the rugged individuals have been honed to a finer edge than the law-enforcement skills of government.

The situation reaches crisis proportions. The American rugged individualists cannot stop their diversionary shipments or their businesses will close down. Illegal business operations have become so endemic that the government cannot deal with these private tyrannies. Foreign governments cannot tolerate the illegal robbery of their resources. The commodity supplier nations of the world combine to form a military force known as the New Peloponnesian League, which suppresses piracy and conquers the United States. The Greek tragedy has been replayed.

View of Florence. *(Photo by Owen Franken/Stock, Boston.)*

Chapter Seven

THE FUTURE OF THE U.S.A.: THE MEDIEVAL REPLAY

Medieval society has perhaps fewer close parallels with American society than do either Greece or Rome, because it differs both in political and economic structure. There is one very interesting resemblance, however, and that is in the dogmatization of belief. Whereas medieval society had dogmatized religion, today we have dogmatized materialism. This suggestion may be contested by some who feel that the Age of Enlightenment relieved the modern mind of dogmas and that we are, indeed, rational and open-minded. However, the McCarthy period, the loyalty oaths, and the 1972 elections remind us how close we can come to inquisition.

SIMILARITIES AND DIFFERENCES BETWEEN
AMERICAN AND MEDIEVAL SOCIETIES

Today in the United States, the materialist doctrine is the principal subject of resistance and unrest by youthful dropouts. Thus, there is a growing body of heretics among us, who may either come to accept some modified materialism under the grinding conditions of deprivation, or who may reformulate the doctrine as did the thinkers of the Renaissance and Reformation. The canonical divisions of the materialist doctrine are many, including economic growth, technology, management, developmentalism, advancement of knowledge, experimentation, and scientism. Of these, science, though slightly tarnished of recent years, perhaps comes the closest to being ensconced as doctrine.

Under conditions of stress and despair, today's doctrine could well become tomorrow's dogma. Certainly it is a path that has been trod before. Let us look down the path by comparing, in Table 7–1, the similarities and differences of the United States and medieval society.

The fealty in the U. S. society is to materialism. That is, one cannot get a job, as so many young people are finding out, without learning something "practical," such as science, economics, management, or (even

TABLE 7-1. Comparison of American and Medieval Societies

Similarities	Differences
1. Settled doctrines	1. Economic structure
2. Fealty	2. Political structure
3. Union-guild system	3. Technology
4. Class-structured society	4. Level of public education
5. Food and material scarcity	5. Printing and news media
6. Foreign threats to supply	
7. Price controls	

TABLE 7-2. Chronological Parallels Between American and Medieval Societies

Event	Medieval date	U.S. date
External threat to supply	4th–12th century	1914–1974
Rise of guilds (unions)	8th–13th century	1900–1950
Compartmentalization of society	5th–13th century	1900–1970
Rise of theocracy	410–1300	1950–1970
Period of invention	1200–1400	1870–1970
Growth of trade	1300–1500	1870–1970
Inquisition	1480	

better) selling. The union structure is part of the class system, which is further defined by technical specialty, by professions, management, proprietors, the rich, the poor, the undereducated, and the under-employed. Moreover, these class distinctions are becoming hereditary, in that the sons of managers tend to become managers, the sons of professionals go into the professions, and some unions are father-son unions.

ANALYSIS OF MEDIEVAL POLICY CHOICES

The feudal mode of survival arose out of the demise of the Roman empire and the threat of the barbarian invaders to life and property. This caused people to band together in mutual defense, and the most defensible sites were the *coloni* estates left over from Roman practice. These were fortified farming communities in which members lived by barter and the exchange of goods for service, after the Diocletian edicts brought the trade economy to a halt with price controls.

On such estates the workers provided fealty and labor to the manor lord in exchange for protection and subsistence. In turn, a manor lord, capable of local defense, might provide fealty, military support, and tribute to a regional liege lord for regional defense. This system of fealty and alliances had the advantages of security, interdependence, and community, with the disadvantages of compulsory servitude.

The medieval economy was land and labor intensive. That is, land was tilled by hand to produce the crops upon which the economy was based. The strength of the defense unit, as well as the wealth of the lord, depended upon (1) the marginal productivity or fertility of the land, (2) the size of the land, and (3) the number of serfs. With these incentives at work, there was a tendency for feudal estates to merge to larger size (just like the American corporate-merger movement) by marriage or conquest. The mode of survival and expansion might then be said to be land intensification and military intensification, both of which required large manpower and were also labor intensive. This was in contrast to the U.S. economy, which is capital intensive and tends to economize on labor (extensive), leading to unemployment.

The feudal system did not have problems with unemployment, though it did with skewed incomes and rich-poor extremes. The income distribution was determined by land holdings, and with few large land-holders (feudal lords), high incomes were distributed to the land owners as rents, leaving subsistence incomes for the serfs.

The policies that made this system work depended heavily on land-holding patterns and worker fealty. The worker fealty was enforced by coercive feudal discipline, and the land-holding patterns were determined by inheritance and conquest. The former required laws and practices of succession. The latter required a code of military behavior (knighthood and chivalry). These practices for the survival of the medieval economy can be compared to our own policy choices if we equate their land-holding customs with our capital-holding customs. However, late medieval times saw the rise of commerce and the textile industry, which was more nearly like our competitive mercantile structure. This mercantilism is reflected in the competitive and pricing policies in Table 7–3, which compares the medieval policy choices with those of the United States.

The medieval policy choices were like those of the U.S.A. in five respects: (1) incomes were skewed to extremes of rich and poor by land holdings, (2) capital (land) was institutionally channeled; (3) poverty costs were externalized and thrown on the charity of the church; (4) technology distribution (in the new sciences and textiles) was narrowly distributed by educating only the elite; and (5) voting was narrow issue based upon the rule of oligarchic councils.

The medieval policy choices differed from those of the United States in that (1) monetary-fiscal balance was achieved through a largely barter economy; (2) competition was open among the new textiles trades with Flanders and the East; (3) prices in the mercentile trades were free; (4) employment was labor intensive, with most production done by handwork through the guilds; (5) education was private and available only to the wealthy; (6) barriers to entry into commerce were low; (7) internal order was maintained coercively by feudal discipline; and (8) international order was dependent upon military prowess and dominance.

We have already seen that the survival vehicle of a civilization has to be intensified as more control over disorder is required. Capital can be intensified, as in the United States, by more savings, technology, and investments. Military intensification can occur, as in Rome, by more conquests, more slaves, more populations, more soldiers. But land intensification as a means of increasing resources, authority, and control is difficult because land is limited.

As a result, medieval times found another means of intensification, the intensification of ideas or dogma. The debacle and collapse of the Roman Empire had given rise to a theocracy (A.D. 410) founded on St. Augustine's *City of God,* written in the years immediately following the sack of Rome. St. Augustine gave to the people, living in chaos, an explanation of the debacle in which they found themselves and also a reason to hope for a better future. The human race, he said, lives in a temporal City of Man, founded on fratricide (Cain killing Abel), given to joys, evils, greed, war, vicissitudes, rising and falling. But the City of

TABLE 7-3. Policy Analysis and Comparison of Thirteen Major Issues Confronting Medieval Society and the United States

	Policy issue	Medieval choice	U.S. choice	Consequence of medieval choice	Consequence of U.S. choice
1.	Monetary-fiscal	Balanced*	Unbalanced	Equilibrium	Inflation
2.	Income distribution	Skewed	Skewed	Rich-poor extremes	Rich-poor extremes
3.	Capital distribution	Institutionally channeled	Institutionally channeled	Capital concentration, in feudal estates	Capital concentration
4.	Competitive distribution	Open*	Oligopolistics	Small units, competitive	Large business, oligopoly
5.	Price policy	Free*	Administered	Competitive, unstable	Profit-maximized, stable
6.	Living standards	Externalize costs	Externalize cost	Less amenities, more government	Less amenities, more government
7.	Employment	Labor intensive*	Labor extensive	Service-oriented economy	Unemployment, capital intensive
8.	Educational distribution	Narrow*	Semiwide	Ruling elite	Specialized techno-structure
9.	Technological distribution	Narrow	Narrow	Fewer firms, oligopoly	Fewer firms, oligopoly
10.	Barriers to entry	Lowered*	Raised	Equalized income	Skewed incomes
11.	Voting	Narrow issue	Narrow issue	Oligarchic	Oligarchic republic
12.	Internal order	Coercive*	Semiparticipative	Feudally policed state	Limited conflict resolution
13.	International order	Coercive*	Semicoercive	Military dominance	Use of economic-military power

*Differences of medieval choices compared to those of U.S.A.

God is ordained by God in a grand design, in which man and nature, joined by peace and love, flourish in plentitude, diversity, and fullness.

St. Augustine linked the City of Man to the City of God by good works and stated that humans could progress by faith, obedience, and good works from this life to the next. This metaphor of human progress became one of the most powerful ideas in Western culture.

The Augustinian theocracy was peculiarly suitable to an age of political instability, economic stagnation (little land to intensify), and serfdom because it helped persons of every station adapt to the present and hope for the future. Such an idea was also a powerful underpinning to the feudal structure; if land intensification (to produce new resources) could not be used to control a restive people, idea intensification could be. This was done by dogmatizing the idea, sanctifying it, socializing the population with it to the end that they might have faith, hope, and charity. The charity in tithes and benefactions increased the resources of the institutionalized theocracy. The feudal theocracy produced a very stable social structure throughout troublous centuries, until 1450, when it began to be disturbed by the rise of mercantilism and intellectualism. This is when our U.S.-medieval scenario begins.

THE FUTURE OF THE U.S.A.—THE MEDIEVAL SCENARIO

Scientific journals carry articles about the "golden age of science" just passed. Physics, the queen of sciences, has reached its zenith in the mid-1960s, biology its apogee a decade later. Eminent scientists write that two or three centuries hence future scientists will still be merely filling in the details of the sweeping theories just wrought. Having achieved all this greatness, science has fallen in general regard. Research funds are being cut. Knowledge is not advancing. Industry is living off previous ideas now being commercially exploited, such as computers, microcircuitry electronic controls, satellites, spacecraft, new carbon compounds.

The United States has reached a slowdown in what had been a great burst of invention, unknown since medieval times when textile dying, cloth looming, pumpmaking, clockmaking, iron and steel smelting, water power, mining and construction tools revolutionzied technology and trade and contributed to the Renaissance. The U.S. renaissance seems to be fading. Faith in science is slipping, among legislators, business people, and, worst of all, students.

The lack of of interest of students in science, learning, and higher education results in dropping enrollments and declining financial support, at the same time that business and government are cutting their research expenditures, owing to the declining marginal returns from research. But the large multiuniversities are still in place, with tenured faculty that cannot be reduced, hoping for a renewal of faith in research and higher learning. The theocratic university structures have a scientific faith, which is looking for a new mission.

Meanwhile, the business community, struggling with inflation, stagnation, and unemployment, has a mission looking for a new faith. The mission of the business corporations is to keep themselves solvent, which is difficult with sales dropping, costs rising, and consumers unable to pay inflationary prices. Inflation, stagnation, and unemployment have eroded faith in the economic system. The American dream, the American way of life, have dimmed.

Heretical views have even emerged. Hippies treat the American dream as a bad trip from the start. Other, less extreme youth merely drop out and ignore the essentials of the social process, by enjoying themselves, not working regularly, and, worst of all, not consuming. The failure to consume is the worst heresy of all, because that could stop the whole production-consumption-expansionist cycle, which has carried us to where we are now.

Into this flux of ideas and economic misalignments comes a political candidate for President who has restructured his party's rules to bring in a broader and more diverse basis of support. His political convention conspicuously displays on television what the grass roots are really like—women, blacks, browns, hippies, intellectuals, scholars, farmers, businessmen, wardheelers, a veritable rabble, as it really is. These delegates not only look like what it really is, they want to talk the way it really is. The impact is so real that it is frightening. Party backers and doctrinnaire voters flee the party as if the pox were upon them, and the candidate is soundly trounced in the election. But the vision lingers, and those in party councils avow that the populace, having once been seen, shall not be seen again.

The new conventions therefore are more properly structured to bring forth before the cameras people of solid appearance and sound views. They look so alike that the California delegation is hard to distinguish from the Illinois delegation. This convention does produce a sound candidate and a sound platform: "Believe in America."

The Believe in America campaign is beautifully packaged by the best New York public relations team. The campaign is touching, and eyes moisten at the thought of what believing in America can do. The candidate is swept into office by voters, who are now bullish on America, and the stock market rises in a show of confidence.

The new President is now in office and faced with doing something about the question: what shall America believe in? But that part of the campaign was not packaged. The President has a medievalist on his staff who speculates that perhaps the American people can be made to believe in what they have always believed in, if it is reinforced from the top and encouraged from the bottom, as in the Middle Ages. The staff man is put to work on the details, which he approaches by reversing those policies contrary to stable ideas. He calls his plan "idea intensification." It consists of the following:

1. The Voluntary Assured Employment Act provides that any worker facing layoff or unemployment may elect to sign an agreement that will continue his work and wages at two-thirds pay, which shall be treated as a loan, debt, or debit. Then during the rehire or reemployment cycle, the employee continues at two-thirds pay until the remaining one-third wages pays off his loan or layoff debits. The act further provides that all employers must accept a pro-rata share of the unemployed, based on the size of their peak work force. Those employers who have insufficient funds to meet their payroll may borrow temporarily from the government, to be repaid from the one-third wages during the period of rehire credits. Since the layoff debits will eventually be paid off by rehired credits, the plan is self-financing, and full employment at a guaranteed annual wage is assured. Employers are also required by payroll taxes to absorb a pro-rata share of welfare for those who cannot work.

2. Since the unemployment problem has been solved, the government then eliminates all welfare and unemployment compensation payments, thus balancing the monetary-fiscal policy and halting inflation.

3. A free-market exchange system is established in which corporations are forbidden to administer a fixed selling price but rather must publish a list of the quantity of products they will offer at varying prices. Every product is age-dated and must be progressively marked down in price, so that it clears the market (is sold) in six months. Since the market is always cleared, business cycles and recessions disappear.

4. The President reestablishes the Science Advisor to the President, whose function is to disseminate technological innovation.

5. No business expenditures for research and development are deductible as a business expense for income-tax purposes, unless the research director is a scientist approved by Science Advisor and participates in the technological innovation exchange program.

6. Higher education is made entirely self-supporting from tuition fees, and in effect it becomes private education available only to those who can afford to pay for it. However, the government sets up a generous fellowship program administered by the Science Ad-

visor, who awards grants for the full cost of education to selected candidates.

7. A new business-development program is set up that lends capital to new businesses. Assistance is also available from the Science Advisor's office in the form of technical innovations and scientific staff. This program lowers barriers to entry and increases competition.

The President announces this new Believe in America program in a low key, except to emphasize that it assures employment and progress. As a good administrator, the President leaves the initiation and implementation of this program to his cabinet, which he relies upon heavily. It becomes a strong cabinet responsible to the President and meets biweekly to report progress.

Every other week, the President and cabinet meet with the Science Advisor in what comes to be called the Seminars on Science and Progress. The agenda for these meetings cover (1) new discoveries in basic science, (2) new applied technical innovations, (3) the progress potential of these discoveries, and (4) the economic implications of the discoveries.

The President lays great stress on these seminars, attends them solemnly without fail, and holds his biweekly press conference immediately following, at which he makes public announcements of new science contributions to progress.

These presidential announcements are followed immediately by a detailed scientific pronouncement from the Science Advisor which gives the technical and economic details of the findings. These Seminar on Science and Progress letters (SSP letters) are limited to an official distribution list that includes only the approved Science Directors of cooperating companies, and Principal Scientists at accredited universities. The Principal Scientists are authorized to hold regional Seminars in Science and Progress in their area, to interpret and disseminate the information to approved participants. No further dissemination is permitted, upon pain of being removed from the approved list.

Principal Scientists are selected from recognized science faculties and are required to take postdoctoral study in the economics of development and the political science of progress specified by the Science Advisor. The posts carry high prestige and emoluments.

The participants allowed to attend the regional Seminars on Science and Progress are business users of technical information. These business people have privileged access to technical, economic, and political developments, which proves essential and invaluable to maintaining competitive position. They are permitted, if they wish to remain on the approved list, to contribute voluntarily 2 percent of their business earnings to the maintenance of the Science and Progress program, which covers support of the salary and staffs of Principal Scientists; the science fellowship program, which trains new scientists in the universities; the information dissemination costs; and a basic research and development program.

The SSP program is used, also, to assist new business development. With selected dissemination of information on technical innovations, capital-assistance loans, and free-market prices, new enterprises invigorate the economy. But this invigoration with new enterprise is kept in nice balance with the prosperous expansion of the existing corporations, through the studies of the Principal Scientists on the economics of development.

University faculties have been invigorated also by the new flow of research funds made possible by the generous contributions of the business users of science. The SSP faculty of the universities are rich and powerful in academic affairs, tending to dominate the temporal faculties in other fields. However, the temporal faculties are not neglected because they provide the private educations to those who can afford it; among these are future business contributors, who must be properly trained in the humanities, arts, and sciences for their role among the elite in running business and government posts of importance.

Among employees, the Voluntary Assured Employment Act has eliminated unemployment. But though everyone is working, it is difficult to get ahead. The layoff debits tend to pile up so high that they are seldom paid off by the rehire credits; thus, the employee is almost always in debt to the Assured Employment Fund and keeps working at two-thirds wages most of the time. The employees and their unions complain these effects leave the worker in indentured servitude. The government and employers are solicitous of this complaint and set up procedures for a union audit to see that business does not abuse the plan by falsely extending the layoff periods or shortening the rehire periods. The definition of the layoff period is that point when business profits fall below a minimum level for survival. Anything above this level must be declared a rehire period in which employees earn rehire credits to pay off their debts. The unions protest that this provision guarantees employers a profit subsidized from wages, whereas before they had had no such profit guarantee. The government negotiator points out that surely the union would not wish to jeopardize survival of the business and the jobs it provides; and in any case the operation of the Assured Employment Fund is by legislation beyond the negotiating jurisdiction of the union because it is a government-supported self-liquidating fund.

The unions and the employees then undertake massive strikes to change these provisions. But there are no unemployment or welfare benefits anymore, so the union strike fund is quickly exhausted. The hungry employees return to work within thirty days.

Then individual workers, piled high with debt from their layoff credits, begin quitting their jobs and seeking other ones. But they are apprehended by the public police and returned to their original employer, who puts them back to work on the Lesson Shift. Employees on the lesson shift work eight hours during the night on the most arduous and disagreable work in the company, and this shift is preceded by a one-hour study period on the Lessons of Progress. The Lesson teaches that science brings new innovations and changes that lead to human progress. The scientific changes themselves may temporarily lead to hardships, in the form of changes in products, sales, profits, and unemployment, but these hardships are shared in the society, and the employees' share, it is pointed out, is their layoff debts, which they eventually pay off. Employees are urged to look, not for happiness now, but to the longer run, to the future—in paying off their debits, in their retirement, in looking back at the progress of society over their lifetimes, in the progress being made available to their children. Therein lies happiness.

After the Lesson Shift, employees are confined to quarters (barracks) on the business grounds, where they may rest, eat, meditate, and contemplate the Lesson. The cost of these rest and retreat periods (for food and lodging) is added to their layoff debits. This puts them more deeply in debt, since they have to pay for their own subsistence at work while still maintaining their families at home. However, the Lesson Shift is voluntary, and employees can go home whenever they wish to resume their normal work under the Voluntary Assured Employment Plan.

Employees stay a very short time on the Lesson Shift. Statistics prove that the learning and rehabilitation rates, without recidivism, are higher under the Lesson Shift than any other form of public correction.

The medievalist on the President's staff now reports that the idea-intensification plan is complete; all the policy choices of 1970 U.S.A., which were adverse to idea intensification, stability, and progress in the future have been reversed. All that needs to be done now is operationally to continue the reinforcement from the top and the encouragement at the bottom. The President continues to enhance the solemnity of the Seminars on Science and Progress. The President, cabinet members, and Science Advisor appear in academic robes of dignified colors. From time to time, a demonstration service is held which brings scientific laboratory equipment before a televised press conference to show an experiment in progress with its human benefits. The televised press conferences become very popular, and the public looks forward to the announcements of new discoveries and the laboratory demonstrations that life will progress and be better in the future. Belief in America and progress is restored among the majority of the population, and those who are obtuse are reminded of their duty on the Lesson Shift.

The society is a marvel of harmony and stability. Capital intensification, along with idea intensification, provides a modicum of progress year by year, with equilibrium. These small steps of progress, it is said, will accumulate to a happier future for all. Meanwhile, business prospers with guaranteed profits, the science hierarchy is rich and influential, politics are stable.

We could hardly design a more substantial society of people with sound views and progressive outlook. Yet despite the beneficence of this society, heresy does emerge. The worst source of heresy are poorly selected candidates for the temporal universities. These are young people of good family background, wealthy enough to pay for their educations, but somewhere they go wrong, perhaps from reading history or literature, or perhaps from surreptitious dissidence within the temporal faculties. These heretics receive their educations and then refuse to sign the Voluntary Assured Employment Plan. They simply drop out of sight. There are no jobs or welfare for them, but they seem to drift from place to place, given food and shelter by disgruntled employees not fully rehabilitated on the Lesson Shift.

These heretics speak of freedom versus thought control, opportunity versus servitude, happiness now instead of progress in the future, human dignity, individual rights, human development, self-fulfillment, and many other unsound ideas. The circulation of unsound ideas has troublesome effects. People go into hiding instead of fulfilling their voluntary agreement to the assured employment plan. Manifestos of human rights are pasted on doors of universities. There is arson in scientific laboratories. Posters appear denouncing SSP as dogma and calling for enlightenment. There is even the burning in effigy of Principal Scientists. The Science Advisor himself has his robes ripped in a scuffle during a Presidential pronouncement, which demeans the dignity of the occasion.

The President consults his medievalist again, who is amazed that such deviants from the beneficial society would emerge in the modern era of enlightened people. Regrettable though it is, he devises a plan to establish Committees for the Examination of Sound Ideas among the SSP faculties at the universities. The temporal faculties are examined thoroughly for the soundness of their ideas, and some seem wanting in their understanding of their disciplines as they relate to SSP. They are removed from their tenured teaching positions on grounds of intellectual turpitude and placed on Lesson Shifts. Other heretics apprehended by police dragnets of the underground communities are also brought before the Committee for the Examination of Sound Ideas. These persons are almost uniformly of unsound thought and are placed for indefinite terms on the Lesson Shifts, subject to reexamination in the future.

The work of the Examination Committees brings an era of peace for a time, but they have rooted out only the most obvious of the disbelievers. The more devious ones continue and use more devious means. The Examination Committees are then forced to use more devious means, sometimes so devious that it is not clear who is a disbeliever and who is not. Suspicion spreads and everyone feels spied upon, informed upon. Distrust within the SSP faculty, between the SSP faculty and the business users of science, and throughout the hierarchy makes it necessary for survival that everyone conspire and counterconspire to prevent denouncement. The internal conspiracy takes so much time that scientific research and dissemination languish. Technical innovation and capital intensification slow down. Business has difficulty surviving and neglects the Lesson Shift. On Independence Day, the populace storms the universities and puts the SSP establishment to flight.

This being the twenty-first century and an age of enlightenment, no retribution is sought against those who fled. The new generation closes the book on the U.S.A.-medieval scenario and considers whether some original scenario might be more livable for the American people. To conceive an original play, they are forced to think about the structure and mission of decisions, and then about a mission for the United States.

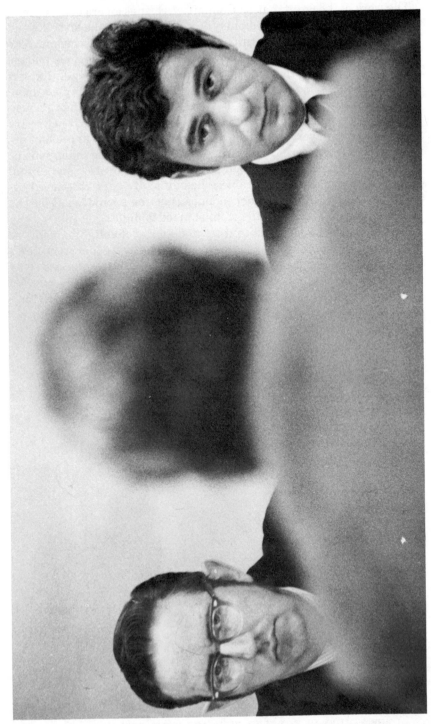

A government hearing. *(Photo by Ellis Herwig/Stock, Boston.)*

Chapter Eight

THE STRUCTURE
AND MISSION
OF DECISIONS

Decisions are frequently looked upon as being of three major types.

The first type is *value oriented,* or the choice among alternative goals. Value-oriented goals are thought to be the domain of legislators and top corporation executives. Generally, such choices are among marginally close values, otherwise the choice would be obvious and need no decision maker. These value choices, moreover, have a relatively short time frame, such as one to ten years, and the time frame is limited by the ceiling on human visibility.

The second type of decisions is *means oriented,* or the choice among the most effective means. These decisions, usually made by technically minded people lower in an organization, involve trade-offs of cost or performance in such a way as to achieve a goal at acceptable cost. These types of decisions are multitudinous, and they involve high skills from the technical and management arts, but their resolution is almost given, within narrow limits, from the statement of the problem and the goal.

The third type is *human oriented;* these decisions have to do with relationships among human beings in the development of goals and means. This field of human relations, organizational development, or consumer attitude is normally viewed as one that seeks maximum accommodation of human satisfactions *within the boundaries of the institution as given.* This class of decisions is usually made in the context of supervisor-employee or seller-client relationships.

These three types of decision making currently make up the bundle of tools in the management arts, but the point of the Roman, Greek, and medieval scenarios I have just presented is that *none* of their outcomes would have been significantly changed by any of these three types of decision making. For example, the value-oriented decisions in each scenario were relatively short (one to ten years) goal choices for achieving the stability of the social institutions as they then existed. The choices were merely incremental extrapolations of present practice, and if present practice were on a collison course with disaster, that would be where the goal choices would lead. Similarly, the means-oriented decisions, in the scenarios and their historical counterparts, were efficient (that is, opportunistic) ways then at hand for discharging the goals. And the human satisfactions were sufficiently attended to, within the boundaries of the institutions, to retain the allegiances of the power structure and many of the adherents with a voice.

Thus, the three scenarios and their historical parallels tend to show that the social process is made up of institutions that have a destiny of their own, regardless of the decision-making arts now in use. Indeed, it is my assertion that present decision-making arts can only make minor perturbations on the social trajectory that have been institutionally cast.

HOW DECISIONS ARE STRUCTURED:
SEVEN QUESTIONS TO ASK

If present decision-making arts are ineffectual and irrelevant to the social evolution of the United States, what about decisions by which we as individuals can influence our own future? To answer this, we must consider the entire context or system in which the decision lies—all of its environment, all of its affected parties, and all of its institutions. A *system* may be defined as an organization of interactive tasks and work functions directed toward a mission of meeting selected human needs. Examples of systems are the nationwide telephone network, the Polaris missile system, the absorption of the sun's energy by plants, the automobile–highway–air pollution system. Decisions in a system have a structure, and it can be determined by answering the following questions:

1. Why is there need for a decision? (That is, what human needs have changed?)
2. What is the system?
3. Who are the decision makers?
4. How is the system now operating (including institutions)?
5. When are needs to be met?
6. Where are needs to be met?
7. How is the institution to be maintained?

The present decision-making process begins with question 4 and asks these questions relative to the institution's needs rather than to individual needs. It assumes that the condition of institutions defines the system. That is, the decision makers are the institution, the sytem is the institution, and the needs are those of the institution. Then the only decision issues are: What needs or goals of the institution should be chosen to be met? When? Where (among whom)? Here are some examples of how questions 4, 1, 2, and 3 are used.

How is business? Business is depressed because sales and profits are down. Why is there a need? To raise sales and profits of the business institution so it can survive. What is the sytem that is to take the action? The business corporation. Who are the decision makers? The business executives.

How is the government? The government is in difficulty because it has huge deficits and lack of public support. Why is there a need? To remove the deficit and increase public support so the government can survive. What is the system to take the action? The federal government. Who are the decision makers? The government officials in Congress, the judiciary, and the Presidency.

How is education? Education is depressed because enrollments are declining and students think schools are irrelevant. What is the need? To increase enrollments so educational institutions can survive. What is the system to take the action? The educational institutions. Who are the decisions makers? The school officials.

Are these not the decision questions of the day? Where in all these decision questions is it asked, what are the individual needs and what should the individual decide? We are great institutionalists, trained, conditioned, and socialized that way, until we are institutionalists first and human beings afterwards.

A systems structure to decision making asks you to be a human being first and an institutionalist afterwards. That sounds very simple, but like all profoundly simple things it is very difficult. Institutions are important to us, because in institutions we find security, support, and protection from the terrors of the world. Besides, institutions perform the role of habit for the individual. With institutions we do not need to think very much, only incrementally, what small little additional thing needs to be done. Without institutions we need to think *de novo*, creatively, originally, into all the ramifications of the idea.

The task of thinking anew, creatively, for all of our acts each day is an obvious impossibility emotionally and physically. We would have to think anew how to breathe, eat, write, see, speak, walk, rather than let our automatic nervous system do that for us. We would need to think anew how to work, buy, sell, govern, settle conflicts and so we let our automatic social habits—institutions—do that for us.

However, as individuals, we often take over from the human automatic nervous system; we paint, write poems, invent machines, choose friends, living style, and other things for our fulfillment. But we can seldom take over from the automatic social institutions because they will not let us. They have goals, needs, and survival and security requirements of their own, which take precedence over our individual needs.

Moreover, we as individuals have, in our desperation to be secure from the terrors of the world, acceded to a social contract in which the delegations of authority to the institutions are practically timeless. Thus, the emergency powers we give the President, once granted, are seldom withdrawn. The appropriation powers of the Congress, however badly used, are seldom modified. The life of the government bureau, however superceded, seldom ends. The role of the school system, however irrelevant, is seldom changed. The powers of business, however massive and usurpatious of capital flows, are seldom controlled. These institutions usually have timeless powers and endless lives. Only human beings die.

The next generation of human beings comes into a life of old social habits and eternal institutions and it seldom gets to ask the question, what is it that I need and how shall it be fulfilled? Present generations have never been asked what form of government they prefer, or how it should be structured. They are only asked, for example, which of two similar candidates they select to place in a given government, with given structure, with given authority, given programs, and given imperatives for reelection and survival. Present generations are seldom asked what form of work they prefer, in what form of enterprises. They are asked mainly to work or not work, to buy or not buy, from given corporations, with given authority, given structure, given products, and given imperatives for maximizing profits whatever its consequences. Present generations have little choice, little expression of individuality of their needs. The eternal institutions already know what is needed, for their own maintenance, and are fulfilling it.

This is why human life is such a repetition of old mistakes, why history becomes a set of fables in which institutions live fabulous lives but human beings do not. This is why also the most revolutionary idea that Thomas Jefferson proposed was that the Constitution be rewritten and American institutions restructured every generation. That idea was a greater stroke for liberty than anything he put into the Declaration of Independence, but this splendid idea for human emancipation has been ignored ever since.

Jefferson's idea was voiced well before its time, for in his generation and a few thereafter, authority did remain diverse, dispersed, and decentralized so that institutions were small and individual authority over one's own life was considerable. Perhaps Jefferson was speaking as a man of vision who had assumed authority, ex cathedra, for the record, to the future—in the same sense that President Eisenhower warned us, ex cathedra, against the military-industrial institutional complex. Then and now, early in the Republic and late, we have been admonished that individuals must recover authority over their own lives even from the best of institutions—even the Constitution that Jefferson helped write—and certainly from the worst of institutions. Such advice tells us that we need to find some change mechanism by which a feasible compromise can be reached between institutional responsibility and individual authority. Institutions should be relegated to the social-habit jobs they do best, which is keeping the store, and individuals should have authority to do what they do best, which is to decide what they need and how to fulfill it.

There is no simple way to achieve this compromise, or earlier civilizations would have found it. But earlier civilizations have never found how to adapt to change, and social change has overcome them. Can we find a change mechanism in our own time before some institutional fable takes us down the dead-end path?

THE ADAPTIVE ORGANISM

An adaptive society, like an adaptive individual, has three characteristics that enable it to change:

1. It has learned how to learn from experience or environment.

2. It has a definable identity, and knows what it is and what it is to do.
3. It is able to test reality, to perceive itself and the world about it correctly.

These characteristics of adaptability are the same as those that define mental health in individuals and organizations.[1] They imply that the adaptive organism have (1) a search capability, (2) an experimental-response capacity, and (3) a reinforcement capacity. That is, first, the organism must be able to seek out new relationships with its environment, their potentialities to meet new needs, the errors of the past, the state of the present, and the combination of possible responses. Second, it must be able to offer an experimental response to test the reality of whether indeed this new possibility is better. Undoubtedly some experimental responses will fail, but then other experiments need to be substituted. Third, once a felicitous response has been recognized, it must be capable of reinforcement and reiteration so that other like needs can be met. The reinforcement is a set of rewards which stimulate learning and repetition.

Now we can begin to see the relationship of the adaptive organism to decision structure and to the elements of social structure and evolutionary periods. These are shown comparatively in Table 8–1.

An adaptive organism asks incessantly the following questions: Are there new human needs? Is there unrest or disorder? Why is a decision needed? Is there a problem? What is the problem? Who is the problem? Where is the problem? What are all the parts to the problem? Why has the problem emerged? Why? These searching questions are inquiry *de novo*, with a fresh eye, a new view, which make up problem definition.

Sensing a new problem or need, the adaptive organism experiments with a response. The response is impossible without knowing the answers to these questions: What is the sytem? What are all the parts of the problem? What are all the interrelationships? Who among animal, mineral, and vegetable are involved? Who am I? What is my identity? What is my purpose? What am I to do? What is my mission? What phenomenon will relate all the parts? What invention will create a new identity? What?

If the experimental response works (probably not the first time), then the adaptive mechanism needs to reinforce the response. The reinforcement is impossible without knowing answers to these: Who are all the decision makers who could respond? Where are they? Are they in some existing institution? Which ones are outside of existing institutions? How can they be encouraged to respond? What authority do they need to respond? How can that authority be delegated to enable them to respond? What changes will have to be made to delegate the authority?

[1] Warren Bennis, *Beyond Bureaucracy* (New York: McGraw-Hill, 1966), pp. 50–55.

TABLE 8-1. The Interrelation of Adaptive Mechanism, Decision Structure, Elements of Social Structure, and Evolutionary Periods.

Adaptive elements	Decision structure	Elements of social structure	Evolutionary periods
1. Search	Questions individuals ask: 1. Why a decision?	1. Needs	1. Fermentation and unrest
2. Experimental response	2. What is the system?	2. Mission	2. "Opportunity-creation-invention" phenomenon
3. Reinforcement	3. Who are the decision makers?	3. Authority	3. Adaptive period
4. Reward and repetition	Questions institutions ask: 4. How is the system now operating?	4. Functions	4. Formulation period
5. Reality testing	5. When are needs to be met?	5. Tasks	5. Development period
6. Reality test and search	6. Where are needs to be met?	6. Allegiance	6. Ideology emerges
7. Nonreality and nonsearch	7. How to maintain the institution?	7. Process	7. Socialization period; later alienation as new needs go unmet—fermentation and unrest
8. Nonreality	8. How to perpetuate the institution?	8. Alienation	8. Disorder

What effects will they have? What struggles for authority will ensue? How can the authority conflicts be anticipated and settled in advance? Who can settle them in advance? Who am I? What do I have to be? What would the system be that would settle these conflicts in advance? Who could settle them? Who?

Individuals and adaptive organisms ask the first three question sets in the table. This is the area of individualism, the necessary requisites of individualism. Institutions seldom ask these questions, and if they do, the answers are preconceived by the imperative of institutional survival and maintenance. Institutions ask only questions 4 through 7 in the question sets. This is the institutional area. They have a truncated, abortive, self-perpetuating decision structure. They do not need to search for needs. Institutions know their need is to survive, and there shall be no needs coming before it. Institutions do not need to ask their identity. They know who they are. Their identity was bequeathed to them from some authority delegation long past which they do not wish to reconsider. Institutions do not need to ask, what is the system and who are the decision makers? The institution *is* the system and its officialdom *are* the decision makers. All the problem-definition parameters are settled before they are asked. There are no problems except whether the institution is surviving and, if not, how to socialize the heretics so it can.

The point is that institutional society has limited adaptive means. Institutions cannot ask the searching questions about individuality. Without the searching questions, they cannot define the problem or the system of relationships involved. Without knowing the personal relationships, they cannot respond experimentally, only with old remedies. Without responding experimentally, they cannot reinforce or learn.

CONFLICTS OF INTEREST: ROLES VS. HUMAN LIFE

In the American system, the President is supposed to be the change agent and thus provide the adaptive role. But the President also wants to be reelected and discharge his office. He cannot be reelected or discharge his office unless there is a Presidency, a Constitution, an executive, the bureaucracy, and the sweeping emergency powers which have never been withdrawn. Therefore, the President has a grave conflict of interest before he performs his first act. If his first act is to abolish the Presidency, because it is potentially despotic and corrupt, then there is no second act as President. If he does not act to abolish the Presidency, then his act must be to preserve it, often regardless of the needs of the people. He may see the need to go to war to preserve the Presidency, regardless of the needs of the people. He may squander resources to be reelected, regardless of the needs of the people. He may merely maintain his salary and those of the bureaucracy, regardless of the unemployment of the people.

The self-perpetuating actions are insidiously required by the mere presence of the office. And this man is supposed to be the change agent in the system? A preposterous idea. Where else? In Congress or in the courts? They are equally constrained to maintain themselves. In business, perhaps, in the search for new market needs? That is more plausible, especially among new enterprises seeking new clients. But by this time we are so far down in the subsystems of the social process that only a few minor demands can be satisfied. The customer of a business cannot sit down and think to himself, "Who am I? What work and things do I need to be fulfilled?" and then go out and buy them. Why not? Because human life is not an assembly line of parts to be picked up in the market. Human life is adaptation, search, relationships, response, reinforcement, and learning—and businesses do not sell that.

Only individuals can adapt, and they have to be the change agents for themselves at the front end of the social systems, instead of in its rear pushing on the hind ends of institutions.

THE MISSION OF DECISIONS: WHO ARE WE?

So far I have discussed the structure of decisions and their relationship to adaptation, social structure, and social evolution, and this discussion has led me to write something close to an intemperate critique of institutions. Now let us look at the mission of decisions, so that we may balance this discussion with an equally severe critique of ourselves as individuals.

The mission of decisions is to answer the question of identity, purpose, and relationships. As individuals we must answer this question in people terms, or we defeat ourselves as individuals. We must respond to questions in terms of human needs—who we are and what our relationships are—otherwise we forfeit choices to institutions by default. When we answer institutionally, as we usually do, we propel the institution another step on its inevitable trajectory. For example:

Who are we? We are the sovereign people of the United States.

That is an institutional response that immediately defines the continental territory of the United States of some 200 million people with a Constitution, a President, a Congress, local government, multinational corporations, and big universities. If that is who we are, the institutions defined in the response will act for us. If that is who we are, let the Roman-replay scenario roll. Now let us ask again:

Who are we? We are 200 million people of diverse backgrounds and needs, filled with unrest over the frustration of meeting those needs, with trade relations with people all over the world, with conflict with those people all over the world over authorities and prices and trade, with four serious wars fought with those people in the past fifty years, with high prosperity among some of us and poverty among others, with conflicts and suppressions on our streets, with sovereignty to solve all these problems if we knew how.

The first institutional answer to the question of identity conjures up the images merely of officials who will act for us. And we know how they are going to act—to take care of the institution and themselves first.

The second, more adaptive response begins to define the system and the problem, which we as individuals ourselves must think through. The system is not the federal government institution of the United States. The system is ourselves and all the people of the world with whom we have relationships. The federal government has no jurisdiction over the other people of the world. Its decision authority is not as large as the system. How can one expect it to govern something over which it has no authority?

The system includes relations among diverse groups at home as well as abroad. The relationships among ourselves are not equitable enough to retain the allegiance (morality) of all. Institutions at home cannot invent new behavior among individuals; they can only reward and suppress what they have already been authorized to reward and suppress. If the system of relationships among us is not working and there are conflicts, more rewards and suppression are not going to resolve the conflicts. More rewards and suppression are merely going to make the rich richer and the suppressed more subjugated. Someone has to invent a new social relationship. An individual has to invent a new social relationship. The individual has to be given authority from an institution to invent the new social relationship. The individual has to be given the resources and the rewards for the new relationship. If the new experimental relationship works, we have a new social invention and a new mission.

Individuals have to invent the new social relations. It is true institutions, today and yesterday, have had the power to stop social inventions, and often have, by the denial of resources, authority, or opportunity. But even granted that, and even remedying that, the social inventions cannot take place unless individuals think individualistically. Too frequently we do not. We think institutionally because we are socialized to do so. For example:

Who am I? I am a professor and dean of a university.

That thought does not get me very far, because it conjures up my daily tasks to operate the university I am in, to respond to its officialdom, to respond to the present students, to meet classes, to grade papers, to maintain all that has always been maintained in universities for six centuries. Now let me ask again:

Who am I? I am a man past middle age who has lived in hope, who felt the reforms of the Depression would meet human needs, who fought in war, who tried many institutional jobs with dubious satisfaction, who raised a family, who saw his children disheartened in their work and with little hope in America, who suffered through the anguish of a Presidency gone wrong, who wonders about the governability of the nation, who sees educational opportunity denied to those who could help themselves and society, who sees work opportunities denied to those who wish satisfying work, who has worked abroad and seen suffering greater than ours, who fears new conflicts and wars with their destructive potential, who fears the Presidency for its destructive potential, who fears the large corporations for their destructive potential, who fears the university for its destructive potential, who fears his own actions for their destructive potential. I am in the same impossible constraint as the President of the United States or any institutional official. Anything I do presents me with a conflict of interest between my institutional loyalties and my humanity. Who am I? I am searching for a new set of relationships, hoping still to find a mission.

Now the first institutional answer got me nowhere. The second, personal, individual answer gets me immediately into a great deal of trouble. It causes me first to endure the pain of thinking. It causes me secondly to be at odds with my institutional loyalties, to criticize those very institutions upon which I depend. I am at war with myself, but I cannot be silent because I do not want my children to end up in a police state handicrafted by General Octavius or whoever the new dictator may be. Nor do I want them to be caught in the economic warfares of self-interest, the tyrannies of the Greeks, nor in the Inquisition. All of these terrors loom in my mind as more probable than that they will be given the opportunity for their own maturation. And what of my students? Although they are not my children, they expect me to guide them, and how shall I do that? Shall I teach them what is acceptable to be taught and help socialize them into the institutional process so that they may have to replay the Roman, Greek, or medieval scenarios? Or shall I try to warn them of the authorities that will rob them of decisions over their own lives?

Most certainly, decisions have mission, movement, destiny, step by step, no matter how small the decisions may be. Just going to work in the morning and doing what one is expected to do moves the social plot one iota more on its destined trajectory. There is no stopping the social process from inevitable ends unless we ask daily, what are those missions and those ends for us as individuals? It is our failure as individuals to ask these questions, or our failure of courage to answer them, which bring destinies that we cannot bear.

A glass office. *(Photo by Robert Eckert.)*

Chapter Nine

THE MISSION OF AMERICA AND THE PLOT MAKER'S GUIDE TO WRITING SCENARIOS

Decisions, everyday decisions, have two aspects: structure and movement. The *structure* of the decisions is concerned with whether they inquire into individual needs and adaptability before they inquire into institutional means. The *movement* of the decisions are in their mission, in who we are and where we are going: Are we going the Roman way, the Greek way, the medieval way, or our own way?

These questions are in our own hands, and we can always ask them. We can ask them of our institutions, although it is true that our institutions in their ubiquitous power can deny the questions or their answers. But it is also true that we as individuals can deny our institutions, ignore them and have as little to do with them as possible. This is what the early Christians did to Rome. This is what youth has done to the United States' institutions recently. Even their job conformance can conceal an erosion of allegiance.

However, there is always the hope that individuals and institutions will learn to live together—to learn that allegiance is a mutual pact and that individuals will grant authority and loyalty to the institution as long as the institution grants the adaptive role of identifying and acting upon their own needs to the individuals. Institutions could make this grant of the adaptive function to individuals in two ways: (1) by giving them the kind of work they wish to define for themselves and (2) by shifting the capital flows so that resources for search, experimentation, and reinforcement go into individual rather than institutional custody.

But, critics might say, this would mean that institutions would no longer set their own goals. Absolutely correct. Then how, they might ask, would they survive? By the support of individuals who like to determine their own identity but not keep their own store. What kind of institutions would these be? More like brokers and bankers and less like the salt mines. What kind of society would it be? More like the society described by the Founders of the United States.

THE MISSION OF THE FOUNDING FATHERS

We hold these truths to be self-evident, that all men are created equal and are endowed by their Creator with certain unalienable rights, that among these are life, liberty, and the pursuit of happiness.

We, the people of the United States, in order to form a more perfect union, establish justice, provide for liberty and the general welfare, do proclaim this Constitution for the defense of the people against tyrannies foreign and domestic, against Octavius Augustus Caesar, against King George III, against the President of the United States, Congress, corporations, schoolmen, dogmas, inquisitions, and all who fail to put the needs of individuals before the maintenance of institutions.

The mission statement of the Founding Fathers is hard to improve upon, even today. It was the ideal, the clarion, the inspiration of liberty and fraternity for Americans and nations around the world for more than a century. The legacy of good will toward Americans around the world still derives from the era of this ideal. But now Americans are not much welcome abroad. The slogans now are Yankee Go Home. Foreigners do not trust the United States any more than blacks or youth at home trust the United States government. How could such a turnabout occur with the same general mission?

The turnabout from allegiance to distrust occurred because the system changed. The system is not the institutions of the United States. The system is the people of the United States—all their needs, identities, purposes, and relationships among themselves, to other people, and to the environment. The system is the distribution of authority among all those relationships, interdependencies, and interactions.

The Founding Fathers worked with a much different system of interactions and authority distribution than we have today. They worked with the authority distribution of agrarian America, where authority was diverse, dispersed, and decentralized, where most families owned their own land and enterprises, where access to capital was amply available. Few of those conditions still prevail. Authority is now concentrated and centralized, family members are mainly employees or unemployed, capital flows are directed away from individuals to institutions. It is not the same system at all.

Under agrarian America, the Founders could superimpose upon the diverse, dispersed, and decentralized authority a structure of government that was small, circumscribed, with limited powers, and representative of those diverse individual authorities. Under postindustrial America, the same governmental structure becomes representative of the concentrated, centralized authorities of large institutions and accrues from them the massive, limitless powers needed to manage large institutional affairs.

ONE WORLD: THE NEW AMERICAN SYSTEM

The system changed and the interactions changed. The interactions in early America were largely local and regional, representing trade among the settlers and among the states. The interactions of present America are worldwide, with trade among all the nations of the world, technical assistance to developing nations, borrowing and lending among advanced nations, cultural exchanges, tourism, airlines, and communication interconnecting everything. It has become One World, but we forgot to change the authority distributions to recognize the new system. The system is all the participants in the interaction. The Arabs are part of the American system, the North Vietnamese, the South Vietnamese—because their decisions require our response, and ours theirs. The Europeans are part of the American system, and the Canadians, Latins, Asians, and Africans, because their prosperity depends upon ours, as surely as American employees at home depend upon it.

Where is the authority distribution in the American system for the Arabs, the Vietnamese, the Europeans, or at home for the blacks, the youth, the aged, the unemployed? What grant of powers and resources has been given to them to help themselves, search for themselves, act for themselves in a mutual pact that will command their allegiance and trust?

The authority distributions went askew from reality. The reality of interactions in the system widened and changed, and authority distribution did not follow. Institutions became mismatched and at odds with the needs.

One fundamental principle of systems analysis is that authority must be coterminous with the system. The system is not, remember, the institutions of the United States, not the federal government, not the corporations. The system is the people of the United States, with all their differences and diversities, with all their interactions with the world, with all their drain upon the ecology. Authority must be coterminous with all those diversities and interactions, else the choices among those diverse interactions will cease to be made, and the system will cease to function as an organism and begin to function more lamely as an institution of limited goals and limited adaptability.

Authority must be diverse, dispersed, and decentralized for a complex system to function, and the more complex the system, the more diverse the distribution. Think of the diversity of our own nervous system as a human organism, how intricate the response capability and interconnection of every cell. Multiply that by three billion people on earth and one gets some idea how big the computer in Washington has to be to adapt to every on-going transaction. Computers are not made that big. Computers are too slow. Leaders are not made that big. Why should we expect so much of them? Leaders, computers, and institutions should be given jobs they can do, such as keeping as tidy as they can the distribution of authority.

DISPERSING POWER AND A NEW SYSTEM OF CHECKS AND BALANCES

The function of the leader is not to exercise authority but to give it away—generously, diversely, to everyone who can use it. The function of the leader is to be a broker and not run the salt mines. This function of giving away and diversifying authority is a role most leaders do not understand, because it makes them feel important to think they are making decisions, to have power. To make decisions and have power, they must maintain their institution of power. That is why it is said that power corrupts, and absolute power corrupts absolutely, and the Presidency of the United States has been afflicted with corruption.

Cleisthenes taught us long ago in Greece that the dispersal of power is maintained by checks and balances, and the drafters of our Constitution repeated that lesson. But the system of interactions changed between their time and ours, so that there are now not enough checks and balances nor enough authority dispersal in the system. Where should the checks be placed?

The placing of checks and balances requires us to return to the system question, who are the decision makers? The decision makers are not the officials of the federal government nor of the corporations. The decision makers are all the participants in the interactive system: the rich and the poor, the black and the white, the old and the young, the employed and the unemployed, the Arbas, the Israelis, the Europeans, the Vietnamese, the Latins, the Asians, the Africans, the endangered species, the food chain, and the ecology upon which all three billion of us depend for our lives. Each of those participants can change our lives. Each of them has a voice, whether it is heard today or not. The whisper today can become the roar of tomorrow, as we have seen from environmental destruction and from the wars of the Middle East. It is a big, big system. It needs a big, big distribution of authority to deal with it, so that organisms can reach decisions on their own how to adapt, just like cells of a body.

The checks and balances have to be placed so all these voices can be heard and not be muffled by institutional imperatives for self-maintenance. Checks are the limitations of authority, or its redistribution. Balances are the provision of voice where it can be heard. Some of the checks and balances that would disperse authority to participants in the present interactive system are as follows.

Checks

1. Checks on the timeless life span of institutions so they correspond more closely to the duration of human lives, and thus to contemporary needs.
2. Checks on the capital access of institutions relative to individuals.
3. Checks on the accumulation of authorities in institutions, either by reason of resources, legislation, or imperfect competition.
4. Checks on the resource drain of human beings upon a limited ecology.
5. Checks on the agents for violence.

6. Checks on the delegations by a sovereign people to Congress and the Presidency.
7. Checks by a sovereign people on the short-run goals of business corporations that cause long-run social costs.
8. Checks by a sovereign people on land use upon which we all depend for our existence.

Balances

1. Voice for the underrepresented in American society to express the needs of youth, minorities, unemployed, aged, and disadvantaged.
2. Voice for change agents seeking to sense and adapt to new needs.
3. Voice for other peoples of the world adversely affected by our actions in trade and foreign policy.
4. Voice for the arts to enrich impoverished cultures.
5. Voice for those who seek ecological balance.
6. Voice for the needy wherever they are.

The invention of checks and balances, which would make retribution of the authorities misplaced, is not the social invention of one man sitting in a study or in the Oval Office. The redefinition of the system and its authority allocations has to be done by all the participants in the social interaction. The means are at hand by the same means that have always been at hand since the days of Solon: arbitrators, referendums, free capital markets, free trade, free prices, and constitutional conventions. It may take time. It may be painful consultation. But it is the only way to change the social trajectory of the United States to put it on a path where the people wish to go.

WRITING YOUR OWN SCENARIO: THE PLOT MAKER'S KIT

There are many possible social inventions and combinations of authority that would provide adaptive change in the United States, restoring hope and allegiance. Some examples of plausible social inventions are given in the next chapter, "The Future of the U.S.A.: An Original Play." However, these illustrations are only meant to suggest rather than prescribe. The scenario is built around three major tools, which make up the plot maker's kit:

1. the structure of an adaptive social system and decision process—see Table 8–1 in Chapter 8;
2. a list of checks and balances over the distribution of authority—see preceding section;
3. a list of the strengths and differences of the United States from other previous societies—see the list of differences in the Roman, Greek, and medieval scenarios.

With these tools from the plot maker's kit, you can write your own future, and should. Here is how:

First, think of the kind of person you would like to be, your own identity, and the kind of world you would like to live in. This gives you a sense of mission.

Second, around the mission construct an inclusive environment of everyone who is affected and interacts in the kind of world you describe. This begins to define the kind and size of system you live in.

Third, construct a structural picture of the typical interactions in that system by allocating the needs, missions, authorities, functions, tasks, and allegiances among the participants. This gives an idealized picture of what the structure of the society might be.

Fourth, of course, you know that people are going to fight with each other over authority, because we are all both good and bad and we are going to stay that way. Thus, you do not want a scenario only for a good world but also for a bad one. This should lead you to think about the strengths of the society we now live in, what makes it enduring, and these are most likely differences from other societies.

Fifth, you must have a list of checks and balances over the use of authority, so that even when the good people are bad, or the bad good, none of them can usurp other's authorities. These checks and balances are most likely to work over a long period of time (even though the Greeks and we have had trouble making them work), if you give the checks and balances to the most enduring characteristics of the social process; you will then have given them to those parts of the social structure that will wield a limited authority continuously, and therefore well. This allocation of checks and balances is a work that the Founding Fathers started and never finished, because it is a continuous job. It is the job of the change agent, or the adaptive organism in the social process.

Now, you are prepared to write your own scenario or fable of the future, in which you can live a fabled life instead of letting some institution live it for you. Do not expect too much of the fable at first, because the fable is an act of social invention, an experimental response to the opportunity-creation-invention phenomenon. The feasible social invention, the new mission, has to interrelate all the interactions that are now out of whack. No one of us is likely to see these many interactions by ourself at first. Thus, a certain amount of fable swapping has to occur before the feasible Great Fable comes to light. Like the New Testament, the Magna Carta, or the Constitution, the Great Fable may have many writers. Still, it is the little fables that become the Great Fable.

Just because a fable is little does not mean it is unimportant. It is important to the writer because it clarifies his or her identity and gives some hope for the future in the miasma of the institutional drag around us. The fable may be important to other fable writers in providing the linchpin that links the myriad other interactions together. And finally, it is important, even if nothing happens, because it is an exercise in adaptation, a learning to learn from experience and experiment. It is an exercise in individualism and some small recovery of humanity in a dehumanized world.

The next chapter is such an exercise; in it I present a little fable that you may use as an example for doing your own.

Flower child. *(Photo by Ed Rice/Courtesy World Health Organization.)*

Chapter Ten

THE FUTURE
OF THE U.S.A.:
AN ORIGINAL PLAY

Suppose we do not wish, as we do not, to relive the Roman, Greek, or medieval experience, nor any of those of the other many civilizations that have come and gone. We have the same genes as our ancient forebears, often quite similar institutions, and very little if any more cranial capacity. History repeats itself, over and over.

How can we expect to escape the inevitable turning of the wheel?

PAST DISSIMILARITIES SUGGESTING ENDURING
ELEMENTS FOR AMERICAN SOCIETY

Perhaps we cannot escape the inevitable turning, but if we can, it will be for two reasons: first, because some differences do exist, if only because nature creates humans in infinite diversity; and, second, because we have somehow introduced more adaptability to change into the American social process. Let us think first of the differences by retabulating the dissimilarities listed earlier in comparing ourselves with Greek, Roman, and medieval societies. These are some differences:

1. family structure
2. local government
3. technology
4. basis for economic growth
5. form of labor contract
6. federalism
7. level of public education
8. printing and news media

Each of these differences is the potential lodging point for a check or balance, if we can think of the social invention to do it. Some of them are already lodged with checks and balances, such as freedom of the press, which has recently revealed corruption of office among elected officials. However, we wish to think about the relative kinds of authority each of these eight social elements now has, has had, and could potentially wield, either as an authority delegation to act or as a check or a balance.

The *American family* is a remarkable unit in itself, with its own internal set of checks and balances, which prevent it from becoming a power usurping agent. For the most part, the American family is tied together by love and cooperation, whereas all other social institutions are formed from the bonds of reward and punishment. The bond of love tempers the good and bad in people, so that conflict is moderated into bickering and need is abetted by nurture. The family is a felicitous organism upon which to build social processes.

The American family has, however, fallen to low estate, become isolated, nuclear, without authority, fragmented by the pull of institutions demanding specialization of labor and separate loyalties. The family finds it difficult to retain unifying purpose among all these conflicting demands and frequently separates or is destroyed. The restoration of the integrity of the family is certainly one of the building blocks upon which the diffusion and dispersal of power can be constructed, by giving the family the unity of economic purpose that it once had in agrarian America, when it was one of the foundations of liberty in the Republic.

Local government is similarly a conflict-resolving institution, because it confronts people and problems face to face in a setting where only eyeball-to-eyeball reconciliation can occur. Local government, too, has fallen into disrepair, through the usurpation of its resources by the federal government, which then has the largesse to return part of them, retaining, of course, a large part for the maintenance of an ungovernable bureaucracy that no one really knows.

Technology is less an institution than a process, in which science and technique discover the interaction of the physical world. Science and technology are essential to the opportunity-creation-invention phenomenon and the operation of the system, but technology is also valueless. It has no sense of purpose, little linkage to human needs, no leadership element. Being valueless, it is therefore in the service of whoever chooses to use the methodology and mounts the resources to marshal its skills. Thus, technology is as equally in the service of those who would kill people by the thousands as of those who would heal them one by one. Technology needs a check on its destructive potential as well as a balance, a strong voice, in the adaptive-discovery process.

The *basis for economic growth* is capital investment in new ideas. Most ideas come from individuals; most of the capital is in the hands of institutions. The matching of ideas with capital is one of the unsolved problems of the social economy. Massive research and development expenditures by large institutions have attempted to solve this problem, but these massive research expenditures have had decreasing returns. The justification of large business institutions, in the first place, was increasing returns with size of capital investment, a condition that exists mainly in factories. This rationale has been greatly overdrawn, because mass-production industries do not predominate in postindustrial societies, service industries do. Service industries, being people intensive, suffer decreasing returns, first in the research, idea-generating process, and second, in the social overhead of managing large people-organizations. A rethinking of the process by which capital is matched to ideas is urgently needed as we move out of the factory age.

The *form of labor contract* in the United States has been used successfully to improve wages, benefits, and working conditions. It may have promise, in the future, for enriching jobs and making them more what the individual would like to do.

Federalism is a concept of pluralism in which many parts have powers that they can jointly use together. By its very nature, federalism implies definitions of authority, and definitions are limiting. This means that the plural parts each have limited powers, and some one place is the sink of residual powers. The Founders thought the residual powers lay with the sovereign people and the states, and that all the other parts (especially the federal government) had limited, circumscribed powers. As matters have worked out, with the escalation of institutional size, the federal government now holds the residual power, and the sovereign people have circumscribed powers. The circumscribed powers of the people are to choose every two years between two like candidates who are financed by special-interest groups. The new election-financing disclosure laws place one check upon this distortion of the election process, but additional checks and balances must be considered in order to restore the residual powers to the sovereign people.

The *level of education* has risen markedly in the last generation, which may indeed contribute in part to the disillusionment with present society. More people are capable of perceiving that something is wrong which prevents their further individuation. Many educated young people are currently underemployed or unemployed. Many employers feel youth are overqualified for the jobs; hence, their talents are underutilized and there is little for them to do. This is an example of institutional thinking, which presupposes that the individuals should shape themselves to fit into the institutionally defined job. But human beings do not exist for institutions, institutions exist to serve human beings. It is the function of a responsible institution to create jobs that fit the skills individuals have and to help develop the individuals onward from there. Checks need to be considered to prevent the abusive function of the job market. The simplest check is to provide the individuals with the means to create their own jobs, at least as a last resort.

Printing and news media have been a bulwark for reality testing in recent elections and public affairs. In one sense, the freedom of the press needs to be strengthened, by checks on the bullying of the press by public officials who are fleeing from hot pursuit. In another sense, however, the freedom of the press needs to be checked from its own abuse. The tendency of news reporters to goad individuals into controversy for the sake of headlines foments conflict and gives platform to the most extreme, rather than representative, views. The journalism profession needs some internal checks of its own to ensure that news is reported rather than "made" at the expense of individuals.

These, then, are the differences and enduring characteristics upon which new checks and balances, and a new scenario, can be built: family, local government, technology, economic base, labor contract, federalism, public education, and freedom of the press. The scenario will seek to strengthen these elements in society, allocate to them new checks and balances, and disperse authorities among them so that our social process, which has become rigidified by institutionalism, becomes more adaptive, individualistic, and humane.

In order to disperse authority with new checks and balances, we need to consider what alternative set of policy choices will effectuate such a dispersal.

ALTERNATIVE POLICY CHOICES

The dispersal of authority cannot be considered separately from the question of where the burden of change will reside. The authority to make changes is also the authority to avoid them. We have seen that institutions have a penchant for avoiding change and insulating themselves against it, which throws the sacrifices involved in change (like unemployment) upon individuals. Individuals have the same penchant, but being many, they have less power to insulate themselves, and thus provide checks and balances upon each other, at least as long as incomes are normally distributed within a narrow range.

A narrow-range, normal distribution of income is, therefore, a cornerstone of the equitable distribution of sacrifice in adapting to change. That is, incentives and taxes can be established that will make the sacrifices (costs of change) proportionate to a normal income distribution.

Free-market prices, freer competition, and freer capital flows are also important means of adapting to change, because (1) they reflect and quickly measure changes in needs, demand, and supply; (2) they adjust capital allocation and supply to new needs; and (3) they distribute the costs (sacrifices) throughout the system.

Wide and free political choice making by individuals on specific issues are an adaptive means to change because such choice making lets individual needs become reflected in the only arena within society where authority can be reallocated.

With these general principles in mind of how the burdens and sacrifices of change will be shared, I offer, in Table 10–1, a comparison of thirteen policy choices for the U.S.A. in 1970 and in the future. This set of policy choices is suggested with the idea that (1) change must come and be provided for in the social process; (2) change requires dispersed authority for experimental response; (3) the sacrifices and costs of change should be equitably distributed; and (4) free prices are the most rapid media for adjusting costs, sacrifices, and demand.

In this comparison between 1970 U.S.A. and future U.S.A., the policy choices are similar but not identical on two issues (educational distribution and internal order) and different on eleven issues. This may seem like a substantial difference, indeed enough to question the feasibility of this alternative. Certainly this degree of policy change would be difficult

TABLE 10-1. Policy Analysis and Comparison of Thirteen Major Issues Confronting the United States in 1970 and in the Future

	Policy issue	1970 choice	Future choice	Consequence of 1970 choice	Consequence of future choice
1.	Monetary-fiscal policy	Unbalanced, expansionist	Balanced*	Inflation	Neutral, equilibrium
2.	Income distribution	Skewed	Normal*	Rich-poor extremes	Equitable
3.	Capital distribution	Institutionally channeled	Open*	Capital concentration	Market/individually channeled, competitive
4.	Competitive distribution	Oligopolistic	Open*	Large business oligopolies	Small units, competitive
5.	Price policy	Administered	Free*	Profit maximized, stable	Competitive, unstable
6.	Living standards	Externalize costs	Internalize costs*	Less amenities, more government	More amenities, less government
7.	Employment	Labor extensive	Labor semiintensive*	Unemployment, capital intensive	Service-oriented economy
8.	Educational distribution	Semiwide	Wide	Specialized technostructure	Adaptable individuals
9.	Technological distribution	Narrow	Wide*	Fewer firms, oligopoly	Competitive
10.	Barriers to entry	Raised	Lowered*	Skewed Incomes	Equalize income
11.	Voting	Narrow issue	Wide issue*	Oligarchic republic	Direct democracy
12.	Internal order	Semiparticipative	Participative	Limited conflict resolution	Restive conflict resolution
13.	International order	Semicoercive	Participative*	Use of economic-military power	Restive conflict resolution

*Differences of 1970 U.S.A. compared to those of future U.S.A.

and would take time. But the United States did it once before, and we can do it again if we are sure of our identity and mission.

The future-U.S.A. set of policy choices is, in fact, very close to those of early America. They are the kind of policy choices and authority distributions upon which the present Constitution is founded and with which the constitutional government is expected to work as a democracy, balancing interests among diversely held power.

Of course, the United States cannot simply turn back the clock. Early America was an agrarian economy and we live in an industrialized service economy. Then technology was relatively simple, now it is complex. Then the population was small, now it is large and densely settled. Then natural resources were overabundant, now they are scarce. These are great differences with which to adjust. Should we try? One thought impels us, at least, to attempt it—namely, that early Americans worked with an adaptiveness, vigor, and individuality that is lacking today. Let us, then, at least examine what this set of policy choices would imply.

As mentioned, the similarities between future U.S.A. and 1970 U.S.A. are only two: wide educational distribution, and participative resolution of internal order. Both of these choices need strengthening, to widen academic range and equality of opportunity, as well as to improve the dispute-settling machinery.

Eleven policy choices would need altering in order to establish (1) balanced monetary-fiscal policy, (2) more equal normal income distribution, (3) open capital flows, (4) open competition, (5) free-market prices, (6) internalized social and environmental costs, (7) stabilized employment by using labor more intensively in services, (8) wider technological distribution, (9) lower barriers to entry, (10) wide voting on specific issues, and (11) participative international-conflict resolution.

There are many ways these policy choices could be altered, all of them controversial because democracy is controversy settling diverse viewpoints. No one individual can foresee and weigh all these diversities of view; hence, controversy has to go to public arenas for debates and choices until resolutions are agreed upon.

This is an uneasy, tumultuous process, from which many today may shrink. But the Founding Fathers did not shirk it; theirs was an uneasy, tumultuous time. The Constitution was uneasily and tumultuously arrived at, and that is the burden of change. If we no longer believe in tumultuous change, we can vote for the stability of an oligarchic republic and follow the Roman road.

We should at least know who we are and where we want to go, and have the ability to vote on our futures. Now let me present my own version (or one of my versions) of Future U.S.A.

THE FUTURE OF THE U.S.A.: AN ORIGINAL PLAY

The closing decades of the twentieth century drag on, with alternating inflation, unemployment, stagnation, slow progress, pollution, corruption, disillusion—all the ailments that surfaced in the 1960s and 1970s getting no better and indeed getting a little worse. But the older generation in institutional positions of centralized authority cannot change. They cannot bear the thought of change, the turmoil, differences, far-out ideas with which they might have to cope; nor are they willing to risk their own prerogatives and preferential incomes. They feel and vote for stability in our time.

Still, what came to be known in the 1960s as The Movement is not dead. Although it never had a form, concept, mission, or leader and wanted none, that is not only its weakness but its strength. It is a weakness because The Movement could not crystallize its diverse emotional base into thought or action. But it is a strength because its emotional diversity and poignancy do not die. There must be, think the brightly educated youth of The Movement, a better way to live, or at least a livable way to live, one where life is wanted, children are wanted, hope is there.

The Movement is still alive in the 1980s and '90s in the hopes of this generation as they come into their age for positions of authority. At least some of these new leaders do not covet their positions mightily, nor the power or materialism that goes with them. Indeed, to Movement members, materialism seems a wasteful pursuit, and they have continued to live and work casually, not coveting much, with stronger interests in authenticity and in each other. They have learned enough about the stress of authority to get along with it minimally in business and government, but their joys are still elsewhere—in their own music, crafts, and talking.

Those in The Movement who are now in authority carry on the business of business and government carefully and efficiently but with an easy sense of participation and compromise. Their own feelings about institutional affairs are ambivalent; institutions are felt to be a necessary means for survival, perhaps, but they are not what life is about. To such individuals, institutional maintenance is not an uppermost thought, but they hear other individuals, if they are authentic, for their feelings and needs. Their needs are thought about, debated, reheard, compromised with other views, and partially settled. Institutional life is not idyllic, nothing is ever really settled, only adjusted, adapted. Change comes rapidly and hard, people disagree. The arguments are as tiresome as they are necessary. Work and public life are tumultuous, stressful, and those in The Movement are not at all loathe to put off the cares of the world into more eager hands so their own lives might be centered on the more enjoyable. Thus, the machinery for participative conflict resolution becomes strengthened in business and government by the desire of leaders to disperse decisions and authority into places of stress.

Still, those in The Movement go along without a conceptual foundation for what they are doing, merely getting along, and feeling a little guilty (from their parents) for casting off their responsibility for decisions upon others. This shirking of authority to seek their own pleasures does not bother them enough to make them change, but it does make them wonder if there is not some way to avoid being loaded with such oppressive institutional responsibilities, which they feel guilty about dispersing, and let people make up their own minds more about what they want to do. However, there does not seem to be any obvious way to change the institutions they man, institutions being what they are, and have always been.

Somehow the feeling grows in The Movement that if people become more able to take care of themselves, they will do so. Then one in authority would not need to make so many decisions for others and could attend more to one's own pursuits. But if people are to be more able to make their decisions, they must be more equally alike in their incomes. The feeling develops in The Movement that a more equal distribution of income would probably do more to disperse authority over individual lives than any other single measure. Had they not all been more or less equal in their means when The Movement started? True, the means had been parental support, but it was fairly equally distributed among them. None had been much richer or poorer than others, and if they were, they shared. So why not try the same thing now, since nothing else has worked?

Now, this is not a concept, policy, or idea, merely a feeling that matters that have distressed them since their youth might be somewhat set aright by normalizing the means (income) for dealing with problems. This generalized feeling probably would not emerge as an issue, except that Congress at this point decides, as it does every ten years or so, to revise the tax structure. The purpose, as usual, is to "simplify" taxes and to "close loopholes." Traditionally, the simplification of taxes has been to reduce the size of the print on Form 1040 and to close a few loopholes while, by the most adroit logrolling, opening others.

The logrolling begins in Congress, and the outlook is promising that a few tidy patches will dispose of the unhappy business for another ten yeas. Then a difficulty arises. It becomes apparent at the hearings that the tax laws are so complex that the Internal Revenue Service does not fully understand them, Congress even less, and the taxpayer least of all. Throughout the country, some old uneasiness and unrest begins to stir, the feeling that maybe the people are not running tax laws but tax laws are running people. One member of Congress from The Movement rises and cries, "Good Heavens, why can't we write a tax law we understand? A really simple tax law, like no deductions at all?"

This idea is put aside by Congress as of little merit, deserving no response, but the comment is given headlines in the news media and the result is that Congress is swamped with mail approving the idea. Then business executives from The Movement begin appearing at Congressional hearings and, flatly contradicting their own paid lobbyists, saying the idea of a tax law with no or few deductions has merit and that incomes should be more nearly equalized. Feeling from The Movement begin emerging, after that, from the Presidential staff, Treasury, Department of Commerce, and even the IRS. Though nonplussed, traditional members of Congress regard the events as freakish and expect old self-interested logrolling to reaffirm itself. But The Movement has a majority on the final vote, and a new tax structure emerges with only a few provisions:

1. Income taxes will be progressive (at reduced rates), with corporations and individuals paying the same tax rates.
2. Low-income families will receive negative tax subsidies below the poverty level, with one dollar of tax subsidy for every dollar earned.
3. No deductions of any kind will be allowed, except savings by individuals invested or reinvested in a family-operated business of which they are active principals.
4. The Executive Branch shall administratively adjust progressive tax rates annually so that they are sufficient to cover all cash expenditures of government and so that they produce a normal income distribution of narrow range.

The new law has so simplified income-tax returns that the return consists only of two figures, plus a supporting list of family-enterprise investments. The results of the law over the next decade are awesome:

Large corporations immediately begin spinning off subsidiaries to disaggregate to smaller size.

Rich families that formerly paid no taxes by using tax-avoidance deductions begin to share the tax burden and life of the rest of the population.

Poor families are able to improve their incomes by their own efforts and achieve a minimally decent living standard.

New family enterprises invigorate the economy by innovating new products and services.

People dissatisfied with the kinds of jobs they have in big institutions go into business for themselves with a job they want to do.

Competition increases as new family enterprises develop and large corporations disaggregate to smaller size.

The increase in competition frees prices and they become more flexible and competitive.

Capital flows are no longer institutionally protected but are competitively channeled through the market and individual investment decisions.

The government budget is balanced and inflation ceases.

Labor is used more intensively because small family enterprises tend to optimize the use of labor in service-oriented activities, rather than channeling funds primarily for capital intensification, institutional expansionism, and economizing on labor.

Technology is more widely distributed because research and development funds are no longer bottled up in the large corporations but are distributed throughout the economy in those units that can achieve a reasonable return on development expenditures.

Barriers to entry are lowered because incomes are more equal, capital flows accessible, prices free, competition open, and technology available.

Even those in The Movement are surprised by what they have done. The economy moves forward, unemployment declines, inflation is gone, people move into the kind of work they want for themselves. Those in The Movement who have positions of institutional authority find they spend less time trying to settle other people's conflicts, as people settle their own. Moreover corporate size is smaller. Business is run by owner-operators, is more creative, and takes more risks. The tendency for rugged individualists to dominate people, markets, or materials is checked by the equalization of incomes; that is, no individual can get so rich and rugged that he can tyrannize. The members of The Movement are tolerably pleased because now people are reasonably well off doing what they want with less effort on the part of institutional managers, and they of The Movement can spend more time on their own pursuits.

Of course even in this society there are some problems. For one thing, prices tend to adjust to change—that is, prices are flexible and unstable—and adjustments tend to come quickly in the economy. That sometimes causes sharp changes in sales, products, profits, and employment. But these adjustments are ameliorated by the negative income tax and especially by the existence of small family enterprises, which tend to take care of their own members. The public accepts these economic adjustments, troublesome though they are, as a necessary sacrifice for adaptation and change. At least, it seems, this adjustment is better than the former pattern of unemployment, inflation, and institutional dominance.

However, there are other kinds of changes that do not occur very easily, especially conflicts among economic groups, ethnic groups, political groups and among nations. The trouble seems to be that issues do not emerge, are not heard, are not confronted until they develop into violence.

Members of the Movement now begin to feel that the old alienations about political power and political structure have not been dealt with. They also have a certain amount of new confidence from their somewhat chance success in restructuring of the socioeconomy. A ferment and many-sided debate begins in the person-to-person talks, meetings, media, and music that Movement members enjoy. A feeling emerges that it has been a long time since they were asked what they preferred in their own governance. Indeed they were never asked. They were not asked about the Vietnam war, what to do with their draft cards, how to make education responsive, or how to settle riots. Some still recall police tactical squads, tear gas, and rifle fire, and they wonder if in their own time they can do better.

If they are to do better, they feel they should talk about it, have a forum, a place to agree and disagree, like a convention—perhaps a Constitutional Convention. A Constitutional Convention has venerable precedence. As a trial balloon, a Movement Congressional representative introduces a resolution calling for a Constitutional Convention. At first nothing seems to happen, and the old guard in Congress prepares to bury the resolution. However, The Movement voice begins to emerge as before—from the Administration, political parties, business, grass roots, wherever those in The Movement ended up. The Movement presents a diverse, tumultuous, impressive display of political power that nudges first the Congress and then the legislatures of the several states to ratify. The call for a Constitutional Convention takes time and is controversial, and it is a little frightening to people in authority to see the public at work forcing ratification, but it happens.

The Constitutional Convention itself is as tumultuous and controversial as the first one. It has trouble organizing itself. There seem few natural coalitions or majorities. The convention delegates are mainly citizens rather than politicians; this adds to the diversity of views, but it also means difficulty in setting an agenda. Slowly a few major issues emerge. War, peace, order, public expression of choice on issues—these become the agenda. The proceeding proves to be long, tedious, raucous, and many persons wonder if democracy can be made to work, it appears so untidy and undignified, with bedlam only just held in check. Finally, however, twelve resolutions emerge from the majority of the Constitutional Convention. They are as follows:

1. We, the sovereign people of the United States, reaffirm the pre-

sent Constitution of the nation, subject to the following modifying amendments:

2. Constitutional conventions shall be faithfully reconvened every twenty years and be known as the Jefferson Memorial Reconventions on the Constitution.

3. Revisions and amendments to the Constitution shall be submitted item by item to the people for majority vote by referendum.

4. Only the sovereign people shall have the right to declare war, by majority on a referendum, and neither the President nor Congress shall conduct military actions outside the territorial limits of the United States without such declaration.

5. Congress shall sit as a Committee of the Whole to recommend revenues and expenditures for the public purpose, but no bills of taxation or expenditure shall have the force and effect of law until a complete balanced budget has been placed before the people annually for approval on referendum, item by item.

6. The Office of Independent Prosecutor is established, the holder to be elected by all the people, who shall investigate violations of law, ethics, and good conduct, reporting such to the people. Any official of government may be removed from office for any reason deemed by the sovereign people to be contrary to the public interest, by a simple majority on a referendum. The Independent Prosecutor shall, upon election, not thereafter be eligible for the office of President.

7. Any group of citizens feeling underrepresented in the Congress, and whose numbers upon petition at least equal the smallest population-to-representative ratio in the Congress, may constitute one of themselves as a member of the Council of Popular Voices, which shall be advisory to the presiding officers of the House and Senate. Such duly constituted members of the Council may present legislation to the presiding officers, upon which it is mandatory that the House and Senate shall vote yea or nay.

8. Local government, in which the residual powers of government lie, other than in the sovereign people, may make drafts for funds upon the approved budgets of state or federal governments on a proportional population or per-capita basis, for all expenditures that do not lie in the specified and limited powers of the federal and state governments as defined in their respective constitutions. The intent of this provision is that federal and state governments shall act as mere fiscal agents for local government, except insofar as specified and limited powers (such as national defense or the regulation of interstate and maritime commerce) are to be executed by federal or state governments.

9. Other nations of the world may join the United States by affirming the Constitution, abandoning their nationalistic government, and dividing themselves into states so that the average population size of their states shall be no smaller than the average size of those already in the Union.

10. Other nations of the world, feeling an affinity for peace and the mission of the United States, but not feeling it to their interest to join the Union, may become Affiliates of the United States by so declaring themselves and merging their military forces into a common defense.

11. The President of the United States shall be elected by popular vote of all the member States of the Union and of all Affiliates for a single term of six years.

12. The President of the United States shall preside over a Council of Heads of State, which will be made up of the Chief of State of every Affiliated Nation. The Council of Heads of State shall be empowered to veto legislation that adversely affects the trade among the several nations. The President is empowered, with the advice and consent of the Council of Heads of State, to make appointments of Cabinet rank to the United States government, and to make treaties that shall be binding upon the United States and all Affiliated Nations.

These resolutions from the Constitutional Convention are received by the public with consternation and puzzlement. The provisions are endlessly analyzed in the press. Great debates errupt in Congress, state legislatures, party meetings, and on television news panels. The protagonists for diverse views are forceful. Debates are prolonged and sometimes acrimonious. Some provisions are bitterly contested by one interest party or another. The combined disagreements appear to be enough to defeat the amendments.

Then the President of the United States, himself now a mellowing member of The Movement, takes to television and the campaign trail. His arguments ultimately ensure the success of the Amendments:

These proposed Amendments may not comprise the best of Constitutions, but then neither do I now preside over the best of governments, nor was the original Constitution regarded as the best of its day. The Constitution then was an experiment in self-government, as is this revision. The division in 1787 was as keen as the division today, but I take it that this keenness of thought is a sign of our maturing and adaptation. Surely now we are capable of adaptation and a trial for twenty years, having retained the basic structure of the original Constitution, until the next Constitutional Convention.

The great merit of these Amendments, compared to the original, is that the Constitution becomes capable in practice of regular and periodic revision as the needs of new generations change. The other great merit of these proposals, however much you may differ from specific items, is that they greatly disperse and decentralize authority back to the people. I do not necessarily agree with all the specific proposals. But I am content with the work that has been done, because it represents the best efforts of a people to recover their sovereignty.

The two great merits of this revised Constitution, the facility for change and the dispersal of power, are sufficient cause for approval, whatever other reservations you may feel. As a President who has wielded massively accumulated power, I can say to you that the temptation to retain power is great, and the opportunity for the people to recover authority over your own lives, which has been lost, comes rarely in history. Seize it, my friends; seize it as it stands, lest it slip from you forever.

Detroit office buildings. *(Photo by Robert Eckert.)*

Chapter Eleven

IS THERE A FUTURE? SOME OTHER SCENARIOS

The scenarios I presented in the previous chapters have necessarily been brief in order to highlight a major option open to use among alternative futures. In this sense, a scenario is like a compass pointing a direction. Once a direction has been selected, a great deal of work may be required to hew out the path to follow. The hewing of the path, or the planning of detailed implementation of these scenarios, involves the collection of data and the definition of measures to realize, for example, equitable tax structure, neutral monetary-fiscal policy, normal income distributions, opening competition, freeing prices and capital flows, et cetera. These are important and difficult problems, but they lie in the area of the known. We can assume that they are feasible. What is being tested in the scenarios, rather, is the plausibility of an adaptive relationship between individuals and institutions.

The scenarios test the feasibility of such alternative relationships, because I regard this as the most severe constraint upon the adaptive process, an assumption based upon my own experience as a student of the sociopolitical economy. Other writers of scenarios make other assumptions about the most severe constraint, and their scenarios have a different context. All scenarios are primarily concerned with identifying and relaxing the most severe constraints in order to make tractable the redirection of the future by human decisions. Some scholars regard the most serious constraints as technological, political, psychological, economic, ecological, or the balance of power. As they seek to relax such constraints, they arrive at different perspectives about the future.

Let us now review some of these other perspectives; they will enrich the scenarios in this book and give us a picture of our other options on the future.

VICTOR FERKISS AND THE FUTURE OF TECHNOLOGICAL CIVILIZATION

Victor Ferkiss, professor of government, Georgetown University, considers the future of technological civilization to be in crisis because excessive growth and expansion threaten social equality, justice, and the destruction of nature.[1] The cause of this crisis lies in rampant individualism, secular materialism, amorality, and the laissez-faire prescriptions of Lockean liberalism. The real problem is seen as extensive, quantitative growth based upon specializaion and ever-increasing technical innovations, which poison the earth but from which there is no exit because to cease technical intensification would cause a collapse of our existing process. In this sense of specialization and overexpansion, we are following the typical history of biological extinction.

Ferkiss's answer to this problem is "ecological humanism," by which he means taking a holistic view of human kind in relation to nature, living within the boundaries of nature, and being conscious of environmental relationships. Ferkiss then sees the need to regulate human activity within the bounds of nature, and this regulation requires a powerful, centralized government, especially a strong President and cooperating Congress. Both President and Congress would be well informed, active, and consciously influencing the public good. In order for the government to operate, it would need a future-oriented information system capable of structuring the relationship of technological society to

[1]Victor Ferkiss, *The Future of Technological Civilization* (New York: George Braziller, 1974).

ecological systems. Behind this knowing and beneficent government would need to be an alert, educated, and participating public.

Critics of the Ferkiss analysis generally agree with his definition of the problem but differ as to the solution. Carroll Quigley doubts that we have the ability to reform our system by conscious choice, because holistic thinkers are too few, and reductionist methods in present decision structures would collapse the system in transition.[2] Carroll Quigley, Georgetown historian, agrees that the public seeks a new sense of community but believes it is more natural to find that community at the local level (even if it is a ghetto) than in a strong national community.

David King, historian at Oregon State University, also feels Ferkiss's optimism is not warranted, because strong central government as a solution in these times of mistrust is not a believable scenario.[3] Futurism in this century, says King, has suffered an unkind fate—namely, a lack of sufficient imagination to think our way out of the technological dilemma.

Ferkiss's response to these comments is that the future is really not in the hands of members of the elite, who may debate cultural options, feasibility, optimism or pessimism.[4] Social change occurs, he says, only when the force of events convinces the general population that old ways will not work, owing to a monumental crisis such as world inflation, food shortages, and the energy crunch which realigns the monetary and political base of the world.

My own view of the environmental crisis is much like that of Ferkiss and since I have addressed it in an earlier book I have not dealt with it here[5]), but my solution lies more in trying to internalize social and environmental costs into the price system, and thus seek an economic rather than a political solution.

The phenomenon Ferkiss describes as technological specialization and suboptimization is the same as what I have described as capital intensification. I have emphasized the capitalization side of technical invention because the organization of massive capital flows is what gives authority and power to institutions. Ferkiss has emphasized the technical reductionism side of the phenomenon to show how the feedback of wastes or deleterious products damage the ecological base on which we live.

The agreement is broad, then, on the nature of the problem in the

[2]Carroll Quigley, David B. King, Victor Ferkiss, "The Search for a Solution to the World Crisis," *The Futurist* 9, no. 1 (February 1975): 38–43.
[3]*Ibid.*
[4]*Ibid.*
[5]Stahrl Edmunds and John Letey, *Environmental Administration* (New York: McGraw-Hill, 1973).

comparative scenarios, but the scenarios part on the political solution. I share Quigley and King's skepticism of the believability in a scenario of a strong, beneficent central government—skepticism based upon the past fifty years of trial of strong central government in the United States which has ended in unmanageable inflation, the 1972 election debacle, and the general lack of confidence in federal governance. The historical unanimity with which strong, central governments become dictatorships, also, is not reassuring. Like Quigley, I find the reaction toward decentralization and local government a more plausible public choice.

Although the scenarios in this book do not treat environmental problems directly, two approaches to solution were implied in my Original Play in the last chapter. The first is that decentralizing capital flows to family-based enterprise will increase the service-oriented and labor-intensive character of economic activity, thus lessening the technical-capital-intensification process, which damages ecology. The second is that freer prices, with ecological costs internalized into the price structure, will shift environmental costs from the public to the private sector, and thus provide an incentive (or penalty) requiring the private decision maker to avoid ecological damage or pay for its abatement.

THE FUTURE OF THE U.S. GOVERNMENT

Since many of the issues of the Ferkiss-Quigley-King debate center on questions of political feasibility in reforming the federal government, we should examine a report of the American Academy of Arts and Sciences on the future of the United States government.[6] Harvey Perloff, dean at the University of California, Los Angeles, who edited the report, states the issues as centering upon (1) pressures on the individual to achieve individual freedom and development within the social order, (2) deterioration of cohesion in society, (3) deterioration of the environment and urban community, and (4) the domestic stress of world order. Among suggested solutions are more public participation in choices, building adaptability into government, and relating financial capability to decentralized (local) delivery of government services.

In the report, Kenneth Karst, law professor at UCLA, notes that centralization of national government power has proceeded apace but that the checks on government are now political rather than constitutional.[7] He sees a tendency toward social accounting, group rights,

---

[6]Harvey S. Perloff, ed., *The Future of the United States Government* (New York: George Braziller, 1971), pp. 3–10.
  [7]*Ibid.*, pp. 39 ff.

and judicial intervention as a means for checks and control. He also observes that market freedoms facilitate adaptation.

Harold Orlans of the Brookings Institution sees a fragmentation of social cohesion, as the nation is beset by excessive protest and dissent and an excess of hatred and murder.[8] The nation stands at a dangerous juncture, he feels, in need of great men to resolve conflict, but great men are rare, cannot be manufactured, and too frequently are assassinated. He sees a need to limit boundless expectations and especially to limit wealth and high incomes.

In the same vein, John Wofford of the Harvard Law School sees the two-party system challenged by alienation from the blacks, upper middle-class youth, lower middle-class workers, and the rigid right wing.[9] While he believes the two-party system can encompass these dissents, he sees anxiety, frustration, and declining national purpose occurring in the process.

John Voss of the American Academy of Arts and Sciences thinks that the political institutions are characterized by a pervasive and elusive sense of powerlessness.[10] The U.S. is an advanced nation with unprecedented economic and military power, unable to use that capability to solve divisive problems at home (poverty, racism) or deal with weak antagonists abroad. This powerlessness can only be remedied, he states, by changes in the political process and our mechanisms for making social choices.

James Barber, political scientist at Yale, sees an attempt to resolve policy issues through pluralism; that is, through the creation of new, interdependent organizational units such as task forces or commissions.[11] Pluralism increases frequency of conflict but decreases its intensity, increases the proposals initiated but reduces those adopted, increases the radical proposals initiated and increases conservatism of those adopted, increases the cost of government plus the number and complexity of formal rules, and increases the power of organized interest groups. The negative feedback from recent pluralistic trends, Barber hopes, will stimulate some corrective invention.

The dominant characteristic of the U.S. Constitution, according to Rexford Tugwell, of the Center for the Study of Democratic Institutions in Santa Barbara, Calif., was protection of individuals from potential encroachment by the government.[12] In early America, he states, equality had been a near-reality, and the present Constitution was designed

---

[8]*Ibid.*, p. 72 ff.
[9]*Ibid.*, p. 100.
[10]*Ibid.*, p. 146.
[11]*Ibid.*, pp. 242 ff.
[12]*Ibid.*, pp. 275 ff.

in this setting for a different kind of democracy. But inequalities now prevail, and the Constitution has congealed government. It needs revision. The constitutional revisions suggested by Tugwell are to restructure the units of government—first, by grouping states into regional republics, and, second, by improving the effectiveness of central government by adding three new branches, political, planning, and internal administration.

The report's analysis of the problems of the federal government are much the same as those presented in the scenarios of this book—namely, the centralization of authority, lack of checks and balances, deterioration in social cohesion and order, alienation, pressures for individuals to achieve freedom and development in a restrictive social order, need for greater equality, powerlessness, and need for constitutional change. The main difference is that the Academy report would seek to remedy these difficulties by restructuring existing organizational units of government, whereas my scenarios seek to disperse authority back to the people. That is, the Academy assumes that reorganizing big government can make it a beneficent, effective government. This is much the same thing that Ferkiss assumes and for essentially the same reasons.

All these writers believe that a socially oriented government is a necessary counterforce to rugged individualism, and that rampant, laissez-faire individualism must be regulated. To some extent, they are fighting old ghosts with Fabian socialism. Laissez-faire individualism died in 1929. Big business is a kept bureaucracy of the federal government—kept by government subsidy, price regulation, and tax devices. Executives move with ease from business to government and back, hardly noticing the difference in risk taking or decision making, except which pocket the money comes from. At last resort, businesses of all kinds look to the government to stay them from bankruptcy. Rugged individualism has disappeared. Big business is a creature and partner of big government. They are one and the same. Government is not a counterforce to business but its cohort. To look to government restructuring as a means of mediating business decisions is futile. The way to take "rugged" out of individualism is to equalize incomes, and the way to give individualism back to people is to return them authority over their own lives by dispersing power from the government-business combine.

Now the issue is clearly drawn: it is confidence in government versus confidence in people. The Academy authors and I see the problems of government, disorder, and alienation in the same way, but the report writers are nineteenth-century liberals who see remedy through the goodness of government. My scenarios represent something closer to middle-America populist, which seeks remedy through individual self-help rather than through either government or business. Nineteenth-century liberalism has had its chance for fifty years, ending up in a powerless, governless, big government that caused a futile war, riots of the 1960s, inflation, and corrupt elections in 1972. Populism worked once, so maybe it can be made to work again. However, Herman Kahn thinks not, so let us turn to him next.

HERMAN KAHN AND THINGS TO COME

Futurist Herman Kahn, director of the New York think tank The Hudson Institute, sees in *Things to Come* more of the same.[13] His long-term, multifold vision of western culture extrapolates present socioeconomic processes into more of everything: growth, centralization, technical knowledge, institutionalization of technology, military capability, industrialization, population, and an increasing tempo of all of the above. He sees this leading to increasing affluence, urbanization, and a topping-off of the second good era (*La Deuxieme Belle Epoque*). Among the things to come in this scenario are sustained economic development, worldwide green revolution, high GNP growth rates, continued growth in trade and communications, and increasing unity in technology-industry-financial institutions. The topping-off is observed in the relative decline of the two superpowers, the rise of Japan as a superstate, the full recovery of both Germanies, persistent trouble in divided regimes (Arab–Israel, India–Pakistan, and Sino–Soviet–U.S.A.–Japan), and some growth in violent, deviant, or criminal behavior.

Kahn's main interest lies in the balance of power in the multipolar world of major nations and alliances. His scenario sees several decades of uneasy peace because (except for Russia and China, who are vitally at odds) the five-variable equation—the United States, Western Europe, Japan, Russia, and China—has no life-or-death economic interests that clash.

What countervailing forces might disturb this scenario resulting in surprise changes? Kahn lists several: the youth counterculture, populism, back to religion, neo-racism, ideologically reactionary governments, and antisemitism. Kahn then advances reasons why none of these surprises are likely to materialize. With respect to the counterculture and populism, he feels that a leadership element is not present to coalesce either interest group.

Populism he defines as a lower-class or mass movement, particularly of people not led by left-wing liberals or upper-class conservatives. Populist movements have emerged suddenly and unexpectedly in both

[13]Herman Kahn and B. Bruce-Briggs, *Things to Come* (New York: Macmillan, 1972).

Europe and America. Today, middle Americans are alienated from liberal intellectuals, and they also feel that they are regressing in economic status relative to the right-wing corporate establishment.

Three possible scenarios exist for the rise of populism, Kahn says. First, a left-wing populism would see middle Americans turning to New Deal liberals to expand government power for the purpose of cutting corporate profits. Second, a right-wing populism would unite the productive middle Americans against the liberals, big spending, corruption, and the welfare poor. Third, a true populism would serve neither of the elite groups (the leftist intellectuals or the rightist corporate establishment) but would seek its own popular individualism and autonomy.

An American populist movement would need as its base the Midwestern farmers, industrial workers of the North, and the small conservative elements of the South. Kahn thinks this group cannot be amalgamated politically. My scenario of the last chapter presumes they can be amalgamated under conditions of persistent inflation-stagnation which convince the populace that the old ways will no longer work. Middle America will blame the leftist-liberals for extravagant government spending programs for fifty years, and blame the rightist corporate establishment for profiteering during inflation. The populist political numbers, which are large, can gain leadership from the youthful counterculture (The Movement), which shares with populists a common lack of interest in technological regimentation and a common interest in doing their own thing. Although this popular revival is plausible only under crisis or protracted frustration of middle America, I regard it as being more likely than a return to nineteenth-century liberalism (as Ferkiss and the Perloff report assume) and also more likely than a return to the cultured Edwardian gentleman, which Kahn assumes in his book *The Year 2000*.

ROBERT THEOBALD AND THE SCENARIO OF SELF-ACTUALIZATION

Socioeconomist Robert Theobald of Spokane has written a scenario for still another alternative future which emphasizes a form of psychological liberation.[14] He sees the economy reaching such techno-managerial efficiency that the abundance of production will make goods free. Even now one-fourth of the population (welfare and dependents) already are freed of work, and their sole role is that of consumer. The advances

[14]Robert Theobald, *An Alternative Future for America* (Chicago: Sevallan Press, 1968).

inherent in automation, servo-controls, and data process will release still more workers to become consumers only, and thus progressively goods will be free. The managerial and technological potentials are unlimited, and hence people can be given the life-style they seek by willing it. We will no longer, says Theobald, need to use the carrot and stick to move people. They will move and be motivated of their own accord and their own interests. In seeking their own interests and development, they will become self-actualizing persons whose lives are mainly devoted to learning rather than to work.

Theobald's scenario is not clear as to how these events occur. He borrows heavily from Abraham Maslow to show the fulfillment of individuality, learning, and self-actualization. His techno-economic scenario has the limitless optimism of the 1955–65 era before shortages, stagnation, and disillusionment with science. Although it is possible that our present era is merely an interlude in the chain of steady technical progress, my own study of environmental problems makes me doubt the realism of such uncontrolled growth, and hence my scenarios regard the environment and the material economy as constraints.

The interesting thing about Theobald's scenario is his view of what the constraint really is. He says the most severe constraint is individual learning and self-actualization, not the economy, not the environment, not technology, not political structures. The severe constraint is in ourselves, our own psyches. In this insight, he may be very profound.

Still, even if the real constraint is psychological, in ourselves, I fail to see how self-actualization can be released by a life of learning. Where is the learning to occur and how? Certainly the near-universal availability of college educations in the past decades has not produced a conspicuous number of self-actualizing people by adaptation in their life interest and life work. That is why they must have authority and resources dispersed back to them, so that they can pursue their life interests free of institutionally defined jobs.

JOHN McHALE AND THE FUTURE OF THE FUTURE

Writer John McHale expresses still another scenario which is that of a technically integrated planetary society.[15] The future of (inherent in) the past is the Industrial Revolution, with the technical capital-intensive organizations it has left to perpetuate themselves. The future of the present, he says, lies in the ecological interactions, the technical envi-

[15]John McHale, *The Future of the Future* (New York: George Braziller, 1969).

ronment, humans plus their sensory extensions, and the new symbiosis of humankind's data augmentation. The future of the future lies in outer-space exploration, inner-space exploration (the sea and earth interior), plus the balancing of the resources of the planet.

McHale's scenario is closest (along with Kahn's) to technological forecasting. The planetary society is seen as being global in scope, and national technological economies require access to material resources of the whole earth. But the use of these resources interferes with the natural cycle of the earth system, and this interference requires world regulatory agencies to absorb some functions from the political nationalisms still remaining. The global circulation of cultural styles, products, and services, McHale says, will create a diversity in life-style everywhere. Worldwide data nets, which transmit and translate symbols and data, will enable individuals to participate in control of complex processes and to interact with each other.

McHale's future is a science-fiction version of a balanced earth concept, which is striking in its imagination and interesting in its technical detail. What McHale treats as the most severe constraint is world resources for technological advancement. What he is silent about is how people interact with each other to make decisions and resolve conflicts. My scenarios are silent on the technological context of the future, mainly because McHale and others can do the technical scenario so much better than I.

However, technical scenarios are, to some extent, orchestrations on a social-organization theme. There was an Industrial Revolution before automobiles, and an electronics industry before computers. Without automobiles, cities would be like New York instead of Los Angeles, but New York before autos was still a massive industrial complex. Technology varies life-styles, but it does not dominate social development.

The ingredients of the Industrial Revolution were iron and steel smelting, coal mining, and textile production. These were all inventions of the fourteenth and fifteenth centuries. The Industrial Revolution came to England in the early nineteenth century and to Germany and the United States late in the same century. Why did it take 400 years for technical inventions to influence the future? The reason is that there were no social inventions (capital accumulation and intensification channels) to utilize the technology. The Industrial Revolution was largely a social revolution and social invention. The future of America will be formed by social inventions and orchestrated by technology. The social invention that is needed is some adaptive change mechanism to separate institutional responsibility from individual self-determination.

FRED POLAK AND THE IMAGES OF THE FUTURE

Fred Polak, professor of sociology at the Netherlands School of Economics, takes perhaps the most profound view of the future by asking what it is.[16] All the other scenario writers (including me) assume that the future represents a chronological difference in time from the present. Polak assumes that the future is a difference in perception, a perceived difference in the state or order of things.

The domain of the future is without boundaries, and it can only be defined in the thought-realm by space-time consciousness. Thus, the future world is an Other world separated by time, space, and state. Spatial images of the Other world include: Before this world; This world; Below this world; Above this world; Outside this world; After this world; Beyond all worlds. The Other world was clear to Hellas, Persia, Israel, Egypt, Christianity, Islam, the Middle Ages, because the Other world was a transcendental state occupied eternally by the gods, while this world was a sensory state occupied by now. These religious-metaphysical images of the future, the Other, were sharply different from now. They differed in bodily-spiritual state, in temporal-eternal time, in bounded-unbounded space, in sensory-symbolic perception. The future was truly a different order of things. As such, the Other world was a powerfully motivating vision, a mobilizer of hope and will.

The modern age of rationalism destroyed the Other world, by defining reality as that testable by the senses, and in the process destroyed the future. If all the world is sensory, the past and the future collapse into the present, because only what one can sense now is ascertainable. The past that persists now can be sensed, but that which is gone cannot. That which is now and will persist in the future can be sensed, but the future that is not now cannot be. Thus, the only perception of the past and the future is now. This world is all worlds, and sensately there is no Other. Since we cannot perceive a different state with our senses until it happens, there can be no future in rationalist thought.

The loss of the future by scientific thought has enslaved science to the present, and scientists must hurry their discoveries into the present so that mass-technicians can press them into use. Failing to fill the present continuously with discovery, scientists fall in status and repute. The exploitation of the subservient scientific intellectual of this age exceeds that of the proletarian worker in the nineteenth century, and this exploitation drives scientists out of the elite into the masses.

[16]Fred Polak, *The Image of the Future* (Amsterdam: Elsevier, 1973).

Some attempts to revive the Other World have been made by thinkers such as Jung and Neumann, who visualize man as a gnostic double-being, the conscious self and the unconscious, which in depth psychology is viewed as being mystically attached to a collective, universal unconscious. But this gnosticism in modern dress yields little perspective on the Other world as a symbolic, future, or different state.

The loss of the future as a powerfully symbolic state of an Other world makes contemporary scenario writing about the future disappointing, wanting, lacking in commanding vision. The future becomes more of the past and present. That is why, in scenario writing, it is hard to depart from old models or images. A caustic critic could say of all the scenarios reviewed in this chapter (plus my own) that they are old images of the future: the model of Ferkiss and of the Perloff report is nineteenth-century Fabian socialism, Kahn's is nineteenth-century Victorian, Theobald's nineteenth-century Freudian, mine nineteenth-century populism, and McHale's nineteenth-century positivism.

The answer to the caustic critic is logically obvious. If the past-present-future are sensately the same, and if the present is in an unsatisfactory state of alienation and disorder, then the future can be found only in the past. The future of the twenty-first century is being forseen through nineteenth-century images. As Polak says, the present has absorbed the past and the future, until they are one and same. This is the severest critique of all.

IS THERE A FUTURE?

I know no way of answering Polak's valid critique short of inventing a new religion or metaphysics. However, new religions are not invented by thinkers at typewriters; they are invented, if at all, by a community of individuals under dire stress through meditation and mystic perception of Other worlds in the inner self. Meditative individuals, suffering disorientation from a temporal world of unhappiness to which they cannot relate, see within themselves dimly a timeless Being, which seems the essence, not only of their own perpetual, motionless selves, but also the essence of all selves, all things, and all worlds. From contemplating this timeless essence they may momentarily see flashes of an Other world, which is an image of the future or their nontemporal state.

What are these images? Depending upon one's frame of reference, they may be hallucination, madness, superstition, subconscious dreams, mystical insights, religious inspiration, or glorious revelation of a great deity. Occasionally in history these images are transmitted by symbolism among a community of individuals, all under the direst stress, who commonly seek surcease in the meditative mode. Then a religious symbol may emerge, filled with powerful feeling of an Other world which is better than the present. This symbolic Other world then crystalizes into a commanding image of the Future, which is infinitely and eternally different in state from the capricious flux of the present.

Is there such an image of the Other world, an image of the future, emerging today? It is hard to know. The old images of a medieval or Protestant hereafter have lost their vitality. The secular religion of a rational, progressive present is found wanting in any future imagery at all. The psychological religion of the unconscious is an amorphous pictureless, primeval state. The one vital set of imagery which may be emerging is the revival of Eastern mysticism within the youthful subculture. The subculture's preoccupation with meditation, mysticism, Zen—sharpened by medieval witchcraft and hallucinatory drugs—is a search for vision and images of the future. If their distress is great enough, if their search is long and deep enough, the subculture may bring forth a new future.

What shall we say, then, about futures? Is there a future? Yes, there are two futures. One is a chronological future that puts the temporal state in sufficient order to make the world livable by the many. The other is a metaphysical future that creates imagery of an Other world or Other state of greater hope and emotional power than the secular world can generate. These two futures are connected, because both futures must have a popular base, if they are to happen at all.

Symbolic futures, religious futures, are popular in origin and popular in extent. Symbolic experience is one way, perhaps the most powerful way, that the populace learns. Images of the Future (Other world) are means of learning and adaptation; they are—for a time, at least, before homeostasis sets in—an adaptive means for change. These religious, symbolic teachings originate in populist men, like Buddha, Jesus, Mohammed, and Luther, who speak in the populace language of parable and vernacular travail. Their teachings are picked up by populist apostles, teachers, and leaders who bring the image to the people at large, mobilizing their interests, stirring their hope, and motivating their wills. When the wills of the populace have been stirred and motivated, a new age has begun, a new *modus operandi* set in motion, and a new Future in the making.

The symbolic Future comes into being when a vision of a new state is accepted (learned) by the populace, and the chronological future can hasten the symbolic Future by releasing the populace to its self-development. Self-development and self-actualization are induced by adaptation, suffering to find one's identity and purpose, meditation, and learning. This is what search and adaptation is all about. Individuals will learn most when they learn for themselves, not as dependents of the state, not as instructed employees of corporations, not as proselytes to university disciplines. They will learn most when they have to make their own work, meet their own environment, make their own decisions, make their own mistakes, suffer their own misfortunes, make their own corrections, learn to avoid their mistakes, reinforce their successes, and learn to deal with their own world. Having searched for their own world here and now, and having learned how to deal with its caprice, they might even discern a less capricious Other world.

Individuals cannot learn the real nature of this world, or an Other world, unless their decisions are in their own hands. To have decisions in their own hands, they must have the authority and resources to try, experiment, fail, succeed, reinforce, learn. Individuals do not have that authority or those resources in an institutional world in which institutional maintenance takes precedence over individual needs. That is why the populist scenario says that all the people must have their chance to try, experiment, fail, succeed, adapt, and learn as they can. If they choose to live under the protection of institutional dependency, then all right, they are not ready to learn. But when they are ready to learn and they do feel suffocated by institutional rules and contraints, individuals should have an easy exit. They should be able to opt out with the means to follow their own pursuits. The exit should be with lights, music, cheers, and a bundle of resources that says, Godspeed, friend, try and learn on your own.

Instead the exit today is slammed, closed, bolted, and nailed with institutional constraints: barriers to entry, oligopolistic competition of the few, closed technological resources, institutionally controlled capital flows, inflationary erosion of individual savings, administered prices, government tax subsidy to existing enterprise, tax disincentives for working individuals, skewed incomes, skewed savings, lagging wages, and no vote or voice on specific issues of governance.

The no-exit door is a form of servitude. The only exit is dissent, disorder, violence, and crime by breaking the door down. The no-exit door gives release only to the most violent among us, who can break it down, and not to the best among us. The best among the populace are confined by institutional constraint, prevented from exit into a world of their own, prevented from exploring, trying, experimenting, adapting, learning.

The chronological future lies in greeting the best among the populace with open doors to their self-development. This means letting down the institutional barriers by the decentralization and dispersal of authority to individuals over their own lives, as I tried to suggest in my own scenario. Through the open door of the chronological future, individuals may learn and adapt sufficiently to find also a popular image of the Other Future, which is not temporally bound but is of a different state. The chronological door is the opening to both futures, which are there.

Appendix

HISTORICAL PROBLEMS
IN AUTHORITY
AND CONSENT

Axioms tell us that history repeats itself; that the past presages the future; that the more things change, the more they remain the same; and that those who do not learn from history are condemned to repeat it. In more academic terms, Hegel speaks of the change process as the historical dialectic and Toynbee calls it the alternation between social drill and schism. Sociologist Robert Nisbet seeks to examine the validity of historical cycles and the developmental metaphor, which he types as one of the master ideas of the Western tradition.[1]

A discussion of the meaning of history or of a theory of history, or even

[1]Robert A. Nisbet, *Social Change and History* (New York: Oxford University Press, 1969), p. 26.

the recounting of significant periods of history is beyond the scope or competence of this book. My concern is with management—how it comes into being and how it is exercised—and it is my assertion that management begins with the distribution of authority to meet individual needs, which is a social process. Management, whether of business, educational, governmental, charitable, or medical institutions, derives from the purpose, mission, and authority allocated to the institution in the social process. In this view, all institutional managements are interrelated in that they are subsystems of one whole social process, which is to distribute the authorities to meet the sum of individual needs.

In turning to history, then, for some guidance on the problems of accession and succession of authority, our goal is the modest one of seeing how previous social structures have distributed authority, functions, allegiance, and tasks and with what consequences. In this appendix, three major historical epochs are examined, each of which ended in some form of dissent and disorder that led to a new social process. These historical cases are the Greek era leading to the imperial state, Roman imperialism leading to medieval society, and the medieval break-up leading to the industrial state. All of these eras are long and complex, and the total influences at work during their times can be adequately studied elsewhere. The usual concept of history is to recount the political and biographical activity of the times, but social histories, economic history, art history, legal history, comparative literature, and philosophy all provide specialized insights into these epochs.

The approach I have taken here is to abstract a chronology of events, which provides a setting, and to present a brief analysis of the authority structure, how it came into being, how accession and succession were managed, and what effects it had. The appendix covers the following:

1. Accession and Succession in Ancient Greece
   a. Chronology
   b. Authority structure
   c. Reforms
   d. From allegiance to disorder
   e. Disorder and the regrouping of authority
2. Authority Problems of the Roman Empire
   a. Chronology
   b. Authority structure and reforms
   c. From allegiance to disorder
   d. Disorder and the regrouping of authority
3. Authority Problems in Medieval Society
   a. Chronology and authority structure
   b. Allegiance, disorder, and the regrouping of authority
4. Summary

ACCESSION AND SUCCESSION IN ANCIENT GREECE

Exhibit A–1 summarizes a system analysis of ancient Greece—that is, the needs, authority distribution, functions, allegiance, and process of the society. The exhibit is followed by a chronology and a narrative of authority structure, reforms, allegiance, and disorder in ancient Greece.

EXHIBIT A-1. Scenario of Authority and System Functions
in Ancient Greece

NEEDS (FUNCTIONS)

1. Provide common defense against Persia and each other.
2. Maintain agricultural output with slave labor despite uprising by slaves.
3. Expand commerce and dominion in Mediterranean colonies as instrument of economic growth.
4. Reduce internal conflict among clans, aristocrats, plutocrats, tyrants, and artisans to workable compromise.

AUTHORITY

1. Initial authority delegated to family head and clan in economic, military, and political affairs.
2. Later, family/clan military and political authority subordinated to aristocrat-king in Sparta and to aristocrat-council in Athens.
3. Economic decision authority delegated to merchant/artisan sector, whose growing wealth later brought political representation in Assembly.

ALLEGIANCE

1. Initial allegiance ran (with authority) to family and clan, later transferred by aristocrats to king or Aeropagus Council.
2. Rising Mediterranean commerce created a working alliance among merchants and artisans, with allegiance to a trade system established in law.

---

3. Economic power of the commercial group brought representation and political allegiance to a democratic assembly.

SYSTEM (FUNCTION NETWORK)

1. Function of king and council was maintenance of internal and external peace, with a military-legal system of order.
2. Trade relations and commercial law (regarding contracts, debt, money, exchange, foreign trade) established a network of economic activity whose function was economic growth.
3. A network of representation based on population and residence established a system of voting choice and political order whose function was resolving conflicts on social issues.

PROCESS (FLOW OF INPUTS AND OUTPUTS)

1. Military inputs were drafts for soldiers on clans, later *demes,* with output of internal and external defense.
2. Input of artisan labor, risk capital, and merchant management resulted in output of international trade upon which national wealth was built.
3. An input of democratic votes, citizen participation in Assembly, and political management by Aeropagus Council produced output of bargaining and conflict resolution on social issues.

Chronology

MINOAN CIVILIZATION, 3000–1400 B.C. The Greek civilization was already more than a thousand years old by the time it arrived at its Golden Age, in the middle of the fifth century B.C., with its flowering of democracy, philosophy, and the arts. The origins of the Greek civilization go back as far as the Minoan culture in 3000 B.C. (see Table A–1), when migrants from Asia established first a pastoral society on Crete and then gradually expanded it by trade to colonize the islands of the

TABLE A-1. Historical Abstract of Civilization of Ancient Greece

Event	Date
Minoan civilization—Crete	3000 B.C.–1400 B.C.
Mycenaean civilization—Peloponnesus	1650 B.C.–1125 B.C.
Dark ages and migrations	1150 B.C.– 900 B.C.
Renaissance and colonization	9th & 8th centuries B.C.
Rise of Sparta, Athens, and the Peloponnesian League	750 B.C.– 466 B.C.
Solon reforms	594 B.C.
Cleisthenes reforms	508 B.C.
Periclean democracy and imperialism	445 B.C.– 431 B.C.
Peloponnesian wars	460 B.C.– 404 B.C.
Socrates	469 B.C.– 399 B.C.
Plato	427 B.C.– 347 B.C.
Aristotle	384 B.C.– 322 B.C.
Sparta and the King's Peace	404 B.C.– 338 B.C.
Macedonian supremacy	338 B.C.– 197 B.C.
Roman imperial rule	1st century B.C.–3rd century A.D.

Aegean Sea. Their Bronze Age skill in metals, textiles, and manufactured goods created an export trade with Greece, Egypt, Syria, and Asia Minor. The intrusion of the Greeks brought an end to Cretian society with the sacking of Cnossus and other major cities.

MYCENAEAN CIVILIZATION, 1650–1125 B.C. The Peloponnesian peninsula, which is connected to southern Greece by the isthmus of Corinth, received an infusion of migrants from the north, from Macedonia and beyond, who were among the first of the Greek-speaking settlers. Though originally cruder in skills than their predecessors, the newcomer Greeks invigorated arts and culture of the Peloponnesus, and in the vicinity of Mycenae, just south of the isthmus of Corinth, a prosperous agricultural community was established and embellished with beautiful cities. The Mycenaean skill in pottery, precious metals, and formal design was exported to Asia Minor. Mycenaean script, adapted from the linear script of Crete, was designed to express the Greek language by syllabic symbols. Trade relations extended to Syria, Palestine, and Egypt and were particularly close with Troy, Thessaly, and Macedonia.

DARK AGES AND MIGRATION, 1150–900 B.C. The eruptions of war and violence after 1300 B.C. led to the fortification of cities, decline in trade, and piracy. The Trojan War brought disaster to all, new waves of barbaric migration, and two centuries of dark ages.

RENAISSANCE AND COLONIZATION, NINTH AND EIGHTH CENTURIES
B.C. The Greek renaissance of the ninth century rediscovered the heroic
era of Mycenaean civilization in the epic poetry of Homer's *The Illiad*
and *The Odyssey* and the religious epics of Hesiod. On the mainland in
Attica and Athens, the political structure of the Mycenaean culture was
preserved, in which citizens belonging to Ionian tribes were loosely
federated in allegiance to a king or later to magistrates.

RISE OF SPARTA AND ATHENS, 750– 466 B.C. The Dorians in Laconia
and Sparta developed a more centralized political system, out of necessity to control the serfs who worked their estates. A system of state
military education took boys from the land-owning tribal families, disciplined them in the arts of war and statehood, and through this discipline granted franchise and citizenship. Throughout its five centuries of
power, Sparta remained an agricultural, land-based military regime
headed by an oligopoly of rich families loyal to a commander-king.

The trade and craft skills of Athens, along with its looser political
structure, led to its development as a commercial and naval power
dominating the Aegean Sea and trading throughout the Mediterranean.
The pioneering Greek colonizers were Ionians of Asia Minor, who
opened the western Mediterranean by planting a colony in the bay of
Naples. Subsequent Greek colonization established such great centers
as Syracuse, Byzantium, and Sicily, until hundreds of colonies spread
from Spain to the Black Sea. Only the rival sea power of Phoenicia and
Egypt limited the realm of this trading empire from dominating the
entire shore of the Mediterranean.

PELOPONNESIAN LEAGUE, 546–466 B.C. During this period, Persia
threatened to conquer Greece and its wealthy trade routes, which led
the city-states of Greece to form the Peloponnesian League. Headed by
Sparta as the strongest land-based military force, the league included
all the major cities of Peloponnesia; later Athens joined. Member states
contracted a defensive coalition, in which all contributed troops under
the command of Sparta, and each city had one vote as to whether or not
to go to war. In exchange, the contracting member state received protection from the league against any aggressor.

The aggression of Persia brought the full military power of the league
into defense of the Greek mainland against the Persian invasion. At
Thermopylae and Plataea, the Greeks fought the Persians to a
standstill, but these defensive victories did not deter Persia, with its
vast resources, from mounting a new attack. Athens wanted to initiate a
counteroffensive against Persia along the coast of Asia Minor, but

Sparta would not agree to fight a foreign campaign. Then, in 477 B.C., Athens formed a naval coalition, the Confederacy of Delos, made up of the Ionian city states in Asia Minor and the islands of the Aegean, in which each state subscribed funds to build a fleet. Athens was to command the fleet and share half of all booty. The coalition won a series of engagements, and then, in 466 B.C., destroyed the Persian fleet and army in Pamphylia.

PERICLEAN DEMOCRACY AND IMPERIALISM, 445–404 B.C. Athens now became the dominant Greek city-state, wealthy from its trade, booty, and custody of the Delos defense fund. This began the era that we now think of as the Golden Age of Greece. Athens used its new wealth, including the naval defense fund of other states, to pay for Athenian government and for the artistic glorification of the city. At this time, Athens was also a democracy, and native citizens shared in the glory and prosperity of the period. The Periclean democracy not only brought a new era of equality, employment, and culture to the city, it also brought new imperial conquests of other city-states. Pericles even attacked and subdued Samos, a member of the Delos Confederacy.

These attacks caused consternation among other Greek states, as it became more clear that the rights of citizenship and the protection of laws applied only to native Athenians and that all others were subject to the will of Athens or to imperial conquest. The Athenians' blindness in failing to extend citizenry and the protection of its laws to others, after forming a successful coalition, led to the Peloponnesian wars and the downfall of Athens. Other Greek states turned to Sparta and the Peloponnesian League for protection, and by 404 B.C. Athens was exhausted, financially and physically, and was defeated.

SPARTA AND THE KING'S PEACE, 404–338 B.C. Sparta kept the King's Peace for another sixty years, but as a provincial agricultural state, it could not keep up the trade and commerce upon which the Greek empire and civilization was built. Athens made a comeback try for empire but failed, and in the end, the whole of Greece was swallowed up, first by the Macedonians and then by the Roman conquest.

Authority Structure

With this historical background, we can now examine some of the authority patterns that accompanied these events (see Table A–2).

TABLE A-2. Authority Patterns of Ancient Greece

Event	Date
Kinship and kingship	3000 B.C.–600 B.C.
Decentralization and individualization	600 B.C.–400 B.C.
Time of troubles and recentralization	400 B.C.–338 B.C.
Authoritarian state	338 B.C. onward

KINSHIP AND KINGSHIP, 3000–600 B.C. The early Greek civilization was founded upon family, tribal, and kinship rule, in which authority was distributed to family members by heredity, seniority, and ability. Hereditary estates were the primary instruments for transferring succession, and seniority reflected experience and expertise. Oligarchies of family kinship, linked by allegiances to a king, formed the established social process. Young noblemen of ability from large families on the fringes of the oligarchy had little hope of acquiring authority except by conspiracy and force. In this they could look for support and allegiance to other disenfranchised men of rank and to the populace.

The results were constant tribal feuds for revenge or over succession to authority and power. The feuding of family and kin was so bad in Sparta that it threatened the social process, by dividing allegiances among the masters so seriously that they could be overthrown by their serfs. It was this threat to the Spartan society which forced the system of state military education, in which the young men of landed families were taken away from their homes and feuds and placed into disciplined men's clubs (*andreion*) to serve the stability of the state. The Spartan state then put down rebellious serfs and intervened in disorders caused by feuds. That is, Sparta solved its disorder problem by centralizing authority in a military regime drawn from the oligarchy. Certainly this has proved to be one of the great and lasting political inventions, for it appears and reappears throughout Western history.

Athens solved its problem of authority distribution in a different way. Athenian trade created a wealthy class of aristocrats who derived their riches from commerce. The claims to authority and power by these wealthy traders disturbed the allegiances of family and clan, and claims of wealth upset claims of birth. The Greek trading states, including Athens, were subjected to tyrannies, during which wealthy aristocrats of trade would seize power to advance their own interests. These tyrants were not revolutionaries, in the sense of seeking to equalize power. They were self-seeking plutocrats who wanted to transfer authority from the landed families to themselves.

SOLON REFORMS, 594 B.C. The disorder and strife caused Athens to put its governance into the hands of an arbitrator, Solon, who divided the citizenry into four classes according to income and ruled that office-holders should be drawn from these four classes. He thus broke the aristocracy of birth and placed governing authority into a narrowly representative council of magistrates, called the Areopagus. Solon's reform of 594 B.C. created a representative plutocracy, which was to become the beginnings of Athenian democracy; this is the second great pattern of social organization that has been passed down throughout Western history in various forms.

DECENTRALIZATION AND INDIVIDUALIZATION, 600–400 B.C. The social organization of Sparta and Athens changed the distribution of authority among their members, as well as among their leaders. The early authority pattern, tribal law, rested heavily on self-help or kinsman-help. That is, aggrieved parties could seek their own redress under sanction of custom, which legitimatized revenge. In the case of homicide, adultery, or rape, the kinsmen of the injured party would exact retribution measure for measure. Fear of vengeance frequently drove the offender into exile. To settle the feud, arbitration was resorted to, in which some compensation (so-called "blood money") might be exacted for the wrong.

By the seventh century B.C., the Greek cities began to write down and codify their laws. This codification, along with the breaking of tribal power in both Sparta and Athens, caused public and private law to come into being, in which the rights and authorities of individual parties were defined in specific cases. Injured parties might seek redress, according to the law, before a magistrate, the Areopagus, or the Assembly of all citizens.

The adoption of coinage and currency by Greece from Lydia in the eighth century B.C., plus the rise of colonization and trade, brought into the legal code whole new classes of cases, particularly the law of debtors under contracts, and international law. Thus, individual businessmen were delegated authority and a set of rights on the collection of debts and the transfer of titles to goods or property. Public law cases were heard by representatives of the Areopagus Council or the Assembly, private-law cases by arbitors, who were citizens sixty years old or older serving by lot. Private litigants were not required to comply with findings of these arbitors, whose competence was very uneven. Hence, the authority system facilitated, but did not compel, settlement of private grievances.

The system of allegiances and delegations, then, ran from the individual to the family to tribal or functional representation to the Assembly, the Council, the magistrates, and the arbitors. The social process left functional decisions over trade and private rights largely in the hands of individuals, with minimal compulsion in private suits. The public interest was more carefully guarded by assembly legislation and magistrate jurors. The public interest was closely related to protection and security, to military regulation and finance, to interstate affairs, and to the police power. Public-law cases were frequently on police, treason, or military matters.

Reforms

Solon Reforms, 594 b.c. The reforms of the Athenian authority structure were largely aimed at equalizing authority and rights. The Solon reforms of 594 b.c., besides breaking the power of landed aristocracy and classifying representation on the Areopagus Council, also benefited the poor. Solon liberated debtors from bondage and slavery, forbade indenture for bankruptcy, revised debt laws, and provided citizen and debtor appeal to the courts. At the same time, he proclaimed freedom for all citizens, equality before the law, and a voice of all citizens in elections, although he left final authority in the hands of the wealthy, who were members of the Areopagus Council.

Despite the decentralization of authority by the Solon reforms, party strife persisted in Athens among the elite, resulting in a series of tyrannies. However, stability in the underlying social processes continued to bring prosperity, particularly in the export trade, which flourished with the supremacy of Athenian pottery and crafts over those of other Greek cities. The family, tribal, economic, and legal linkages established community despite turbulence at the top of power groups.

Cleisthenes Reforms, 508 b.c. The townspeople, craft, and guildsmen gained in political experience under the Solon reforms, as well as in wealth by trade. The rivalry among the aristocrats for power at the top became an intolerable, unstable influence to the interest of the whole community. This instability led to the Cleisthenes reforms in 508 b.c. Like Solon, Cleisthenes was an arbitrator called upon to settle differences, and he was authorized to draw up a constitution. He then proceeded to distribute more governing authority to the guildsmen, tradesmen, and townspeople at the expense of members of the clans, who had abused their power by aristocratic rivalry.

The basic reform was to create an electoral system based on location of residence, instead of upon clan. The area of residency was called a *deme,* from which we derive the word democracy. The *demes* elected representatives to a new council, which prepared agenda for the Assembly and carried out routine administration. The *demes* also raised military contingents and elected their own generals. However, Cleisthenes retained the Areopagus Council as guardian of the constitution, by giving it veto power over the Assembly and the trying of all treason cases. The Cleisthenes reforms were a series of checks and balances, which decentralized authority to diverse social groups and compartmentalized power so neither the tribes, the Assembly, nor the Areopagus Council could dominate.

The Cleisthenes solution to the authority problem, plus the great wealth that came into Athens with the defense fund of the Delos Confederacy, laid the foundation for the Periclean democracy and the final glory of Greek civilization. Pride, loyalty, and allegiance to the city-state of Athens was at its height among the citizenry, as all men participated in its economic, political, and social processes. The arts flourished. Architecture, sculpture, drama, oratory, and literature reached a pinnacle. Athenian trade dominated the Aegean Sea and Mediterranean.

Then, in a matter of three decades, Athens committed a kind of social suicide by its venture into imperialism and the Peloponnesian wars. The Athenians used the Delos fund and their own wealth to dominate neighboring city-states, creating fear and distrust. Citizenship, representation, access to the law, and the decentralization of authority were never extended to anyone other than Athenians. While Athens took pride in democracy at home, its policy abroad was authoritarian. This authoritarian inequality, plus the aggressions of Athens, led other members of the Peloponnesian League to invoke Sparta's aid to help defeat Athens, which was achieved in 404 B.C.

From Allegiance to Disorder

The catastrophic defeat of Athens, after such a glorious period of achievement, brought into being an age of pessimism and what the British historian Sir Gilbert Murray called a "failure of nerve." The discontinuity of moving from wealth and democratic freedoms to bankruptcy and social disarray left Athens adrift and in doubt. Filling the vacuum, the aristocratic families seized the government and returned to power an oligarchy that was ruthless with its enemies—among them the gadfly, critic, and individualist Socrates.

SOCRATES AND THE DECLINE OF INDIVIDUALISM, 469–399 B.C. Socrates was charged with impiety to the gods and with corrupting the youth. Given the privilege of proposing an alternate sentence to that of death, he refused to ask for mitigation. During his trial, he said:

> Men of Athens, I honor and love you; but I shall obey God rather than you, and while I have life and strength I shall never cease from the practice of teaching my philosophy, exhorting anyone whom I meet, after my manner, and convincing him, saying: O my friend, why do you, who are a citizen of the great and mighty and wise city of Athens, care so much about laying up the greatest amount of money and honor and reputation, and so little about wisdom and truth? Wherefore, O men of Athens, I say to you, do as Anytus bids, and either acquit me or not; but whatever you do, know that I shall never alter my ways, not even if I have to die many times.[2]

Socrates' martydom was the defiance of individual freedom of thought against oligarchic centralization of power. The regrouping of authority into the hands of a few put Socrates' life at issue, and he preferred to die rather than be denied his individuality. This schism between political authority and personal rights caused Plato to observe: "A man who really fights for what is right must lead a private, not a public, life, if he hopes to survive, even for a short time."[3]

TIME OF TROUBLES AND RECENTRALIZATION, 400–338 B.C. The schism between public and private authority, dramatized by Socrates' martyrdom, persisted for a century. The time of trouble was upon Greece, with individualism weakening as the power of the state increased in the form of oligarchy in city-states, of the authority pattern of Sparta as peacekeeper, and finally of Macedonian imperialism.

The social structure of Macedonia was feudal, unlike that of other Greek city-states. The king was elected by the people and could be deposed by vote. Once elected, however, he held title to all land and property and conducted state affairs solely at his discretion. He chose his own nobles as companions, advisors, and comrades at arms. All citizens were freemen who owed the king personal service, allegiance, and taxes.

[2]Plato, *Apology*, p. 38.
[3]*Ibid.*, p. 32.

There were no serfs or slaves. As free men, Madedonians delegated all authority to the king voluntarily. Their access to the king or his heirarchy was easy, because the people had theoretically the right to try the king for treason or to depose him. The king, therefore, represented the public interest as long as consent persisted.

The Macedonian form of citizenship was highly disciplined in a centralized state; but it held one advantage over the citizenship of Athens—namely, Philip of Macedonia extended citizenship to the Greek states he absorbed. Some Greek states were persuaded by bribery to join, others by the appeal Philip's orderly governance had to unstable oligarchies, and the rest were acquired by conquest.

PLATO, 427–347 B.C. Plato was a student of Socrates, Aristotle a student of Plato, and Alexander the Great a student of Aristotle. From this family of thought came most of the concepts that prevailed for the next 2,000 years. Plato's solution to the problem of the social disorder observable in his time was not democracy, as implied by the title *The Republic* in his *Dialogues,* but a benevolent form of authoritarian state governed by guardians of the state, similar to the aristocratic Areopagus Council, and headed by a philosopher-king, trained perhaps as Alexander was. Plato turned from the individualism of Socrates to an ideal of governance by men, without property or wives, devoted to plain living and high philosophy, not unlike what later became the *City of God*, the monastic life, and clerical rule. Plato was a rich conservative, who scorned the untidyness of democracy, and who proposed instead a communistic aristocracy, which was a forerunner to such diverse, but commonly authoritarian, social structures as the French Revolution, Marxism, and facism.

ARISTOTLE, 384–322 B.C. Plato's metaphysics rests on a theory of Ideas, an Absolute of eternal laws, forms, and prototypes. This hierarchy of the *Logos,* or divine mind of God, became the cornerstone of medieval scholasticism. Combined with the taxonomies in the natural science of Aristotle, the idealism of Plato and Aristotle became the Great Chain of Being, which influenced natural science and scientific thinking for 2,000 years.

Alexander himself contributed no philosophy or writing, but he accomplished something perhaps even more lasting in tangible social organization—namely, he defined the boundaries of empire and created a prototype for the Roman Imperial State.

The disorder of the fourth century B.C. increased as poverty deepened in the midst of growing wealth. Sparta's destruction of Athens had ruined the olive groves and farms of small landowners. Agriculture moved into the hands of few families working large estates with serfs. Silver was mined in abundance by wealthy families with slaves. Industry and trade, as they were restored, relied more on credit and exchange to buy or sell services and commodities. The small craftsmen had less access to credit, and commercial wealth began to concentrate in fewer hands.

DEMORALIZATION, FOURTH CENTURY B.C. As the poor increased in number, they tried to use their democratic rights in the Assembly to redress the inequality. The poor gained a majority in the Assembly in Athens and voted the property of the rich into the city treasury. Elsewhere less legal methods were used. In Mytilene, debtors massacred their creditors, and the democrats of Argos killed 1,200 of the rich and confiscated their property.

Moral disorder accompanied the troubled times. Educated classes disavowed the state religion, denied parental authority, and discouraged males from marriage and females from motherhood. Free unions, sexual liberty, avoidance of political and economic responsibility became commonplace. Military service was avoided, and people bought their way out of liturgy or service to the public. Athletics became professionalized, war became mercenary, politics became intrigue, and routes to succession became conspiratorial.

Conservative intellectuals like Plato, Aristophanes, Xenophon, and Isocrates deplored this degeneration of order and toyed with the idea of restoring order through an aristocratic communism.

MACEDONIAN SUPREMACY, 338–197 B.C. The weakening of Athens brought the rise of Syracuse into power in the west. Caught between Syracuse and Macedonia, the central Greek city-states quarreled among themselves, fought wars with each other, were torn by internal dissensions, and practiced intrigue with their powerful neighbors.

Philip of Macedonia, who had lived as a hostage among the Greeks, knew their diplomacy, disorders, and methods of war, and he exploited the greed of the rich oligarchies by bribery and exploited the disorder by offering stability and cooperation. He identified himself as Greek; claimed descent from Heracles, the son of Zeus; put Heracles and Zeus on his coinage; and promised independence to Greek cities that came voluntarily under his protection. The rest of the city-states he conquered. The Greek oligarchs were no match for Philip's intrigue or military strategy, and besides they yearned for a return of order.

In 338 B.C., Philip defeated the Boeotian League and Athens. Isocrates, who had seen almost constant war, imperialism, and disorder in his ninety-eight years, petitioned Philip to form an association of Greek states based upon cooperation, rather than to force hegemony by imperial rule. Philip, who had previously shown generosity in victory toward Thessaly, chose a course of coalition and negotiation, which formed all of Greece into the League of Corinth, bound in offensive and defensive alliance for all time "with Philip and his descendants." When Philip was assassinated two years later, the young Alexander went on as head of the league to conquer Persia and all of the eastern Mediterranean.

AUTHORITARIAN STATE, 338 B.C. ONWARD. The circle was now complete. Greece had restored order, limited individual liberty, returned unlimited authority to a king surrounded by feudal allegiances of nobles, and created an imperial state. Alexander had the same power as Minos had had in Crete several millennia earlier, only over a vaster territory. The Greek states even granted Alexander, at his own request, "godlike honors"—and the pattern was set for the next era of imperial rule by divine authority.

AUTHORITY PROBLEMS OF THE ROMAN EMPIRE

The main features of the Roman society are shown in Exhibit A–2, which provides a brief system analysis of the needs, authority distribution, allegiances, functions, and process of the society. The exhibit is elaborated on in the discussion that follows, which gives a chronology of the Roman Empire, its authority structure, reforms, and the movement from allegiance to disorder.

Chronology

The Roman epoch differs from that of Greece in its authority and managerial patterns in two important respects—first, in the central focus on patrician authority, and, second, in the scale of organizational structure, which could be managed only by formalizing policy into law. A historical abstract of these authority changes is shown in Table A–3.

NEEDS (FUNCTIONS)

1. Provide for military supremacy over Etruscan kings, later over all Italy and the Mediterranean.
2. Sustain food output by independent farmer-soldiers during period of conquest, later by slave estates.
3. Expand economic wealth of Rome by military spoils and tribute.
4. Manage conflict among aristocrats of Senate, slaves, agrarian rebels, and plebes.

AUTHORITY

1. *Patria potestas* delegated all authority over persons and property to family head, later to be usurped by *tribunicia potestas* giving Caesar all power and reducing family to dependence on state.
2. Aristocratic family heads delegated military and order keeping to Senate and consuls.
3. Farmers and plebes wrested functions of king's mercy from Senate and vested them in tribunes.
4. Codified law enabled tribune to protect citizen rights in court.
5. Power of tribunes aided farmers and plebes to achieve representative political vote in Assembly.

ALLEGIANCE

1. Individual allegiance ran to family head.
2. Allegiance of family head given to Senate and consuls.
3. Allegiance of farmers and plebes placed in tribunes and Assembly.

SYSTEM (FUNCTION NETWORK)

1. Functions of Senate and consuls were to raise legions, conquer Mediterranean world, and suppress internal disorder.
2. Functions of Caesar were to intercede on side of Senate aristocrats to suppress internal rebellion, manage the colonial empire by municipal law, and extort tribute from colonies for enrichment of Rome.

PROCESS (FLOW OF INPUTS AND OUTPUTS)

1. The military inputs were drafts on clans and property-owning farmers for legions with output of conquering Mediterranean.
2. The input of military consuls and aristocratic procurators established control over colonies by administering municipal and military law to exact tribute.
3. An input of Assembly representative voting and Tribune intercession resolved political conflicts until 118 B.C., when military intercession and *tribunicia potestas* restored absolute monarchy as final arbiter of conflict.

TABLE A-3. Historical Abstract of Roman Civilization

Event	Date
Villanova tribal life	2000 B.C.–800 B.C.
Etruscan kings	800 B.C.–509 B.C.
Roman republic	509 B.C.–265 B.C.
Roman conquest of Mediterranean	265 B.C.–146 B.C.
The Agrarian Revolt	143 B.C.– 30 B.C.
Return to monarchy—the Principate	30 B.C.–A.D. 192
Roman Imperial State	A.D. 192–A.D. 305
Diocletian edicts	A.D. 294–A.D. 305
Division of the empire	A.D. 305–A.D. 476

VILLANOVA TRIBAL LIFE, 2000–800 B.C. The focus on head-of-family (patrician) authority was derived from the custom of the Villanova tribes, which migrated from the north to settle the area of the Roman hills. A distinctive characteristic of the Roman family was the absolute, private law-making authority, known as *patria potestas*, which the father had over wife, children, remote descendants of the male line, slaves, and adopted members of the household. He assigned use of property, gave members in marraige, meted out punishment (including capital punishment) for crimes committed within the family, and led the vendetta of revenge against those who wronged the family. The mother's merciful ministrations were co-extensive with the father's punitive ones, and this strength of family was one of the foundations of Roman society.

All property-owning males of a tribe constituted a town meeting and the army. The property owners annually elected two consuls or praetors, who administered tribal rules on the advice of elected elders (senators). Most villages were independently governed, and land was privately held except for common pasture.

ETRUSCAN KINGS, 800–509 B.C. The Etruscan kings imposed classes or orders on the decentralized Roman society in order to conscript a military force. Property owners made up the first class, and all were liable for military service. The other four classes had lesser military responsibilities. Under the Etruscan kings, trade with other Mediterranean centers was established, and finely wrought Etruscan art appeared in Greece and Asia monor.

ROMAN REPUBLIC, 509–265 B.C. The expulsion of the Etruscan kings returned Roman society to its more provincial and pastoral interests, and also returned authority to patricians and consuls in a republican form of government. However, some families had become large landowners or wealthy traders under the Etruscan kings, with the result that the republic was more nearly an aristocratic oligarchy ruled by rich patricians in the Senate.

The common classes, or plebes, were numerous and important to the society as soldiers and farm laborers (this being prior to extensive slavery), and the plebes clamored for more equal distribution of authority. The plebes seceded to Mons Sacer when called for military service against Etruscans, and by their demonstration and dissent they won the right to elect advocates of the people (tribunes), to prevent arbitrary arrest under the harsh debtor laws, and to enter pleas for them in court.

As a social institution, the tribunate had no legal precedent elsewhere, and it was a distinctive Roman invention. The tribune had to perform his duty of intervention in person and within the city, and in performance of his duty, he was sacrosanct and exercised what had previously been regal powers of clemency. Because tribunes were effective protectors of the oppressed, they became powerful officials who gradually intervened in all the functions of state.

CODIFIED LAW, 450 B.C. The tribunes were hampered by courts rendering judgments according to unwritten custom, and the judgments, as to the rights of individuals, might vary according to interpretation and recollection. The result was a demand for and eventual passage of (450 B.C.) codified law, in the form of the Twelve Tables, which enscribed customary practice into written law.

The needs of the plebian class for some voice in changing laws was also recognized in the next year by granting that plebiscites, passed by the plebian Assembly, would become law upon acceptance by the patrician Senate. Thus appeared bicameral legislatures, which Western democracies have used extensively ever since. The constitutional change also made the authority of tribunes inviolate and gave every citizen the right to appeal a death sentence to the Assembly. These constitutional distributions of authority to the common people and their representatives gave Rome a functional republic under which the allegiance of the plebes was assured and strengthened sufficiently for Rome to draw large legions from small-farmer and plebian classes. With these legions, Rome proceeded to conquer an empire.

CONQUEST OF MEDITERRANEAN, 265–146 B.C. Rome first consolidated its power on the Italian peninsula by the Latin and three Samnite wars between 423 B.C. and 265 B.C. The three Punic wars with Carthage, from 265 B.C. to 146 B.C., put all of the western Mediterranean under Roman rule. The three Macedonian wars, from 200 B.C. to 168 B.C., placed all of the East under Roman protectorate.

These 300 years of war, from the time of the constitutional reform of 449 B.C. to the end of the eastern wars in 168 B.C., also brought profound internal changes within the Roman society at home. Generations of warfare had severed small farmers from their land, either through protracted military service or through indebtedness. The distressed land was bought up by the rich and worked in large, slave-operated estates called *latifundia*. The slaves were captured freemen from conquered territories, and they lived lives without hope, toiling from dawn to sunset with only enough food and clothing to stay alive. Absentee owners left estates in the hands of overseers, who quelled reluctance or disobedience with whiplash, worked slaves in chains, and often locked them in dungeons at night. The patrician owners preferred slave workers to Roman freemen, because slaves were not subject to military service, and slave labor cost less. Yet slavery was very inefficient in that the land supported only about one-twentieth of the population it had under freeman farming.

AGRARIAN REVOLT, 143–30 B.C. Dispossessed small farmers migrated to the city, augmenting the unemployed among the plebian order. Craft and trade workers also suffered unemployment because, with the rise of empire, trade and commerce were neglected. Government did little to encourage development of industry, trade, or its own resources. Businessmen became less concerned with commerce and more with the business of empire, such as lending money at higher interest rates in the colonies or acting as *procurators* for military or civil functions abroad. Businessmen also preferred to use slaves to Roman freemen, thus aggravating the unemployment.

The Agrarian Revolt (143–30 B.C.) was a reaction by the dispossessed and the unemployed to their loss of authority and rights during the growth of empire. The brothers Tiberius and Caius Gracchus were elected tribunes to carry out land reform and redistribution. Tiberius proceeded aggressively to enact such legislation, which the Senate denounced as confiscatory, and was assassinated. Caius, acting more cautiously, won over the soldiers by providing them with free clothing, businessmen by giving them trade concessions in the colonies, and the masses by providing corn at half price, and he made voting more democratic in the Assembly. The influence of Caius was short-lived, however, and the Senate found the means to oust him from office. The only permanent impact on Roman society was that his corn laws became a permanent dole for the poor.

RETURN TO MONARCHY, 30 B.C.–A.D. 192. Slave revolts, colonial uprisings, plebian discontent, a social war over Italian enfranchisement, and clashes between the Senate and the commerical classes, led to a breakdown in the effectivensss of civil authority. Repeatedly, military leaders had to intervene to support the Senate, first Marius, then Sulla, Pompey, and Caesar, until it became clear that military authority was essential to rule. The dictatorship of Julius Caesar and the coming of Caesar Augustus marked the end of democracy and the rise of monarchy.

The monarchy, or principate, deferred to ceremonial prerogatives of the Senate for a time, but between A.D. 70 and A.D. 180 the emperors were deified and became absolute rulers with succession by heredity.

Diocletian, as emperor from A.D. 284 to A.D. 305, eliminated all constitutional limitations and vestiges of the republic and made the monarchy divine and absolute, in the Oriental fashion.

Authority Structure and Reforms

The authority patterns in Rome evolved through four distinct phases: patriarchy, representation, law-making, and monarchy (Table A–4).

PATRIARCHAL AND ELECTED TRIBAL AUTHORITY, 2000–800 B.C. The patriarchal authority, *patria potestas,* rested on the placement of all property rights and all rule making for the family in the father. He, in turn, as a property holder delegated to a Senate of elders and a common town meeting all rule making for the tribe or village. In earliest Roman society, the common assembly could not initiate proposals, only the elders in the Senate could. The consuls, elected annually, took administrative action only upon advice of the elders. The elders, then, held much the same authority over the tribe as the father did to the family. The tribal organization also held sacred land used in the worship of their dieties—Jupiter, Mars, Juno, Minerva, and so on.

REPUBLICAN REPRESENTATION, 509–265 B.C. The Republic formalized these same tribal authorities into a city state in 509 B.C., and the patrician aristocrats dominated the society through the Senate. The secession of the plebes in 471 B.C. won them the right to a tribune to represent them, particularly upon arrest. The assembly was also authorized to

TABLE A-4. The Authority Patterns of Rome

Event	Date
Patriarchal and elected tribal authority	2000 B.C.–800 B.C.
Kingship—Etruscan	800 B.C.–509 B.C.
Republican representation	509 B.C.–265 B.C.
Senatorial oligarchy	509 B.C.
Plebian assembly and tribunes	471 B.C.
The Twelve Tables of law	450 B.C.
Rise of municipal law	396 B.C.
Lician constitutional reforms	367 B.C.
Gracchan reforms	133 B.C.–121 B.C.
Military support of Senate oligarchy	118 B.C.– 30 B.C.
Monarchy	30 B.C.– A.D. 476

instruct tribunes by resolution, and tribunes might also place proposals before the assembly. The Twelve Tables of written law code, which codified the law of persons and civil law, assured reasonable uniformity of court judgments in cases brought by the tribune on behalf of plebes.

LICIAN REFORMS, 367 B.C. The rise of wealthy plebians who aspired to high office led in 367 B.C. to the Lician constitutional reforms, which limited land holdings and interest payments and which required that one elected consul must be plebian. With a plebian consul presiding at elections, the obstacles to plebian officeholding were removed. As plebian authority increased, the assembly was also authorized to initiate legislation with the force of law, without senatorial approval, although subject to Senate veto. The legislative independence of the plebian assembly secured representational democracy for the lower classes in Rome, as a city-state.

The conquest of Italy led to new problems, both of citizenship and of administration. The centralization of government in Rome made colonies impossible to administer, and authority had to be decentralized. Different provinces had differing citizenship rights, depending upon their treaty arrangements with Rome, or on whether they were conquered.

RISE OF MUNICIPAL LAW, 396 B.C. ONWARD. The colonial organization of government was by a local constitution or charter to the municipium, carefully subordinated to higher authority in Rome. Municipia had local assemblies, senates, magistrates, and courts, and citizens had right of appeal to Rome in a capital case. Roman civil and municipal law applied in the colonies, and prefects were sent out from Rome to administer justice uniformly.

GRACCHAN REFORMS, 133–121 B.C. These were the main authority patterns and institutions that pertained during the rise of Rome and its democratic period. By the end of the conquest of empire, in 168 B.C., the democracy had been weakened by the impoverishment of the plebes. Gracchus' attempts at land reform and reducing the power of the Senate over appointments and veto led to the Agrarian Revolt.

MILITARY SUPPORT OF SENATE OLIGARCHY, 118–30 B.C. As military leaders were called in to support the Senate in quelling revolts, military patronage and authority increased under Marius and Sulla. Julius

Caesar's dictatorship was based, in part, on the municipalization of the empire; that is, on making the municipal administrative authorities responsible to himself rather than to the Senate or consuls.

MONARCHY, 30 B.C.–A.D. 476. Caesar Augustus converted the nominal republic into an operating monarchy by several constitutional reforms: one naming him *princeps senatus,* or first in presiding over the senate; another designating him *imperium pro consule,* which declared him to be equal and superior to elected consuls; still another by designating himself, *tribunicia potestas,* so he could initiate reforms on behalf of the people. Augustus then proceeded to divide the colonies into "unarmed" colonies, which the Senate could rule, and "imperial provinces," which needed the protection of the army and reported to Caesar. Thus, Augustus kept control of the army and the richest colonies. From these authorities, the power of successive Caesars grew until it became absolute under Diocletian.

The *tribunicia potestas* displaced *patria potestas* in the life of Roman society, and the *familia* as a corporate organizational unit of persons and property under authority of the household head was reduced to connubial and child-care functions. One of the chief objectives of the Caesar emperors was to isolate the individual, reduce the family, cut moral ties of man to man, prevent new associations, and make the individual utterly dependent upon the state. This isolation and lack of community ties prevented individuals from combining to oppose the state and gave the emperor absolute authority. Centralization of power was achieved by stripping the individual of all associations, allegiances, and human ties that might provide him with decision choices alternative to those of the state.

From Allegiance to Disorder

Under the Roman Republic from 471 B.C. to 265 B.C., the individual had lived in a society of diversified and decentralized authority, with substantial personal authority in his own decision process. The distribution of authority and rights throughout society to the plebes, by representation and law making, created a social order in which there was wide participation in authority, checks and balances, and individual rights. The property-owning peasantry, assured in their personal and civil rights, formed the backbone of the legions that conquered Italy, Carthage, and then the East. Their allegiance and stake in the society was high as long as they were participants.

TIME OF TROUBLES, 143–30 B.C. By the end of the conquests in the East, the peasantry had become dispossessed, through debt or military service. Lack of property rights was one loss, disparity in wealth another, and the peasant and plebian classes no longer had the means to exercise their political rights. By 104 B.C., only 2,000 Romans owned property, according to Cicero. Appian reported that the plebians lost everything, and the condition of the poor became even worse than before.

DEMORALIZATION. While part of Roman society was being impoverished, the elite were flooded with new wealth and new ideas. The new wealth came from Egypt and the eastern Mediterranean. The ideas came from new learning with the conquest of Greece. It is hard to say whether the wealth or the learning had the more devastating effect on Rome. Cato in his lifetime (234 to 149 B.C.) observed an almost complete transformation of Roman society from stoic simplicity to reckless luxury. Houses became spacious and lavish; exotic foods from throughout the empire became a luxurious pretense; women turned to rich adornment. Belief in the old gods was denied, sexual practices became promiscuous. Homosexuality and bisexuality became fashionable among Roman men; adultery, free love, and divorce among aristocratic women. Everyone was judged by money, greed was rampant, and corruption was ignored. Votes were bought, justice bribed. Men avoided military duty and work. Women avoided motherhood, and the population declined.

The breakdown in Roman morality, family, and patriarchal authority required new authority in their place. Old allegiances to the democratic process weakened as the Assembly failed to deal with poverty, with the Senate, and with the problems of the times following the Agrarian Revolt and the social wars. The unemployed were put on a dole and became dependent upon the head of the state, whoever and whatever he was.

RECENTRALIZATION AND MONARCHY, 30 B.C.–A.D. 293. The new authority that emerged to take the place of old allegiances was the military and dictatorial power of the emperor. The military rule of the emperor lasted for two centuries and then began to topple from its own authoritarianism. The depopulation of the Roman citizenry by low birth rates created a very mixed and heterogeneous population, largely slave. Rome never did develop an economic and agricultural base in Italy but depended upon its colonies. The colonial mines began to run out, making Rome short of minerals. The end of conquest stopped the influx of slaves, and the agricultural estates produced less food as the slave-labor supply diminished. Exports from Italy failed to keep pace with imports from the colonies, and trade began to languish. The poor became poorer, and the class struggle became more violent. The army, now recruited from provincial poor, often joined in attacks upon the wealthy.

With the decline in economic and military strength of Rome, the outlying provinces rebelled. In the thirty-five years between A.D. 235 and A.D. 270, thirty-seven emperors were proclaimed, many of whom were murdered or slain by their troops. When Valerian became emperor in A.D. 253, he faced war simultaneously on almost all the Roman frontiers—with the Franks, Alemanni, Marcomanni, Goths, Sythians, Persians, and Mesopotamians.

The empire was collapsing from external threats, largely because it had already collapsed within. There was no longer a broad Roman citizenry with rights, property, and participation in governance giving allegiance to the cause of Rome. Instead, there were a wealthy few who avoided military duty, the poor on a dole with no rights or authority or allegiance, the slaves, legions drawn from the provinces, and Christians passively resisting Roman authority. On all sides, land was running to waste, cities and towns were decaying, and commerce was paralyzed. Rome had depopulated itself by infanticide and birth control, and then the provinces were depopulated by war, plague, and famine. Taxes to support the army produced less revenue, and financial support to protect the frontiers became precarious.

Disorder and the Regrouping of Authority

The disorder and financial distress of the empire caused Diocletian as emperor (A.D. 293 to A.D. 305) to decree the absolute power of the emperor and his own divine authority.

FISCAL ORDER TO DISORDER. Even more far-reaching in its effects was the Diocletian edict that sought to deal with the financial crisis by price controls and payment of taxes in kind. The poverty of the provinces had made the collection of money taxes difficult. Food, mineral, and manufacturing production were declining and support of the army diminished along with the economy. Diocletian required that taxes not collectible in money be paid in kind for logistical support of the army. In practice, this edict took the empire out of a money economy into a barter economy and made tax collection a more local function. Transportation limited the boundaries of practical administration. If a tax was collected as grain, then the taxed estate had to meet a grain allotment, and the tax collector became a kind of local warehouse for the army.

ECONOMIC DISORDER. Lack of sufficient slave labor and the general depopulation compelled landowners to lure workers back to the land to meet their tax allotment. They changed the *latifundia,* or slave, estate into a *coloni,* or cultivators', estate. Freemen were brought from the city and treated as tenants paying rent, or a tenth of the produce. Some landowners changed slaves to *coloni* tenants to improve production on the land.

The local nature of supply and tax collection, plus the threats on the frontier, made the regional military commander a more vital and independent figure in the Roman Empire. The peasants and landowners needed the military commander for protection from barbarian raids, and the military commander needed the peasants and landowners for taxes in kind, materials, and manpower. Neither needed Rome, as Rome ceased to provide order and management. The Roman provincial rulers became self-sufficient, but even they could not check the increase of waste lands left by landowners and peasants who fled to escape the tax collector, nor the declining population, the infanticide, fewer taxpayers, fewer soldiers, economic depression, and collapse of trade. In this weakened state, the Roman Empire fell under the attacks of barbaric invasion and came to an end.

THE COLONI AND EMERGENT FEUDALISM. The last Roman institution to survive was the *coloni* estate, worked by tenants and serfs who yielded their allegiance, produce, and labor to the landlord for protection. The landlord in turn used his local produce to maintain a military contingent on the estate. This was the beginning of the feudal system, which was to survive as the bastion of medieval society. The centralized, authoritarian regime of the Roman Empire, which was remote and impersonal to the average citizen, was unable to maintain order and allegiance. The feudal system that took its place, whatever its other faults in constraining individual freedom, was the antithesis of Rome. The feudal system was based upon close personal relationships, allegiances, and loyalties, and these ties became the cement of the medieval world.

The other great legacy of the Roman Empire was its system of law making, the written legal code, administration of decentralized municipia by public law, uniform judicial administration, and a bicameral legislature. We still use these powerful legal inventions today in public law, public administration, and private business administration. Business corporation law is derived from the law of municipal corporations or municipia. Hence, much of our present authority structure, which is embedded in law, is derived from Roman civilization.

AUTHORITY PROBLEMS IN MEDIEVAL SOCIETY

Exhibit A–3 summarizes the medieval social system, its major needs, authority distribution, allegiance, functions, and process. The exhibit is explained in the text that follows, which covers the chronology of medieval society, its authority structure, its basis in Augustinian theocracy, and the movement from allegiance to disorder during the fifteenth and sixteenth centuries. The regrouping of authority from this period of disorder led to the Enlightenment, science, and the present modern age.

EXHIBIT A-3. Scenario of Authority and System Functions in Middle Ages

NEEDS (FUNCTIONS)

1. Reestablish order and confidence (faith) after the Roman debacle.
2. Protect local food production against marauding barbarians.
3. Reopen trade with Middle East after Crusaders and expand textile industry as means for economic growth.
4. Reduce conflict among feudal principalities to a manageable level.

AUTHORITY

1. Primary authority lay in the Church and the City of God.
2. Feudal lords were delegated authority to protect manoral food supply and to regulate serfs.
3. Merchant princes held authority to develop textile trade, mining, and construction under commercial law.
4. Political authority was partioned among merchants for trade, guilds for production, aristocracy for land agriculture, and divine king for defense.

ALLEGIANCE

1. Primary allegiances ran from serf or freeman to the manoral lord for protection, from lord to king, and king to church.

---

2. Emergence of technology and trade in fourteenth through seventeenth centuries disturbed the network of allegiances by injecting independent merchants, guildsmen, and princes who needed neither lord, king, nor church.
3. Realigned allegiances ran from tradesman to guild, guildsman and merchant to legislative representatives who formed a power block leading to reformation, representative government, and limited monarchy.

SYSTEM (FUNCTION NETWORK)

1. King and lord maintained defense against marauders, principalities, and rising nationalisms.
2. Guilds and later legislatures made trade regulations upon which textile trade and industry could expand.
3. Church administered canon law to regulate spiritual grace, conflict among principalities, and temporal affairs in marriage and morality.

PROCESS (FLOW OF INPUTS AND OUTPUTS)

1. The input of serf labor was utilized for military and agricultural outputs.
2. The fealty input of feudal barons was used to protect and enrich the king (as well as the barons).
3. The work and voting input of guildsmen and merchants was utilized for economic outputs as well as to resolve trade issues and political conflicts in the legislatures.
4. The input of piety was used to produce outputs of salvation and moral behavior.

Chronology and Authority Structure

The economic organization of medieval society was based upon feudal agriculture, the products of which were traded in handicraft villages with such cottage industries as spinning, sewing, cobbling, baking, and simple food processing. The peasants were under the protection of the feudal lord, and the three main authority figures were the lord, the parish priest, and a local magistrate. This social organization was an outgrowth of the *coloni* formed during the latter part of the Roman Empire, and it had restored many of the communal social ties that the

Roman Empire had broken. The patriarchal family and tribal rule were gone, but in their place came a kind of community based upon economic and military necessity. The community performed the functions of sustenance of its members, protection of their safety, and custody of their spiritual needs. These are, indeed, powerful needs and functions, which made the society cohesive and enduring. The medieval society itself endured for a thousand years after the sacking of Rome by Aleric in 410 B.C. (see tables A–5 and A–6), and a traditional society, closely resembling the medieval one, persisted for another four centuries before being destroyed by the French Revolution.

TABLE A-5. Historical Abstract of Medieval Civilization

Event	Date (A.D.)
Augustinian theocracy	410–1378
Moslem domination of Mediterranean	620–1270
End of Crusades and opening of East	1270
Invention of the clock	1271
Black Plague and manoral reform	14th & 15th centuries
Invention of pumps, iron and steel casting	14th century
Guilds and mercantilism	800–1600
Rise of the textile industry	1300–1600
Italian Renaissance	1378–1534
Invention of printing press	1454
Reformation	1517–1564
New World colonial expansion	1535–1776
Copernican revolution	1543
Bacon and scientific method	1620
Application of machines to industry	1500–1700
Thirty Years War	1618–1648
Statute of Tenures	1660
Adam Smith and economic individualism	1776
Enclosure Acts and agrarian reform	1785
French Revolution	1787–1814
Industrial Revolution	1790
British Corn Laws	1815–1846

TABLE A-6. Authority Patterns of Medieval Civilization

Event	Date (A.D.)
Central theocratic, with decentralized feudal authoritarianism	410–1378
Decentralized bourgeois merchant economy	1378–1776
Nationalistic monarchies	13th–18th centuries
Dissident religious and economic minorities	1517–1648
American, French, industrial revolutions creating representative plutocracies	1776–1815

AUGUSTINIAN THEOCRACY, 410–1378. The second main foundation of medieval society was the Catholic Church, which preserved much of the Roman law and administrative structure in the canon law and organizational hierarchy of the Church. The administrative potential of canon law and organizational hierarchy made the Church the only institution capable of large-scale social management. With law and hierarchy, the Church, like Rome, was able to decentralize local ministerial functions to the parish, while still maintaining policy and financial control at the top.

Perhaps even more important than the administrative skills inherited from Rome, however, was the policy-making genius of St. Augustine in conceiving a theology that knit all the functions of the individual, feudalism, village life, and the Church into a comprehensive world view, which became the basis for implicit faith.

St. Augustine's *City of God,* written in the years immediately following the sack of Rome, gave to the people, living in chaos, an explanation of the debacle in which they found themselves and also a reason to hope for a better future. He characterized the human race as living in two cities, a City of Man, and a City of God. The City of Man, he said, was founded on fratricide (Cain killing Abel) and was subject to war, greed, and vicissitudes but also joys. The joys were those of nature, humanity, companionship, and love among men; but there was also hate and greed leading to wars. It was not surprising, then, that temporal cities might rise and fall. But the City of God, Augustine said, was one of a great design ordained by God, in which the plentitude, diversity, and fullness of nature and man flourished, joined to each other in the peace and love of God.

St. Augustine then linked the City of Man to the City of God by creating the metaphor of human progress, which has been one of the most powerful ideas of Western culture. There is no inherent reason why Augustine should have introduced the idea of human progress into Christian doctrine, other perhaps than that he sensed its inherent appeal. The Greek civilization had a historical view of life as cyclical birth and decay, or *physis,* after the manner of plant life, and Rome, too, adopted the same view. Oriental philosophy has tended to view life as an endless round, the wheel of fate. St. Augustine argued against the idea of cycle, birth and decay, by positing that God has preordained the scheme of the world and the entire history of the human race.[4] In this design, the human being, seeking the City of God, progresses to perfection and redemption by his Savior.

[4]Robert A. Nisbet, *Social Change and History* (New York: Oxford University Press, 1969), pp. 63–98.

With St. Augustine began the distinctively Western idea of the unity of man, his works, civilization, and religion. Such unity of purpose proved to be a magnificently supportive idea in chaotic times, and this unifying idea proved to be a world view around which the medieval world was built. The Church, with the Pope as emissary of the City of God, became the final arbitor of all things religious, temporal, and political, until the Papal Schism occurred in 1378.

END OF THE CRUSADES AND OPENING OF THE EAST, 1270. The Papal Schism, in which the French and Roman branches of the Church each elected their own Pope, was an outgrowth of the changing authority and society that came with the rise of merchant princes. Europe had been a closed feudal society, cut off from trade and outside influence during the period from 620 to 1270, when Moslems dominated the Mediterranean. The end of the Crusades opened the East to trade in silks and dyestuffs, and this trade centered in Florence, Milan, and Genoa. In 1300 a Florentine, Federigo Oricellarii, brought home the secret of extracting purple dye from lichens from the Middle East. The dye industry revolutionized the textile industry, and Florence became preeminent in textile manufacture as well as in the East-West trade.

RISE OF THE TEXTILE TRADE, 1300–1600. The East-West trade exchanged silk and dyestuffs from Persia and Constantinople with wool, linen, and fuller's earth from England, Flanders, and Germany. The northern Italian cities were the focal point of this trade. Florence became a financial center, with eighty banks. Modern financial techniques such as bank deposits, check cashing, letters of credit, insurance, double-entry bookkeeping, foreign exchange, and merchandise exchanges came into being. Florence had over two hundred textile mills and one-fourth of the population consisted of industrial workers.

THE ITALIAN RENAISSANCE, 1387–1534. The bankers, merchants, craftsmen, manufacturers, and professional men were organized into guilds. Seven trade guilds made up the *popolo grasso* ("fat people") and fourteen artisan guilds made up the *popolo minuto* ("little people"). Every voter had to be a member of a guild because the nobles had been disenfranchised in 1282 by a bourgeois revolution. The guilds elected a municipal council and a chief magistrate, who managed the city-state. The victory of the business classes over the landed aristocracy in Italy was the first breakup of the traditional society, and the political history of the Italian Renaissance is of a struggle of the wealthy to control the government. The society was a thriving plutocracy, and with wealth the arts were cultivated as creatively as in ancient Greece. Great names like Leonardo de Vinci, Michelangelo, Botticelli, Donatello, Fra Filippo Lippi, Verocchio, Titian, Petrarch, and Boccaccio all flourished in this wealthy enlightenment.

GUILDS AND MERCANTILE SYSTEM, 800–1600. The East-West trade also invigorated the economies of Germany, Belgium, France, and England, which first supplied materials in the wool trade and then became major textile manufacturers in wool, silk, linen, and tapestries themselves. The guilds and mercantile system owe some of their distinctive characteristics to their English and German origins. Guilds derive in part from sworn brotherhoods in early Germanic or Scandanavian sacrificial banquets. An artificial blood bond or kinship was established between two or more persons by comingling their blood in earth. Guild merchants set up foster brotherhoods for their mutual protection, in the same sense that feudal lords protected agriculture. The Church fostered guilds as a form of brotherhood of man. After the Norman Conquest in England, the kings also encouraged merchant guilds, by granting them royal charters that gave them a trade monopoly within a village or for a specific product. The merchant guilds formed a kind of insurance group for its members, aiding them in sickness, age, poverty, murder, or loss of property by robbery, shipwreck, or conflagration.

INVENTIONS AND TECHNOLOGY, FOURTEENTH CENTURY. The invention of the pump, waterwheel, and steel casting in the fourteenth century caused England and Germany to emerge as economic powers to rival Florence. The pump made possible the mining of coal and iron in shafts that previously had been unworkable from water seepage. The waterwheel created a vast dispersion of small textile mills throughout England on its many streams. Iron and steel casting technology brought Germany to the fore in blast furnaces and steel making. The trade that emerged from these developments created the Hanseatic League among German states as a major economic block and turned England and the Netherlands into major maritime nations.

From Allegiance to Disorder and the Regrouping of Authority

During the sixteenth century there were five major economic powers in Europe: Italy as financier of the East-West trade, France as an agriculture and textile center, the German Hanseatic League, the England-Netherlands trading axis, and Spain with gold from the New World. Much of the turmoil and war of the next century stemmed from the rivalry for power of these groups: France conquering Italy and the Papal Schism; the English rivalry with France and Spain; the Protestant wars of the German states against the Roman Church.

TURBULENCE FROM SCIENCE, PRINTING, AND THE REFORMATION, SIX-TEENTH CENTURY. The turmoil of the fifteenth and sixteenth century was intertwined on economic, political, intellectual, scientific, religious, and technological levels. The invention of the printing press made Europe one open society of ideas at the same time that it was a closed society politically and religiously. The experimental method, founded by Copernicus and proclaimed as a new secular salvation by Bacon, brought invention and technology, which began a mechanical and mercantile revolution. The power of the merchants and their guilds made claims for political authority in England and on the Continent, just as they had earlier in Florence. The political convenience of German princes and merchants was served by the Reformation and the Thirty Years War, which broke the power of the Papacy and began to redistribute the authority the medieval society had placed in feudal lords and in the Church. The Statute of Tenures (1660) in Britain recognized the need for producing food for Britain's growing town populations and for engaging in manufacture and trade, by converting feudal estates into a manoral (tenant farmer) system.

NEW WORLD COLONIAL EXPANSION, SEVENTEENTH CENTURY. The period 1660 to 1776 were years of continued mercantile growth and a marked colonial expansion of all the European nations. The wealth of the colonies and trade was squandered partly on war and mostly on luxurious living by upper classes in the traditional society, but there was a quiescence in the class struggle between the merchants and landed gentry. The excesses of luxury, taxes, and arrogance of members of the aristocracy, who made few moves to distribute authority to either the merchants or common people, led to the American and French revolutions.

THE FRENCH REVOLUTION, 1787–1814. The French Revolution resulted in the destruction of the traditional society in France. In Britain, however, where the Industrial Revolution began with the application of coal-fired steam engines to textile manufacture in 1790, the transition of authority was more gradual and legalistic. The Enclosure Acts of 1785 and the repeal of the Corn Laws in 1846 ended the domination of politics by the landed gentry and shifted authority to the new industrialists (or Manchester School).

THE INDUSTRIAL REVOLUTION, 1790 ONWARDS. The ideological spokesman for the Manchester School and the new industrialists was Adam Smith, whose *Wealth of Nations* appeared in 1776. The last of the physiocrats or mercantilists, Smith fastened upon the partially mechanized wool trade as a conceptual paradigm (although it was in fact an anachronism at the time he wrote about it). The economic analysis of Smith is an apt description of sixteenth-century England, with many producers (wool farmers) and innumerable small mills along each stream. In this period, Adam Smith's three conditions for economic equilibrium prevailed: (1) divisible capital, (2) competition, and (3) free-market exchange. With these three presumptions, Smith could posit a closed economic model with all the balance of a clockwork.

The clock as an intellectual model is certainly among the most significant inventions of the Middle Ages. Western thought has since created five pervasive theories on clockwork principles—celestial mechanics, Newtonian physics, logical positivism, behavioral psychology, and Smith's economics. The clock is a closed system, once the spring is wound. Who winds the spring? The "invisible hand," as Smith called it. Actually, society is not a closed but an open system, and a closed-system paradigm prevents managers from understanding the dynamics of the change process they are seeking to control.

The first thing that went wrong, for Adam Smith's paradigm, was the Industrial Revolution, which started three years after *The Wealth of Nations* appeared. By definition, an industrial revolution has high capital requirements for energy and mechanization. The high capital requirements in large, technologically indivisible units destroyed Smith's first premise. The tendency of managers, faced with high risks of large investment, to combine and avoid competition destroyed his second premise. The ability of combined oligopolistic enterprises to influence and administer prices vitiated his third and last premise. While the paradigm was drained of its reality by technological events, the advocacy and idealization of laissez-faire and economic individualism was good politics for the Manchester industrialists, because it rationalized their seizing power from the landed gentry.

SUMMARY

Historical epochs exhibit marked shifts in the pattern of authority distribution. In those eras that open society, through trade, discovery, new territory, or exploration (for example, Greece in the eighth century B.C., Rome in the fifth century B.C., Europe in the fourteenth century A.D.), authority tends to become dispersed, decentralized, and diverse. The dispersal of authority gives individuals a wide range of judgment in their own decision process, and an era of creativity in a participative society follows (Greece, fifth century B.C.; Rome, third and fourth centuries B.C.; Europe, fifteenth and sixteenth centuries A.D.). Under the dispersal of authority, new power groups arise seeking to assure the continuance or succession of their authority by fixing it in institutional procedures. In this rivalry, disorder occurs and society, which abhors disorder (because it vitiates individual decision making), allows power to centralize in a dominant group (Greece, fourth century B.C.; Rome first century B.C.; Europe, fifth through eleventh centuries A.D.). The consequence of centralizing authority in a dominant institution is to stultify the society, diminish individual decision authority and freedom to a neglible range, weaken allegiances, and set the stage for a new cycle of rivalry for authority.

The most important thing managers need to know is where their society and institution stand in the cycle of order-disorder or dispersed versus centralized authority. Unless they know this, they can have no control over the dynamics of the social processes that affect them or their institutions. Unless managers are conscious of the dispersal centralization phenomenon in the organizational process, they will be unable to manage change—and the management of change is the first requirement of an administrator in any institution.

Past societies have been unable to manage the change process, which is why the cycle of order to disorder repeats itself. It is questionable whether contemporary managers today know how to manage the change process, and we may indeed be on the order to disorder trajectory ourselves. To know where we are today on the trajectory requires that we examine ourselves and the events of recent decades to see where the authority patterns lie and what changes are now under way.

BIBLIOGRAPHY

Ackoff, Russell. *Redesigning the Future*. New York: John Wiley & Sons, 1974.

Ashford, Douglas E. "Political Science and Policy Studies: Toward a Structural Solution," *Policy Studies Journal* 5 (1977): 570–82.

Bagley, Edward R. *Beyond the Conglomerates: The Impact of the Supercorporation on the Future of Life and Business*. New York: American Management Association, 1975.

Baier, Kurt, and Rescher, Nicholas. *Values and the Future*. New York: The Free Press, 1969.

Bauer, Raymond, and Gergen, Kenneth. *Policy Formation*. New York: The Free Press, 1968.

Beckwith, Burnham P. *The Next 500 Years*. New York: Exposition Press, 1967.

Bell, Daniel, ed. "Toward the Year 2000," *Daedalus, Journal of the American Academy of Arts and Sciences* 96, no. 3 (Summer 1967): 639–977.

————. *The Coming of Post-Industrial Society: A Venture in Social Forecasting*. New York: Basic Books, 1973.

Bell, Wendell, and Mau, James, eds. *The Sociology of the Future*. New York: Russell Sage Foundation, 1971.

Bertalanffy, L. V. *General Systems Theory*. New York: George Braziller, 1968.

Brewer, Garry D., and Brunner, Ronald D., eds. *A Policy Approach to the Study of Political Development and Change*. New York: The Free Press, 1975.

Brameld, Theodore. *The Teacher as a World Citizen: A Scenario of the 21st Century*. Palm Springs, Calif.: ETC Publications, 1976.

Brubaker, Stirling. *In Command of Tomorrow: Resources and Environmental Strategies for Americans*. Baltimore: The Johns Hopkins University Press, 1975.

Buffa, Elwood. *Operations Management: The Management of Productive Systems*. New York: John Wiley & Sons, 1976.

Bundy, Robert. *Images of the Future: The Twenty-first Century and Beyond*. Buffalo, N.Y.: Prometheus, 1976.

Cary, Charles. "An Introductory Course in Evaluative Research," *Policy Analysis* 3 (Summer 1977): 429–44.

Clarke, Arthur C. *Profiles of the Future: An Inquiry into the Limits of the Possible*. New York: Harper & Row, 1973.

Churchman, C. A. *The Systems Approach*. New York: Delacorte Press, 1968.

deLeon, Peter. "Public Policy and Political Development," *Policy Studies Journal* 5 (1977): 596–615.

Durant, Will. *The Story of Civilization*. New York: Simon & Schuster, 1939, 1944, 1957.

Easton, D. *Systems Analysis of Political Life*. New York: John Wiley & Sons, 1965.

Edmunds, Stahrl W. *Basics of Private and Public Management*. Lexington, Mass.: D. C. Heath, 1978.

————. "Social Responsibility, Neglects, and Reticulation," *Business and Society* 16 (Spring 1976): 38–45.

Falk, Richard A. *A Study of Future Worlds*. New York: The Free Press, 1975.

Ferkiss, Victor. *The Future of Technological Civilization*. New York: George Braziller, 1974.

Fuller, R. Buckminster, and Marks, Robert. *The Dymaxion World of Buckminster Fuller*. Garden City, N.Y.: Doubleday, 1973.

Hellman, Hal. *The City in the World of the Future*. New York: M. Evans, 1970.

Jantsch, Erich. *Design for Evolution: Self-Organization and Planning in the Life of Human Systems*. New York: George Braziller, 1975.

deJouvenel, Bertrand. *The Art of Conjecture*. New York: Basic Books, 1967.

Jungk, Robert, and Gultung, Johan. *Mankind 2000*. Oslo: University of Oslo Press, 1969.

Kahn, Herman. *The Future of the Corporation*. New York: Mason and Lipscomb, 1974.

Kahn, Herman, and Wiener, Anthony. *The Year 2000*. New York: Macmillan, 1967.

Kauffman, Draper L., Jr. *Futurism and Future Studies*. Washington, D.C.: National Education Association, 1976.

Kothari, Rajni. *Footsteps into the Future*. New York: The Free Press, 1974.

Lasswell, Harold D. "The Policy Orientation." In Daniel Lerner and Harold D. Lasswell, eds. *The Policy Sciences*. Stanford, Calif.: Stanford University Press, 1951.

———. *A Preview of Policy Sciences*. New York: American Elsevier, 1971.

Lazlo, Ervin. *The Systems View of the World*. New York: George Braziller, 1972.

Leavitt, Harold, ed. *Organizations of the Future: Interaction with the External Environment*. New York: Praeger, 1974.

McHale, John. *The Future of the Future*. New York: George Braziller, 1971.

Martino, Joseph. *Technological Forecasting for Decision Making*. New York: American Elsevier, 1972.

Meadows, Dennis L.; Behrens III, William B.; Meadows, Donella H.; Naill, Roger F.; Randers, Jorgen; and Zahn, Erich K. O. *Dynamics of Growth in a Finite World*. Cambridge, Mass.: Wright-Allen Press, 1974.

Mendlovitz, Saul H. *On the Creation of a Just World Order*. New York: The Free Press, 1975.

Mesarovic, Mihajlo, and Pestel, Eduard. *Mankind at the Turning Point: The Second Report of the Club of Rome*. New York: E. P. Dutton, 1974.

Moffitt, Donald. *The Wall Street Journal Views America Tomorrow.* New York: American Management Association, 1977.

Nadler, G. *Work Design.* Homewood, Ill.: Richard D. Irwin, 1970.

Perloff, Harvey S., ed. *The Future of the U.S. Government: Toward the Year 2000.* Englewood Cliffs, N.J.: Prentice-Hall, 1971.

Peters, B. Guy. "Developments in Comparative Policy Studies," *Policy Studies Journal* 5 (1977): 616–28.

Polak, Fred. *The Image of the Future.* Amsterdam: Elsevier, 1973.

———. *Prognostics: A Science in the Making of Surveys of the Future.* New York: Elsevier, 1971.

Rosenfeld, Albert. *The Second Genesis: The Coming Control of Life.* New York: Vintage Press, 1969.

Sheffer, Gabriel. "Reversibility of Policies and Patterns of Politics," *Policy Studies Journal* 5 (1977): 535–53.

Small, Glen. "Land in the Sky: Visions of a Megastructure," *The Futurist, Journal of the World Future Society* 11 (June 1977): 150–56.

Spengler, Joseph J. *Population and America's Future.* San Francisco: W. H. Freeman, 1975.

Theobald, Robert. *An Alternative Future for America's Third Century.* Chicago: Swallow Press, 1976.

Toffler, Alvin. *Future Shock.* New York: Random House, 1970.

Tugwell, Franklin. *Search for Alternatives: Public Policy and the Study of the Future.* Englewood Cliffs, N.J.: Winthrop, 1973.

INDEX

Roman empire:
  authority problems of, 187
  collapse of, 197
Roman republic, 59, 190, 193
Roman society, 69
Rostow, Walter, 42

Saint Augustine, 42, 106, 202
Science, medieval, 205
Search capability, 122
Self-actualization, 164
Senate, Roman, 59
Slavery, 182
Smith, Adam, 206
Scenario: 54, 136
  plot-maker's guide to, 137
Social contract, 120
Social evolution, 42
Social organizations, 42
Social structure, 174
Social trajectory, 125
Socialization, 48
Socrates, 89, 184
Solon, 18, 88, 181
  reforms of, 182
Sparta, 89, 178
Spengler, Oswald, 42
Standard Oil decision, 76
Statue of Tenures, 205
Succession, in Greece, 175
Sulla, 75
System:
  defined, 118, 126
  functions of, 25, 44, 47
  interactions with, 135
  relationships in, 126
  structure of, 119–20
  U.S., 133
System analysis:
  of Greece, 175

of medieval society, 199
of Rome, 187

Tasks, 25
Tax structure, 150
Taxation, in Rome, 197
Technology, 13, 73, 143
  medieval, 204
Technological civilization, 158
Technological progress, 27
Theobald, Robert, 164
Theocracy, 108, 202
Time of troubles:
  in Greece, 184
  in Rome, 196
Title, property, 87
Trade:
  in medieval society, 203
  in Rome, 197
Trajectory, social, 125
Transfer payments, 6
Tribune, 59, 72
Tribunicia potestas, 195
Tugwell, Rexford, 161

Unemployment, 30, 79
Underemployment, 28
Unions, 97
United Nations, 18
Unity of purpose, medieval, 203

Villanova tribal life, 189
Voice, 135
Voluntary institutions, 33, 34
Voss, John, 161
Voters, medieval, 203
Voting, 15

Wars, 29
Wofford, John, 161
World Court, 18